TRAVELLING
to
TOMORROW

YVES REES (they/them) is a writer, historian and podcaster based on unceded Wurundjeri land. Yves is a Senior Lecturer in History at La Trobe University, the co-host of Archive Fever history podcast (with Clare Wright), and author of the memoir *All About Yves: Notes from a Transition*. They are also co-editor of *Nothing to Hide: Voices of Trans and Gender-Diverse Australia*.

'Thoughtful and curious, critical and kind, Yves Rees's study of these globetrotting Australian women richly renders their lives and times, as well as contemplating how we reach across time to read them today.'

ANNA CLARK, Australian Research Council Future Fellow, University of Technology Sydney

'Fresh, captivating, and full of fantastic women. Yves has somehow managed to assemble the greatest fantasy dinner party you never knew you needed, whilst also uncovering a fascinating and untold side of our history. A real treat.'

ZOË COOMBS MARR, comedian, performer and actor

'Yves Rees has the remarkable ability to bring history into the present, reminding us all that the only thing that really separates the generations is a linear notion of time. *Travelling to Tomorrow* gives voice to the women at the forefront of Australia's own "American Revolution". What I love most about Yves is how they bring an unwavering commitment to human rights in their exploration of history, the language of equality ever-present in their handling of the past. In Rees, we have found a historian of rare skill – they possess the ability to tell us something we didn't know about something we thought we did.'

CLEMENTINE FORD, feminist writer, columnist and broadcaster

'This book is a knockout. Yves Rees is that rare historian who thinks like a scholar and writes like a dream – the literary equivalent to floating like a butterfly and stinging like a bee. You will want to meet these fearless and feisty women: women not only before their time in forging new geocultural paths to independence but also making their times by putting flesh to the bones of modernity. Rees gives us their stories in full-bodied, hot-blooded fashion. A sheer delight.'

PROFESSOR CLARE WRIGHT OAM, Professor of History, La Trobe University

TRAVELLING
to
TOMORROW

THE MODERN WOMEN WHO SPARKED AUSTRALIA'S ROMANCE WITH AMERICA

YVES REES

NEWSOUTH

UNSW Press acknowledges the Bedegal people, the Traditional Owners of the unceded territory on which the Randwick and Kensington campuses of UNSW are situated, and recognises the continuing connection to Country and culture. We pay our respects to Bedegal Elders past and present.

A NewSouth book
Published by
NewSouth Publishing
University of New South Wales Press Ltd
University of New South Wales
Sydney NSW 2052
AUSTRALIA
https://unsw.press/

© Yves Rees 2024
First published 2024

10 9 8 7 6 5 4 3 2 1

This book is copyright. Apart from any fair dealing for the purpose of private study, research, criticism or review, as permitted under the *Copyright Act*, no part of this book may be reproduced by any process without written permission. Inquiries should be addressed to the publisher.

A catalogue record for this book is available from the National Library of Australia

ISBN: 9781742238135 (paperback)
       9781742239057 (ebook)
       9781761178023 (ePDF)

Design Josephine Pajor-Markus
Cover design and illustration Mika Tabata

All reasonable efforts were taken to obtain permission to use copyright material reproduced in this book, but in some cases copyright could not be traced. The author welcomes information in this regard.

CONTENTS

Cast of characters	viii
Preface. California calling, *San Francisco, 2011*	ix
Introduction. Light years ahead, *New York, 1927*	1

PART I: ACROSS THE PACIFIC

1	Seeking fame and fortune in America *The lawyer, Los Angeles, 1910*	13
2	The vocation of glamour *The decorator, New York City, 1917*	26
3	Freshwater mermaid does Hollywood *The swimmer, Honolulu, 1918*	38
4	Decorator to the stars *The decorator, New York City, 1923*	50
5	Herstory, whose story	60
6	Getting modern with natation *The swimmer, San Francisco, 1923*	65
7	A new comet in fiction *The writer, Central Queensland, 1927*	76
8	A city of dreams *The artist, New York City, 1927*	87
9	We do not teach ladies *The swimmer, Sydney, 1927*	97
10	An atmosphere for excellence *The pianist, Chicago, 1928*	106

PART II: THE WORLD OF TOMORROW

11	Our only woman judge *The lawyer, Los Angeles, 1928*	119
12	Passports	129
13	The religion of progress *The economist, Seattle, 1929*	134
14	Boom to bust *The writer, Southern California, 1929*	144
15	People over profits *The economist, New York City, 1931*	152
16	Why should we hate each other? *The pianist, Chicago, 1932*	160
17	A philosophy of nakedness *The health guru, Chesapeake Bay, 1933*	168
18	From colonial girl to fierce feminist *The dentist, Melbourne, 1934*	176
19	The Yanks are on the right track *The nurse, Chicago, 1935*	185

PART III: LESSONS

20	An unfortunate addiction to modernism *The artist, Melbourne, 1935*	197
21	The pernicious virus of American hooey *The health guru, Perth, 1937*	207
22	Hard to take after America *The nurse, London, 1937*	215
23	Making Australia modern *The pianist, Melbourne, 1938*	222

24	Lessons from Australia *The economist, Washington DC, 1939*	228
25	Anti-English and pro-American *The nurse, New York City, 1940*	237
26	Selling Australia *The decorator, New York City, 1942*	242
27	A better world for women *The lawyer, Los Angeles, 1945*	251
28	Democracy itself	261
29	US women have more freedom *The dentist, Perth, 1947*	264
30	The greatest aquatic show *The swimmer, Sydney, 1948*	271
31	How to wear a wheelchair *The writer, Miami, 1950*	278
32	The tyranny of American abstraction *The artist, Melbourne, 1960*	284
33	When Persia met POTUS *The economist, Washington DC, 1962*	291
34	Isabel's ashes *The swimmer, Sydney, 2023*	298

Endings	301
Notes	304
Select bibliography	321
Acknowledgments	329
Index	333

CAST OF CHARACTERS

The lawyer: May Lahey (1888–1984), attorney and judge.
The decorator: Rose Cumming (1884–1968), interior decorator and socialite.
The swimmer: Isabel Letham (1899–1995), surf pioneer and swim teacher.
The writer: Dorothy Cottrell (1902–1957), novelist and story writer.
The artist: Mary Cecil Allen (1893–1962), painter and art educator.
The pianist: Vera Bradford (1904–2004), concert pianist and music teacher.
The economist: Persia Campbell (1898–1974), academic and consumer activist.
The health guru: Alice Caporn (1875–1969), nudist and health entrepreneur.
The dentist: Dorothy Waugh (1894–1983), academic and feminist.
The nurse: Cynthia Reed (1908–1976), nursing student and novelist.

PREFACE
CALIFORNIA CALLING
SAN FRANCISCO, 2011

When I was 23, I farewelled my mother at Melbourne Airport, on unceded Wurundjeri land, and boarded United Flight 840 to San Francisco. My then-partner had scored a gig at a Silicon Valley start-up, and I – a recent history grad – found an internship at a nearby museum. We were two wide-eyed young Australians, ambitious provincials keen to make our mark in the metropole, headed to Obama's America, land of hope and opportunity. It was before Trump, before George Floyd, before Facebook white-anted democracy and *Roe v Wade* was overturned – back when white progressives could still, if we squinted hard enough, glimpse the American dream.

In San Fran, ferries criss-crossed a giant bowl of a bay and eucalypts stretched up to blue skies. We lived in the Mission, a fast-gentrifying Latino neighbourhood, where organic grocers and hipster cafes sprouted up among traditional taquerias. By night, we feasted on guacamole alongside tech tycoons plotting disruption in their teenage-boy uniform of sneakers and hoodies. It was there I caught my first Uber, saw my first bluetooth headphones. It felt, quite literally, like the future. Even the Occupy protests that flooded the streets that fall seemed a harbinger of a better world just around the corner.

It was a stark contrast to London, where I'd studied the previous year. I'd arrived in England a cringing colonial, a wannabe scholar following in the footsteps of generations of settler

Australians who'd undertaken what historian Angela Woollacott calls the 'secular pilgrimage' back to the mother country. It was meant to be a spiritual homecoming, a return Home. Yet I found myself adrift in a cold and alien city, huddled in my coat as I trudged home through the 4 pm twilight after the daily onslaught of convict jokes. Contrary to expectations, my British heritage did not translate into any sense of belonging in London. This grey capital was no home of mine.

But now, in California, I'd found an alternative metropole that pulsed with vivid life. At my internship, I worked on an exhibition for the 75th anniversary of the Golden Gate Bridge. The museum director repainted the downtown exhibition space the same burnt orange as the bridge itself, and later thanked me with a leather wallet in an identical hue. There was no reserve here. The bolder, the better.

For the holidays, we flew to New York. On New Year's Eve, we ended up at a warehouse party in lower Manhattan where beautiful people undulated to Foster the People's 'Pumped Up Kicks'. Now, finally, I'd made it. I'd left the sleepy coal-mining Newcastle of my childhood far behind; I'd arrived at the beating heart of the universe. Later that evening, I lost my coat and my friend misplaced one silver stiletto, but we didn't mind because we were bright young things in NYC on NYE, high on our delusions of destiny. Out with the Old World, in with the New.

By this point New York had its own 'Little Australia'. In thanks for Australian participation in the early 2000s 'War on Terror', the Bush administration had introduced the E-3 visa program, a scheme that made special provision for Australians to work and live in the United States. As a result, the Australian population of NYC exploded – from 5000 in 2005 to 20 000 by 2011. You could now visit Australian cafes that sold flat whites and smashed avo. My presence there was unexceptional.

But the historian in me wondered how this all began. For how long had Australians been seeking their fortune in the United States? My generation was surely not the first to discover the charms of an American adventure. When and why did Australians start crossing the Pacific?

We already knew about the long line of Australians who'd tried their luck in London. There was Barry Humphries and Germaine Greer and Clive James, Patrick White and Kathy Lette and Margaret Preston and PL Travers (author of *Mary Poppins*) – not to mention the iconic ocker Barry McKenzie, fictional protagonist of Barry Humphries' 1972 hit comedy *The Adventures of Barry McKenzie*. Their stories had already been told. Thanks to countless novels and memoirs and histories, the ritual of 'going home' to London had taken hold in the cultural imagination. It was an endless quest to outrun the cultural cringe, a compulsive return to ground zero of empire.

But what of those who, like me, were seduced by the United States instead? The Australians who chose New York or Los Angeles over London? Surely there had been other antipodeans drawn to a global superpower that defined itself through modernity instead of tradition. As a historian, I knew better than to assume anything was original. But just how far back did this history go? And what could this alternative travel trajectory tell us about Australia's place in the world?

INTRODUCTION
LIGHT YEARS AHEAD
NEW YORK, 1927

After a rough crossing of the Atlantic, the last day dawned calm and still. On 30 September 1927, a sparkling morning that felt like midsummer, the *Aquitania* entered the mouth of the Hudson River for the final leg of its journey. Up on deck, a gangly figure leant over the ship's railing, taking in the scene while the breeze tossed her corn-coloured hair. As she surveyed the waters with an artists' gaze, Mary Cecil Allen was reminded of Sydney Harbour. This landscape was not so wild, not so beautiful as Gadigal Country, but it had the same blue and silver tones, the same warm clear air.

Up ahead, she observed a great white bird resting on the water. What strange American creature was this? As they approached, Mary realised she was looking at the Statue of Liberty. Although made of bronze, Lady Liberty had been weathered by the ocean air into a silvery green, so pale it was almost white. Behind the statue rose what looked like a range of icebergs, huge monoliths reaching to the sky, their peaks gilded by the sun. Here it was at last: the New York skyline, those iconic skyscrapers. Was this a city or a fairyland? 'I can't describe how incredible and dreamlike it looked,' Mary wrote of her arrival.

Twelve months earlier, Mary had been a rising star of the Melbourne art world. She was a professor's daughter who'd topped the National Gallery Art School, and became the first woman to give public lectures on art. She was appointed art critic for the *Sun*. Her paintings were cautiously modern; her fashions more boldly so. She knew everyone. Dame Nellie Melba opened her 1921 solo exhibition; Ivy Brookes, daughter of ex-Prime Minister Alfred Deakin, was a close friend.

In September 1927, after eight months touring Europe, Mary arrived in New York City. She was immediately head over heels. The city was 'extraordinarily stimulating'; there was 'no other place in the world where it was possible to live so complete a life'. She settled in and began lecturing on modern art. Soon, other opportunities arose. There was a studio in Greenwich Village, rumoured lovers, summers painting in the countryside. There was little reason to go home, so she didn't.

Or at least not until 1935, after almost a decade away. That year, Mary visited Melbourne to see family and spread the word about the latest trends in modern art. To the horror of the conservative art establishment, she flaunted her abstract canvases and lectured on modernist painting to sell-out crowds. Her 'unfortunate addiction to modernism' dismayed local critics, who cried 'distortion' and were not sorry to see her return to New York the following year. But this hostile reception didn't stop Mary coming back to Melbourne in 1950 and again in 1960 once more to evangelise the American avant-garde.

In retrospect, Mary was a woman ahead of her time. As well as a modernist painter and educator, she was a geopolitical avant-gardist who anticipated the 'special relationship' between Australia and the United States that continues – for good or ill – into the 2020s. Long before the transpacific alliance was formalised from the 1940s, she challenged the traditional gravitation towards Britain and nudged Australia into the American orbit.

Mary may have been unusual, but she was far from alone. From 1875, regular steamship services connected Sydney to San Francisco. By 1920, annual departures of Australian women to the United States numbered 1000. By 1960, this number had tripled. Thousands more entered the United States via Canada and Britain. Most were short-term tourists, but many stayed for months or years. By 1940, US census data showed that more than 12 000 Australians were resident in the United States, 50 per cent of whom were female.

Who were these women? For years I searched out their stories in archives big and small, tracking them down everywhere from Perth to Los Angeles to rural Illinois. I squinted over faded handwriting on letters yellowed with time, breathing in century-old dust, and spent thousands of hours trawling old newspapers.

The stories I found were electrifying. There was a celebrity decorator with blue hair. A single mother who advised JFK in the Oval Office. A Christian nudist with a passion for almond milk. A wheelchair user who wrote bestselling novels and a cigarette-loving nurse who dodged immigration control. In total, I found around 700 characters – a raucous compendium that ranged from militant temperance campaigners to an aviatrix embroiled in a murder and a savvy businesswoman who ran an Australian restaurant in Jazz Age Manhattan.

A century ago, back when most women remained tethered to the kitchen sink, these Australians did something remarkable. Throwing convention to the wind, they packed up a suitcase and set sail. Unlike their contemporaries in search of wider horizons who gravitated to London, they headed across the Pacific to make their fortune. Decades before Prime Minister John Curtin announced Australia's turn to America in 1941, and the ANZUS treaty was signed in 1951, these Australian women sparked Australia's romance with America. They were rebels, they were trailblazers, they were disruptors who pushed the boundaries of what women could do and be. Individually, they have remarkable stories. Collectively, they offer a new history of Australia's turn to the United States – a history that rewrites women into international relations and emphasises that Australians looked to America from the first decades of the 20th century. More than just passive recipients of American mass culture, ordinary Australians were active participants in reorienting their nation towards an emergent global superpower.

These days, Australia–US relations is commonly imagined as a story that began in World War II – a male-dominated saga of diplomacy, war and empire. This narrative positions Australia as a pawn in global geopolitical dramas not of our making. It is history from the top down, the record of decisions made in parliaments and boardrooms. But relations between nations are not only wrangled by politicians; they also take place on the ground, in the realm of culture and ideas and everyday encounters between individuals. At this level, the travels and enthusiasms of women like Mary Cecil Allen influenced how one nation imagined and interacted with the other. Before we even had an ambassador in Washington DC, Mary and other modern Australian women were drawing the two societies together via their own ambition, agency and desire.

Why don't we know their names?

Mary Cecil Allen's destination was unusual, but her departure was not. Australia's aspirational settlers had been setting sail since the 19th century. Born on stolen land on the outer rim of the British Empire, the hungry artists, ambitious professionals and social climbers gravitated towards the centre. The expat author Sumner Locke Elliott, who migrated to New York in 1949, captured this mood in *Fairyland* (1990), an autobiographical novel of growing up in interwar Sydney. As the narrator writes, anyone with an ounce of taste or ambition 'intended to shake off the dust of Aussie forever just the minute [they] had the fare'.

For women, there was added incentive to leave. Although Australia's white women were, in 1902, the world's first to get the vote and the right to stand for parliament, formal equality at the ballot box did not dislodge an underlying atmosphere of misogyny and discrimination. In this colonial nation forged in the traumas of convictism and dispossession, on a continent remade by white male violence, the subjugation of women and femininity was baked into settler culture. Women were not elected to federal parliament until 1943. The female basic wage was half the male rate until 1950. Married women were barred from the public service until 1966. In the professions, sexism was rife.

Faced with this hostile environment, departure could appear the best choice. As the historian Ros Pesman puts it in *Duty Free*, 'More constrained at home, women had more reason to flee and more to gain by flight.'

The question was not *if to flee* but *where to go*.

To most, the answer was obvious: London. The mother country, imperial metropole, de facto Home. In 1925, according to *Australian Demography Bulletin*, almost 17 000 Australians sailed to Britain, from a population of only six million. That number rose to 20 000 in 1930 and 30 000 in 1950. As the playwright Doris Hayball put it in *Strawberries in the Jam* (1940), 'all good Australians hope to go to London before they die'.

By contrast, the United States was a little-known quantity. Although Australians were exposed to American popular entertainments like vaudeville from the 19th century, there was comparatively little direct contact between the two nations. In the 1910s and 1920s, most Australians had never even met an American. There was no cable or wireless link between the two countries, no formal diplomatic ties. It was even hard to access American books (unless they were published in Britain) or magazines. Only at the picture palace did US culture occupy central stage. A 1927 Royal Commission found that Hollywood imports made up 90 per cent of films screened in Australian cinemas, which sold 110 million tickets per annum among a population of only six million. As a result, Hollywood did more than anything to shape

Australian images of 'America'. The United States came to be associated with the blonde bombshells, cops and gangsters of the silver screen – a seedy image that fuelled anti-American sentiment.

In this climate, to head to America was to swim against the tide. It was an unlikely destination, a leap into the dark, a black box that drew the rebels and outliers and moderns who wanted to shake things up. '[Americans] are light years ahead of us,' actress and journalist Dorothy Jenner told fellow Australians in her 1975 memoir, *Darlings, I've Had a Ball!*. 'Sometimes on the wrong foot, but more often on the right one.' Dorothy, also known by her pen name 'Andrea', was a journalist and actress who sojourned in the States five times between 1915 and 1967. She was convinced the United States was the future, and only wished that Australia would stop dragging its heels and get with the program. As she wrote of coming home to Sydney in 1925: 'I had changed so completely during those ten years in the United States. Australia seemed to have stood still. It was all steak and eggs and ladies' afternoon tea parties.'

The Australian women who gravitated stateside were those who, like Dorothy, were impatient for the world of tomorrow. They were modern women with little patience for tradition, for doing things as they'd always been done. Long before 'disruption' became a buzzword, these women were progressives with an appetite for the new – whether in the realm of art, entertainment, science, education or simply the perennial question of how to live. They were women frustrated with the limited scope of female endeavour in Australia, and excited by the modern manners and machines of the United States. For those who sought a life beyond the kitchen sink, America seemed a portal into a brave new world – a world in which women could reach their full potential.

Indeed, gender was key here. The ultimate sign of America's modernity? Its emancipated modern women. Time and again, Australians returned home with the news that 'Australia is still very much a man's country when compared with the United States.' In 1923, Sydney journalist Helen Jerome declared the United States a 'matriarchate'. 'Nowhere in the world are men so kind to women, nowhere are women taken so seriously,' she observed. Others called the United States a 'land of matriarchs', a 'woman's paradise', a 'woman's country'.

As late as the 1970s, Sydney writer Kate Jennings found life across the Pacific a welcome reprieve from the 'misogyny' that prevailed at home. 'I shall never forget my early years in New York and finding for the first time that I didn't have to defend my ambitions or be on the defensive or the offensive as a woman,' Jennings wrote.

Viewed with a sober eye, these utopian visions contain a strong dose of fantasy. The United States is still not a woman's country – even affluent white women can't secure equal pay or reproductive rights or access to the Oval Office. A century ago, the idea of the States as a feminist utopia is almost laughable. American women did not gain the right to vote until 1920. True, throughout the early 1900s, they did boast higher rates of tertiary education and professional employment than their Australian (and British) counterparts. There was also more widespread ownership of labour-saving devices like washing machines and refrigerators and vacuums.

But a vacuum cleaner does not equality make. A slightly bigger female minority is still a minority. The United States was better on some measures than Australia – but that says more about the dire situation in Australia than anything paradisiacal about the United States. Moreover, the few opportunities that did exist were largely restricted to affluent white women. Black women, First Nations women, immigrants, rural women and the working class often existed in conditions that better approximated hell than paradise.

But white Australians did not see that sobering reality. They saw things they personally lacked – washing machines and university degrees – and drew sweeping conclusions about freedom and equality. Australians also found emancipation in the United States precisely because it was a long way from home. Away from domestic obligations and familial scrutiny, life would have indeed felt more open – irrespective of the actual conditions on the ground. Their America was an America of adventure and anonymity; a place where they could reinvent themselves. Of course it tasted like freedom; for them, it was freedom.

So, no, the United States was not a fairyland of female emancipation – at least, not for most women. But these cold hard facts are beside the point. The mere impression that American women were living the dream was enough to make their Australian counterparts 'realise what we are missing'. It was a fantasy, no doubt, but one with very real consequences. The story of a 'woman's paradise' across the Pacific took on a life of its own. In some cases, it kindled a feminist politics, prompting Australian women to better see and strain against their constraints back home. More broadly, it fuelled a love affair with the United States, a passionate liaison that changed women's individual lives and the trajectory of Australia.

Travelling to Tomorrow tells the story of Australian women whose aspirations for a larger life led them across the Pacific, and in doing so reoriented Australia towards the United States. The majority returned home – either temporarily or permanently – and they brought back with them new ideas about life and work, and growing doubts about the wisdom of emulating the British model. Perhaps it was the United States that had the most to teach Australia? For the artist Mary Cecil Allen, this meant spreading the word about American abstract expressionism. For the health guru Alice Caporn, it meant evangelising fruit juices and salads. For the swimmer Isabel Letham, it was teaching synchronised swimming. Others imported the latest thinking in dentistry, fashion, music, medicine and more. Less often, Australians facilitated exchange in the opposite direction, spreading antipodean innovations within the United States. Having spun threads between Sydney and San Francisco and New York and Los Angeles by traversing the Pacific, these women later tugged on those threads to bring Australia and America into a tight embrace.

If these women were so remarkable, why don't we already know their stories? In part, it's because Australia is a nation that defines itself through male icons: the Gallipoli digger, the bushranger, the bronzed lifesaver, the cricketer. But this forgetting also stems from the biases of history itself. By and large, we tell histories of nations: Australian history, French history, Indian history. When an individual leaves their homeland to live abroad, they can drop off the historical map. Over in New York, someone like Mary Cecil Allen had left the main arc of Australian history, but – as a foreigner – she wasn't quite part of American history either. She did not neatly belong to either national narrative. Caught between histories, it is easy for someone to fall through the cracks.

In this book, I delve into the cracks between national narratives, and offer a new history of Australia's turn to America through the interwoven lives of transnational Australian women. From my initial cohort of 700, I have chosen to focus on 10 women – a sample whose stories collectively represent broader experiences and themes. In telling this story, I show that the United States was an empire-by-attraction, a global honeypot that seduced white Australian women, selling them a streamlined future easy to get excited about. Above all, this history is a romance, a love story between Uncle Sam and modern women from Down Under, fuelled by a distinctive 20th-century faith in progress and modernity.

These days, that romance has lost its lustre. From the vantage point of 2024 – indeed, from as early as the countercultural 1960s – it's clear the American century was not all it was cracked up to be. It promised progress and affluence, a better life for all. In practice, it was built on colonisation and slavery, and seeded war, violence, environmental destruction, economic inequality and white supremacy. It was sold as a shiny utopia but gave us a planet on fire. It also corrupted those who bought into its agenda. As historian Emma Shortis argues in her 2021 book *Our Exceptional Friend*, Australia's alliance with the United States is 'based on shared whiteness' and infused with 'fear and hatred and death' that 'constrains our morality, our imaginations, and our humanity'.

A bad romance, by any measure.

Yet no matter how illusory, no matter how destructive, the utopian promise of modern America is worth remembering. It may have been a mirage, but it still made history. As we confront the ruins of the American century, we must recall that the United States didn't become a global hegemon through brute force alone. It also attracted foreigners to its shores and sold them the American Dream. At a time when Britain was pummelled by two world wars and cracks emerged in its empire, the United States emerged as a glamorous alternative. It was highways and skyscrapers, washing machines and career women. Bottomless coffee and endless possibility. An idea that won converts in droves. I drank the Kool Aid as late as 2011; countless others had done so before. Mary Cecil Allen was one; Dorothy Jenner was another. There were hundreds – likely thousands – more like them.

Let's peek into their passports.

PART I
ACROSS THE PACIFIC

1
SEEKING FAME AND FORTUNE IN AMERICA
THE LAWYER, LOS ANGELES, 1910

In a classroom stands a woman. She's young, barely 23, and sports a shock of curly red hair. Her milky skin and blue eyes betray Irish heritage, but her voice carries the distinctive intonation of the Antipodes. She's no ill-spoken hick, to be sure; she's trained in elocution and has been giving recitations since girlhood. But still, as soon as she opens her mouth, there's no hiding her Queensland origins. It's become a joke among her fellow students. For months now, they've mocked her habit of saying 'tomarto' instead of 'tomayto' and 'clark' rather than 'clerk'. After her first debate, she was brought to tears by their ridicule.

Today, she must brave the podium once again. She's due to give a speech in front of her fellow students. This morning, before class, she was sick with butterflies, and sought comfort from her elder sister. Ida, six years her senior, is a nurse who can be relied upon to soothe the most agitated nerves.

But now she steels herself to speak. The prescribed topic: The Constitution of Arizona. Arizona, a few hundred miles to the east, just over the Colorado River, is about to become the 48th state of the Union. A place she's never been – a place she'd barely heard of before arriving in this country last year.

Her audience stretches out before her, 56 fellow students, almost all of them men. There are 20 women enrolled in the Law

School, but only one or two in this room. She knows she enjoys a tenuous welcome in this space; she knows she has a lot to prove.

Outside these four walls, it's almost summer. Blue skies and balmy temperatures remind her of home. Down on the sidewalk, where Broadway meets First Street, the clanging streetcars are not so different from the trams she rode as a schoolgirl in Brisbane. The mild air is perfumed with eucalyptus and the faint whiff of salt. It's all so familiar, she can almost forget her parents are 7000 miles away. Back across that great expanse of ocean, on the other side of the Pacific.

But here, inside this university classroom, she's very much the foreigner. Too Australian, too female, too pretty. She needs to silence the naysayers with a knockout performance.

Luckily, performing is something that comes naturally. She's always loved the limelight. Her girlhood ambition was to walk the boards as an actress. At family gatherings, she would hold forth on all sorts of topics, even challenging the men on their views. Like her Irish father, she has the gift of the gab, an effortless charm that often allows her to get away with 'unwomanly' behaviour. Like her father, she colours outside the lines with such aplomb that her transgressions are rapidly forgiven.

She'll have to channel all that charisma to win over this sceptical audience.

She looks down at her notes, takes a breath, and begins.

May Darlington Lahey was the third Lahey sister to try her luck in America. Ida the nurse went first. Ida left Brisbane in February 1906, just shy of her 24th birthday, and three weeks later entered the United States. Two years later, in 1908, Ida was joined by Eva, the middle sister, also aged 24 when she arrived.

Then, in 1910, it was May's turn.

May was the youngest of five surviving Lahey siblings, the precocious baby sister. The redhead with the fine contralto voice. She'd spent her earliest years on Queensland's lush Gold Coast hinterland, a bush girl living among the Yugambeh people on the front line of colonisation. There'd been massacres in the area in the 1850s and 1860s, around the time the Laheys joined the first wave of settlers.

The Lahey clan were Irish migrants who ran a sawmill at Canungra, a tiny dot in the green hills behind the coastline south of Brisbane. May was born in Canungra on 23 May 1888, just in time for the centenary of European invasion. Her middle name was a tribute to the nearby Darlington Range.

A spirited child, May's earliest ambition was to be a 'bullocky' – a bullock team driver. Much to her grandmother's horror, the little girl emulated the bullocky's curses and rough speech. But words, not animals, were May's greatest love. She adored poetry and was a passionate talker. Once, her mother offered May a shilling if she remained silent through dinner; despite her best efforts, May failed to claim the money. Later, she gained some spit and polish as a scholarship girl at the Grammar school in Brisbane, the colonial – and later, state – capital 50 miles to the north. May matriculated in 1906, the same year that Ida left for America.

Four years later, May set sail from Brisbane, aged 22, travelling eastwards on the *Makura* along the All-Red Route, so named because it linked the British dominions (painted red on world maps) of Australia and Canada. The ship stopped at New Zealand, then Fiji and Hawai'i, before docking at Vancouver. It had been winter when May left home in July, but she arrived at the height of a northern summer. The sun didn't set until 10 pm as the *Makura* steamed into the Strait of Georgia. From the ship's deck, May would have seen the fir-covered slopes of Vancouver Island. Once she made landfall in British Columbia, May crossed the land border into the United States and headed south to join her sisters.

The Lahey sisters were reunited. As a Brisbane newspaper put it, all three Misses Lahey had now ventured 'to seek fame and fortune in America'.

Since their arrival in the States several years earlier, Ida and Eva had been on the move. Chicago, North Dakota, Michigan. But after May joined them, they all settled in Los Angeles where they lived with an aunt and uncle – their mother's sister and her husband. The brothers remained in Australia with their parents. The Lahey children were now separated by the Pacific Ocean. When, in 1914, their mother, Emily, joined her daughters in Los Angeles the gender divide was complete.

Why did the Lahey clan cleave in two? The evidence is murky, but it's likely alcohol was a factor. May's father, James, known as Jim, was the larger-than-life black sheep of a big Irish clan, the seventh child of 11. While his brothers built up the family sawmill business, Jim hit the bottle, causing no end of chaos for his wife and offspring. Family historian Shirley Lahey speculates that Jim's drinking drove his daughters – and later his wife – overseas. At a time before no-fault divorce, this was a quasi-respectable means to get away from a difficult man.

Later, when she became famous, May would spin other tales about why she ended up in California – stories that made no mention of a drunk father.

One story involved a chance meeting with a young Herbert Hoover, later elected Republican president of the United States. As a young man, in the 1890s, Hoover worked in mining in the Australian colonies, at a time when May's father was a prospector. May claimed Hoover came to dine at the Lahey family home. Bewitched by this exotic specimen, the first American she'd ever met, May henceforth harboured a desire to see the United States for herself. In one version of the story, May challenged Hoover on his dismissive views of American suffragists and was later horsewhipped for her unladylike behaviour.

An apocryphal story, perhaps. It certainly reads like a Hollywood plot: plucky Queensland girl drawn to the US of A via a fiery encounter with a charismatic future president. Whatever the truth of this tale, May did campaign for Hoover in Los Angeles in 1928, when he was running for President. It's just possible she was helping out a man she'd met as a schoolgirl on Yugambeh Country.

In a third story about May's departure to California, the crucial figure was her uncle William Lindsay, a Canadian who came out to Queensland to work for the Intercolonial Well Boring Company in the 1890s. Lindsay married May's maternal aunt, Sarah Wiley, in Brisbane in 1902. May went for an extended visit at the Lindsay residence in Coolangatta after she matriculated in 1906.

Uncle William was impressed with what he saw. At the dinner table, May spoke her mind and could mount a formidable argument. To his mind, this confident little redhead had all the makings of a successful lawyer. There'd never been a woman lawyer in Queensland, but it was the start of a new century and white women had just won the vote. Surely they would enter the legal profession before long.

In 1907, May's aunt and uncle relocated across the Pacific and, so the story goes, Uncle William wrote to the Laheys with an offer they couldn't refuse. If they sent May out to Los Angeles, he would pay for her tuition at the University of Southern California (USC) Law School. The Law School was new, the first of its kind in Southern California, but already it had a reputation as a progressive institution with a diverse student body. Under the leadership of Dean Frank M Porter, USC Law welcomed women students, as well as Black, Japanese and Filipino Americans.

It seemed the perfect fit for May.

In this story, the Laheys jumped at William's offer and sent May off 'like a package'. Never mind that she had no knowledge of or interest in the law. For all her bold speechifying, May, a dutiful daughter, did what her parents told her.

Which of these stories should we believe? Escaping a drunk father, a childhood encounter with President Hoover, an uncle with big ambitions for his niece – each can explain why May crossed the Pacific in 1910. Perhaps all are partially true; perhaps none is. Perhaps she simply wanted to reunite with her two older sisters.

At any rate, one fact is certain: from that fall, May was enrolled at the University of Southern California Law School.

Los Angeles was still a quiet frontier town on the lands of the Gabrielino/Tongva and Tataviam people. Not yet the slick home of Hollywood, in 1910 it was a smaller and younger sibling to venerable San Francisco, the colonial metropole up the coast that had occupied Ohlone/Costanoan land since the 1770s.

Over the next decade, however, everything changed. In 1910, director DW Griffith made the first film in the city, and soon the US film industry relocated there from New York, drawn by a mild climate that enabled year-round filming. By 1920, Los Angeles was responsible for 85 per cent of US movies and two-thirds of global film production.

With the birth of Hollywood, the city exploded. Los Angeles was remade into a boom town that attracted fortune seekers from around the country and the world. Young women flocked to this western metropolis, fuelled by dreams of movie stardom, or hopes of work in pink-collar industries clustered around the film studios like publicity, fashion and beauty. Hollywood was the world's glamour factory and young girls everywhere wanted in on the action. As a result, by the 1920s, Los Angeles had transformed into a city of women, described by historian Hilary Hallett as an 'urban El Dorado for intrepid female migrants'.

The Lahey sisters were there to see it. They'd arrived at the start of the wave.

At first glance, May could be mistaken for one of these Hollywood aspirants. A fresh-faced young woman, new in town, bursting with charm and ambition, she had all the trappings of a hungry starlet. But her El Dorado was not a Hollywood lot; rather, her energies were channelled into the classrooms of the University of Southern California.

The main USC campus was at University Park, southwest of downtown, but the Law School made its home in the heart of the downtown legal district. From 1911, law students attended classes in the Tajo Building, a five-storey office block on the corner of Broadway and First Street. The US District Court, the US Marshal and the US District Attorney all had offices in the building, as did the Los Angeles Stock Exchange.

In the Tajo Building May learnt the intricacies of the US legal system. She was now a Trojan, the name given to USC students. For her first year, she enrolled in bailments, negligence, agency and domestic relations. Each subject came with an encyclopaedia-size textbook, and she pored over these pages at night.

She needed to burn the midnight oil to prove herself, because the legal world remained a boys' club. Although women had studied and practised law in the United States since the 1870s, they were still only a tiny minority of the profession – less than 2 per cent in 1920. The few women who managed to carve out legal careers battled hostility and discrimination.

Even at USC Law School, a national leader in women's inclusion, students in skirts were a small minority. The first woman had entered the school in 1908, only two years before May arrived. By the time she commenced, there were 20 women law students. In her graduating class, women made up 5 of the 19 students – and they were still addressed as 'mister'.

Nevertheless, this situation was better than in Australia,

where not a single woman worked in the law until Flos Greig was admitted to the Victorian bar in 1905. Women were not even entitled to practise law in New South Wales until 1918. Lahey was the first woman from Queensland to embark on a legal career. Not until 1926, when Katharine McGregor became the first woman admitted to legal practice in the state, did Queensland have a local female lawyer.

From the start, May excelled at her legal studies. Despite the culture shock and gender bias, she was soon the top of her class. At the end of her first year, she scored one mark of 94 per cent. In her second year, she did even better. In addition to several marks in the 90s, she scored one 100 per cent, beating all the men in her cohort.

And the speech on the Constitution of Arizona? May nailed it. When she finished, the teacher offered congratulations. In front of the whole class, May was told she was the standout orator of the group.

Afterwards, she packed up her papers and rushed home to tell her sisters the good news. We can imagine her, tapping down the stairs of the Tajo, plunging out onto the sidewalk, her face flushed with glee. Perhaps she scanned up and down the street, searching for a cable car to carry her home. Perhaps she looked up and felt the sun on her face, savouring her moment of victory. This would be the first of many. May Lahey was on her way.

A hundred years later, in March 2013, I planted my feet at the same intersection. I'd come to Broadway and First to visit the Los Angeles Law Library as part of my quest to uncover May's life. I'd been corresponding with a librarian, who'd promised to plumb the institution's holdings for traces of the red-headed Queenslander. Now I was here to view the evidence.

That semester, I was living in Washington DC, but had flown over to California on a budget redeye for a fortnight of research. After an interminable east coast winter, a trudge through frigid grey days, I shrugged off my puffer jacket and bared my limbs to the air. I strolled beneath palm trees and remembered what it was like to squint into the sun. Los Angeles was more akin to Sydney than the snow-dusted city I'd left on the other side of the country. My body uncoiled, awash with the familiar. It was easy to imagine how a Queenslander like May would feel at home.

Now, after catching the bus downtown, I stood outside the Law Library, daunted by the squat modernist building stuffed with papers covered in impenetrable legalese. I didn't realise it then, but the library occupied the very same site as the Tajo Building where May had learnt her trade a century earlier. After serving as the base for USC Law from 1911 to 1925, the Tajo was demolished in the late 1930s when First Street was widened. In the early 1950s, the Law Library was built on the same intersection. In 2013, as I sifted through fragments of May's life, I occupied the exact patch of earth where her foreign vowels attracted mockery from her fellow students.

Los Angeles of 2013 was unrecognisable from the city May made home. By the 21st century, the city was an unwieldy megalopolis, strangled by highways and shrouded by smog. Downtown was a rundown area only gradually emerging from a long decline, after decades of white flight to the suburbs.

When May arrived, downtown was still a stranger to crowds and pollution. Although it would soon become 'the first great metropolis of the twentieth century', Los Angeles had yet to acquire the metropolitan buzz of Chicago or New York. As historian Hilary Hallett puts it in *Go West!*, the city in 1910 was a 'dusty backwater'.

Yet scale is always relative. A backwater for the United States could still be the big smoke for someone from Australia. For the Lahey sisters, fresh from sleepy Brisbane and even sleepier Canungra, the 1910 version of Los Angeles was a modern marvel. Automobiles sped along miles and miles of fully asphalted roads. The city was dotted with public parks and gardens. Especially exciting were the public libraries, where the latest books and magazines could be borrowed for free.

'What wonderful people Americans are – so progressive!' May's sister Ida reported back home.

Most thrilling of all was the cinema. Although motion pictures had screened in Australia since 1896, the medium was not yet an entrenched part of the local leisure scene. In the young Commonwealth in 1910, most cinemas were still open-air or tent operations, flimsy set-ups exposed to the weather, with dubious respectability.

Over in Los Angeles, by contrast, cinema going was a weekly ritual. Every Saturday afternoon, the Lahey sisters visited a picture palace. They would watch a 90-minute show, sometimes two. In terms of venues, they were spoiled for choice. One option was the Glendale Theatre, a cinema on East Broadway that opened around 1910 to entertain the public with 'moving pictures' and 'illustrated songs'. Another possibility was Tally's, a cinema on Broadway between Eighth and Ninth, a two-storey brick edifice erected in only 30 days in April 1910. Tally's boasted a live orchestra and seated up to 900 patrons. After watching a moving picture, the Laheys could've gone window-shopping at the nearby Hamburger's Department Store.

But such delights were for the weekend. During the week, while May attended law classes downtown, Ida and Eva also kept busy. Unusually for white women of their class, all three Lahey sisters pursued skilled work outside the home. Ida was studying nursing and in 1912 won a prize for the most proficient nurse in her year. Eva, the middle sister, served as secretary to Professor Henry Bolley, an eminent botanist. Yet while all three Laheys were modern career women, May was the star who would remake expectations of what women could do and be.

Once she'd found her feet at Law School, there was no holding May back. In 1912, she was invited to join the world's first legal sorority. Founded at USC in 1911, Phi Delta Delta was a professional organisation for legal women. The following year, May was vice-president. Still in her 20s, she had a bent for leadership. She may have been young and feminine, the kind of woman usually dismissed as merely decorative, but when May spoke people listened. That Irish gift of the gab had its uses.

The year 1913 was also momentous for another reason: May took out American citizenship. After only three years in the United States, and with the bulk of her family still in Queensland, the erstwhile Australian was willing to declare she was gone for good. This change of citizenship may have been a pragmatic decision to aid her legal career. But it can also be interpreted as a vote of confidence in the life on offer to women in a California on the rise. Here in the Los Angeles of early Hollywood, May could carve out a life and career that was frankly unimaginable in Brisbane. The thrills were bigger, the opportunities greater, the horizons wider.

Though not in every respect.

On one front, May lost rights when she switched citizenship. As a female citizen of the United States, she didn't have the right to vote or stand for parliament. The franchise in America was still a male prerogative, and it would be another seven years before women could cast their ballots. In the 1910s, Australia was the toast of the world when it came to women's rights. As historians Clare Wright and Marilyn Lake have shown, American suffragists looked in envy at the political rights boasted by their white

Australian sisters. Even though Los Angeles was fast becoming the headquarters of modern life, in this respect it trailed Australia.

May had deemed it worthwhile to disenfranchise herself to gain the benefits of US citizenship. This must have been a difficult decision. Yet May's ability to make this hard choice was itself a privilege that few could then enjoy. In the first decades of the 20th century, only women understood as 'white' could even imagine freedoms like casting a ballot or moving across borders with ease.

In Australia, whiteness defined the limits of the citizenship. The same legislation that gave the Lahey sisters the franchise had disenfranchised First Nations women. Meanwhile, women of colour were excluded from the nation altogether under the *Immigration Restriction Act 1901* that formed the backbone of the White Australia policy. Whiteness was also a currency that allowed Australians to find welcome in the United States. At this point, both Australia and the United States imagined themselves as 'white man's countries' that needed to band together to protect the 'white race' against the 'rising tide of colour'. In this context, white Australians like May were ideal immigrants, imagined as close kin or 'blood brothers' to the much-fetishised white American of 'British stock'.

Other foreigners, however, were increasingly unwelcome. The United States had banned most Chinese migrants in 1882, and in 1917 would create an 'Asiatic Exclusion Zone' that locked the door to much of Asia. Soon after, even southern and eastern Europeans were deemed 'undesirable' migrants, not white enough to make the cut. In the supposed 'land of liberty', belonging was contingent upon race.

This context ensured May was at home in California. Thanks to her whiteness, this fresh-off-the-boat Queenslander would enjoy greater welcome in Los Angeles than a Chinese woman whose family had lived in California for generations. US citizen or not, May 'belonged' from the moment of arrival. The formal citizenship papers were just the icing on the cake, the addendum to a racial citizenship she'd enjoyed from birth.

Twelve months after becoming an American citizen, May graduated from USC Law at the top of her class. She was now a fully-fledged attorney.

June 1914. In the last months of peace before World War I tore up Europe, May was admitted to practise. The first Queensland-born woman lawyer, and still one of only a handful in California.

She'd made it into the boys' club of the legal profession, but how far would the boys allow her to rise? For even in modern California, even for a well-heeled white woman, the fight for equality was only just beginning. Being teased about her accent was nothing compared to the challenges awaiting ahead.

2
THE VOCATION OF GLAMOUR

THE DECORATOR, NEW YORK CITY, 1917

There were few better people to lunch with. If you wanted to be someone in New York City, Frank Crowninshield was the man to make it happen. As the editor of *Vanity Fair*, Crowninshield – known as Crownie – was an urbane taste maker, an 'old New Yorker' renowned for nurturing young talent. Over the past three years, he'd transformed *Vanity Fair* from an obscure fashion magazine into a hotbed of modern literature and art. Dorothy Porter, F Scott Fitzgerald, TS Eliot, Gertrude Stein, Matisse and Picasso were just some of the luminaries to grace his pages.

One day in spring 1917, the season the United States entered the Great War, Crownie's date for lunch at the Plaza Hotel was a striking young woman impatient to be discovered. Fresh off the boat from Sydney, she'd been hobnobbing with literary types at the Algonquin Hotel and helping fundraise for the war effort. But she was fast growing weary of socialising and good works, and now wanted some kind of career.

Her sister Dorothy, a rising star of the silver screen, had suggested that the *Vanity Fair* editor might offer some advice. Ever the networker, this young Australian leapt at the chance to seek guidance from the great man. Whatever happened next, it couldn't hurt to be seen with Crownie at the Plaza, New York's most fashionable venue.

Down in the Plaza's Grill Room, men in uniform ordered champagne and steak. Just a few weeks earlier, the German ambassador Count von Bernstorff had been a guest of the Fifth Avenue hotel. Now, it was full of soldiers preparing to fight the Germans in Europe. The kitchen was still serving its full opulent menu despite rumours that restrictions and rationing were around the corner.

Amid the lunch rush, Crownie and the young Australian settled at their table for two. Over a meal, she explained her predicament. She was at a loose end, she needed some purpose. What on earth should she do with herself?

What happened next became the stuff of legend, a story retold so often that it assumed a mythic quality. It is likely embellished, perhaps entirely apocryphal, but that's almost beside the point. The story of this encounter took on a life of its own.

'Well, what would you like to do?' Crownie asked.

'I'm perfectly useless. I don't know how to do anything,' the woman replied in her elocution-trained voice. Like most Australian girls of her class and generation, she'd been raised to speak like a proper Englishwoman.

Crownie took the young woman's measure. She was undeniably fascinating, a full-figured beauty with dramatic eyebrows and a generous mouth, an exotic arriviste from the Antipodes who injected sparkle into every space she entered. Raw yet chic, with a brazen quality that evoked a wild colonial youth. The editor's sixth sense for talent picked up a whiff of something special. After a moment or two, he proffered a suggestion.

'Well, perhaps you would like to become a decorator?'

It was a shrewd idea. Decorating was fast becoming a fashionable profession for young women, popularised in the early 1900s by actress Elsie de Wolfe and novelist Edith Wharton. In 1906, the New York School of Art (now Parsons) established the nation's first department of interior decoration. By April 1917, just as

Crownie and the Australian sat down to lunch, the magazine *House & Garden* had published its first 'Interior Decoration' issue. Decorating was the talk of the town.

In response to Crownie's suggestion, however, the woman only frowned. Decorating? She'd never heard of such a thing. There were no decorators back in Sydney. There were only upholsterers who secured fabrics to furniture.

'Perhaps I would like to be a decorator,' she answered, 'but first tell me what it is?'

And just like that, one of the most iconic decorators of the 20th century found her vocation.

Rose Cumming played the role of colonial ingenue, but she was cannier than she looked. Behind her famed decolletage and beguiling smile was a woman of no small ambition, whose protestations need to be taken with a grain of salt. 'She was like Coco Chanel – a self-invented character,' a colleague later observed. In the work of art that was her life, Rose never let the truth get in the way of a good story.

Of her many inventions, the most flagrant was her age. Upon arrival in New York in December 1916, Rose announced herself as a girl of 20. By her own account, she was a veritable debutante, a provincial lass unformed by the world. But that was a convenient fiction. According to her birth certificate, Rose's true age was well past 30. Born into a New South Wales landholding family in 1884, she'd been navigating the social whirl of Edwardian Sydney for nigh on 15 years. By 1916, Rose was an old hand at flirtation, had broken more than her fair share of hearts, and notched up visits to New Zealand, England and Ceylon. Now she was ready to conquer New York.

Rose told everyone she'd ended up in New York by accident. She had a fiancé in London, she explained, and was travelling to meet him via the United States. She sailed from Sydney on the *Niagara* on 23 November 1916, travelling northeast across the Pacific, with the idea to traverse North America before sailing on to England. In Manhattan, however, Rose discovered that civilian transatlantic travel was suspended by the war. Stranded, she lingered in New York, without purpose or occupation. Eventually, the fiancé became impatient and broke off the engagement. And Frank Crowninshield stepped in to offer Rose career advice.

This was the official Rose Cumming origin story. A colonial lass thwarted in love by a world war, washed up in New York like a piece of flotsam carried by the tides. But just like her purported youthfulness, the London fiancé was likely a romantic fiction. He is never named, was little mourned, and makes no appearance in her personal archive. Rose kept letters from countless beaux, but there is no London fiancé among her many lovelorn correspondents. Did he exist, or was he a convenient invention to legitimate a most unwomanly wanderlust?

An alternative explanation for Rose's arrival in New York is her sister. Dorothy was the youngest of the Cumming siblings, but the first to find fame and fortune. Born in 1894, a decade after Rose, Dorothy was an actress already making waves in the United States. After signing with theatrical impresario JC Williamson in 1911, aged only 17, Dorothy toured Australia and New Zealand, before making her screen debut in *Within Our Gates* – a 1915 silent film about the Gallipoli campaign. By July 1916, Dorothy embarked on the well-worn path of JC Williamson starlets: like her better-known contemporary Judith Anderson, she left Sydney to try her luck in America. In the early 1900s, Williamson's eponymous firm dominated the Australian stage, but the man behind the brand was an American who maintained strong links with the

United States. As historian Desley Deacon has documented, his transpacific networks helped innumerable Australian thespians break into the American industry.

Within months, Dorothy had been joined in New York by her big sister Rose. Had Rose been lured across the Pacific by Dorothy's reports of glamour and excitement in the big smoke? The sisters were reportedly 'wild to get away' from wartime Australia, as they 'felt so bottled up there'. With Dorothy already in New York, it would have been easy for Rose to make the leap. At any rate, Rose arrived in New York in December 1916 and, fiancé or no fiancé, she never left.

Following their lunch, Crowninshield introduced Rose to decorator Mary Buel, who hired the Australian as her assistant. Soon after, Rose moved on to the department store Wanamaker's, a temple to style that occupied a full city block at 770 Broadway. Since opening in 1896, during the golden age of department stores, the store had become one of the city's top shopping landmarks. Rose joined the staff of Au Quatrième, Wanamaker's dedicated decorating service – the first of its kind in the United States. Thanks to Crowninshield's patronage, Rose was apprenticed to the best in the business.

Although untrained in art or design, Rose had an immediate knack for decorating work and soon realised decoration was her 'greatest love'. Men would come and go, but curating beautiful spaces was her one constant. Born with a romantic sensibility, Rose had strong opinions and an eye for beauty. That, in her opinion, was the essential prerequisite for being a decorator. 'Either you have flair or you haven't', she was wont to remark. Rose most definitely had it.

To her mind, this flair stemmed from childhood. Rose's father,

Victor Cumming, was the proprietor of Narrangullen Station, a 10 000-acre sheep run on Ngunnawal Country, 20 miles from Yass. The property's homestead was stuffed with 18th-century furniture, a collection acquired from the departing governor of New South Wales just prior to Rose's birth. As a result, Rose grew up surrounded by fine antiques. 'When I was a girl, I dwelt in beauty', she wrote. 'There wasn't a single object in the house that wasn't an antique or a lovely old possession.'

Rose was the eldest of three girls. Dorothy, the actress, was the youngest. The middle child Eileen was born in 1890. Eileen was the steady ballast that grounded Rose and Dorothy, two more-riotous souls. Their father, Victor, was a gambler, and family finances were erratic, but in general the Cumming girls enjoyed a charmed youth in the upper echelons of colonial society. Alongside Narrangullen, the family also occupied Hurstville, a Goulburn mansion built in the 1860s by Methodist minister Reverend Hurst. Later, the girls attended Sydney's elite Ascham School, then located in Darling Point.

Despite their age difference, the three sisters roamed early 1900s Sydney as a tight trio. The family photograph album resembles a series of stills from *Picnic at Hanging Rock* or *My Brilliant Career*. Picnics, amateur theatricals, outings to the beach, balls at the Town Hall. Young girls in virginal white dresses and oversized hats. All was gaiety and youthful exuberance. This was the wilfully innocent Australia of the Federation moment, a sun-drenched new nation drunk on its own potential, a land of 'better Britons' committed to the conceit of *terra nullius*. If you believe the jolly photographs, nothing bad had ever happened here.

After their close-knit childhood, the Cumming girls could not bear to be apart for long. By 1918, Eileen and their mother, Sarah, had joined Rose and Dorothy in New York. Victor, the patriarch, soon followed. From 1920, he divided his time between New York and the south of France.

Having launched Rose as a decorator, Frank Crowninshield also took an interest in Eileen and set her up with a job as decorating editor at *Vogue* magazine. *Vogue*, like Crowninshield's *Vanity Fair*, was part of the Condé Nast stable, and the Cumming sisters moved in the same social orbit as Nast himself. Later, Eileen worked as advertising director at Franklin Simon, a New York department store chain, before being recruited by Saks. When the new Saks flagship opened at 611 Fifth Avenue in 1924, Eileen was hired as advertising and fashion director. There, she helped establish the department store as a byword for taste and elegance.

Dorothy, meanwhile, made strides in the film industry. After several stage roles in New York, she made her North American film debut in *Snow White* (1916), in which the gamine starlet Marguerite Clark played the titular role. During 1917, Dorothy toured the United States and Australia as the female lead in *Grumpy*, a hit stage comedy starring English actor Cyril Maude. After the tour, Dorothy settled into cinema work.

By this time, the United States film industry had migrated from New York to Hollywood. Over in California, where May Lahey was embarking on a legal career, Dorothy was one of several Australian actresses who carved out steady film work in the 1910s and 1920s. The first was Lilie Leslie, a veteran of the Sydney stage, who claimed the title of Australia's first US film star when she appeared in *The Third Degree* in 1913.

In the following years, it became a rite of passage for Australian thespians to try their luck in Hollywood. The success stories accumulated: Enid Bennett, Sylvia Bremer, Helen Holmes – all silent screen stars in the 1910s. The most successful was Louise Lovely, a Sydney actress who arrived in California in December 1914, aged 19. Louise was contracted to Universal Studios and was soon one of the highest paid actors in Hollywood. Transformed into a pin-up with peroxided blonde ringlets, she became a household name around the United States.

Although never a fully-fledged star like Lovely, Dorothy Cumming also became a familiar face on the silent screen. In 1920, she appeared in six films and accrued 39 film credits across a short but prolific career. Too tall and striking to be a girlish starlet in the vein of 'America's Sweetheart', Mary Pickford, she was cast in supporting roles as the 'bad woman' or 'vamp'. In 1922, Dorothy married fellow actor Frank Elliott, and soon had two children.

As a trio of foreign career women, all beautiful and charming, the Cumming sisters made quite an impression in New York. Thanks to Dorothy's film industry contacts, the three were soon a fixture in high society. They summered in the Hamptons, on the east end of Long Island, Shinnecock and Montaukett land that from the 1870s had developed into a holiday playground for New York's movers and shakers. Later, Rose and Dorothy purchased their own residence on Southampton's South Main Street, an 18th-century weatherboard cottage known as Green Shutters. Rose, of course, took charge of the decoration.

Although the Cumming sisters were hailed as a novelty, they were in fact doing something quite commonplace: living abroad as a sibling group. When unmarried Australian women travelled abroad in the first decades of the 20th century, they frequently did so with a sister or two as companion/s. The examples are legion. There was lawyer May Lahey and her two sisters; the 1930s film star Mary Maguire and her sisters Patricia and Joan; and Constance and Gwyneth Little, Australian-born sisters who, from 1938, co-authored detective fiction from their homes in New Jersey. Then there was Rachel, Edith and David Grieve – a Melbourne-born trio who together migrated to Detroit in the early 1920s, where Edith worked as an illustrator, Rachel as a weaver, and David as a jeweller and metalworker.

The appeal of sibling travel is not hard to understand. In the early 20th century, travelling solo was still beset by moral hazards for middle-class white women, and existed in a grey zone of dubious respectability. Ideally, a family member or friend would act as a chaperone. A sister offered the ideal balance of propriety and freedom. She offered real and symbolic fortification against the insults of the world but was also an equal of sorts, with limited authority to censure or command. When accompanied by a parent or husband, a young woman could be bound by convention to subordinate her own desires; with a sister, the door was open to greater autonomy.

For the Cumming sisters, it was not enough to travel together; they also worked in aligned fields. As the war ended and the Jazz Age began, the sibling trio found themselves working in a family business: the business of glamour. Rose was in decorating, Eileen in magazines and marketing, and Dorothy was in the movies, but each was part of a broader rise in pink-collar industries that commoditised the newfound emphasis on visual spectacle and women's physical appearance. Fashion, beauty, design, cosmetics – all were new frontiers in consumer capitalism that responded to a Hollywood-fuelled impetus to craft an alluring spectacle of the self. As historian Hilary Hallett writes, these were feminised industries 'made more romantic by Hollywood's reflected glow', a new arena for women to carve out careers for themselves.

By working in these glamour industries, Rose and her sisters marked themselves out as quintessential creatures of the modern age. The jolly Edwardian girls of the Sydney years were no longer; the Cumming sisters were chic and modern now. They were also part of a global influx of labour to the new creative industries headquartered in the United States. Although hardly prototypical 'workers', Rose and her sisters were nonetheless participants in a process of female labour migration that fuelled new frontiers of culture and economic life.

By 1921, Rose was somebody in New York. In April, her work was featured in *Vogue*, part of a wedding design spread shot by celebrity photographer Adolph de Meyer. Around the same time, her friend Nellie Leach, visiting from Sydney, reported that 'Miss Rose Cumming is considered one of the smartest interior decorators in New York.' According to Nellie, Rose was 'absolutely' part of the Four Hundred – a term, dating from the 1890s, used to describe the upper echelons of New York society.

It was time to strike out on her own. That year, Rose opened her own decoration boutique on Madison Avenue, constructing a treasure trove based around her signature style of vivid colour and camp excess. Rose detested the clean lines and austerity of modernist design; she preferred curves and whimsy and drama. The 18th century was her aesthetic home. Blues and purples were her preferred palate; browns were anathema. The result was an eccentric melange of contrasting styles that somehow came together into a glamorous whole. Good lighting was essential to set off the ensemble. Rose preferred the romance of candlelight to the harsh glare of a naked bulb. However, while she was dubious of electricity, she did use electric lights to illuminate her shop windows overnight, an innovation at the time. When most shopfronts went dark, Rose Cumming's glowing windows became famous as a New York destination for evening flâneurs to marvel over.

How did Rose obtain the capital to set up this business? By her own telling, Dorothy, flush from working in Hollywood, lent her the money. Other documents in the Cumming archive suggest Eileen provided the necessary funds. Given their close bond, it's credible that either or both sisters would help Rose get on her feet. A third possibility is a much-disputed tale concerning Otto Kahn, a banker and patron of the arts, colloquially known as 'the King of New York'. Kahn was, rumour had it, Rose Cumming's long-term lover and the financial backer of her decorating enterprise. According to some sources, their relationship was an open secret in

New York society. Mark Hampton wrote in *Legendary Decorators of the Twentieth Century*, Rose was 'the mistress of a titanically rich financier whose largesse kept her in business'.

Eileen Cumming, however, denied the liaison. After the *New York Times* referenced the affair in a 1979 article, Eileen wrote an outraged letter to the editor. 'Rose Cumming never even met Mr Kahn,' she insisted. By her account, Rose did some decorating work for Kahn's wife, who sent flowers in thanks. Rose told visitors the opulent bouquets came from the 'Kahn greenhouses' – sparking unfounded rumours she was romantically involved with Otto. But that, Eileen emphasised, was the full extent of Rose's contact with the family. A 1988 biography of Kahn takes a similar line, concluding that Rose and Otto had no connection.

Yet it's doubtful the pair were strangers. Kahn was a close friend of Frank Crowninshield and media mogul Condé Nast, both of whom socialised with Rose and Eileen. As a prominent arts patron, it would be natural for Kahn to take an interest in these young creatives. If Rose truly was part of the Four Hundred, then she and Kahn would have been in the same social orbit. Moreover, in 1926, Kahn visited the set of *King of Kings*, a film starring Dorothy Cumming, and almost certainly met the actress that day. At some point, then, Rose and Kahn surely crossed paths. If anything happened beyond a mere meeting, it's impossible to say. Rose was not averse to extramarital liaisons. Although she remained unmarried, the decorator was a prodigious flirt who adored men and took lovers during the 1920s and beyond. Kahn may have been one of them, or not.

Whatever the truth of the matter, Rose did well for herself. She was an artist who had found her métier, a bohemian creative spirit who – through a mix of luck, privilege, and ingenuity – had built the kind of life almost unthinkable for an Australian girl born in the backblocks in 1884. She was mistress of her own household, answered to no one, made her own money, lived and breathed creativity, and took lovers to boot. Not a husband or a baby or a stove in sight. No wonder that, even as the war ended and travel resumed, Rose showed no inclination to move on from New York. At any rate, she was too busy: the Jazz Age was beginning, money was flowing, and Hollywood had come knocking. The new breed of screen stars needed luxe interiors, and Rose was the woman for the job.

3

FRESHWATER MERMAID DOES HOLLYWOOD

THE SWIMMER, HONOLULU, 1918

Isabel stepped off the gangplank, clutching her towel and bathers. The *Niagara* would only be in Honolulu for the day; there was no time to waste. She was determined to taste those famed waves – the ones Duke had raved about.

Down on the dock, a reporter rushed forward.

'Miss Letham! Miss Letham!'

He announced himself as Mike Jay from the *Honolulu Star-Bulletin*. Could Australia's famous surfboard rider spare a moment?

She could. A taxi was booked to drive her down to Waikiki, but until it arrived, she was happy to talk to the press. Who knew, a Hawai'i news clipping might come in handy in Hollywood, help get her foot in the door.

Isabel smiled at the reporter, turning on the charm.

'Yes, this is my first visit here and I'm just dying to get into this bathing suit and have a plunge at Waikiki.'

The reporter ran his eyes along Isabel's person. The young Australian was dressed all in white: ankle-length dress, light coat, gloves, low heels and stockings, topped with a cylindrical hat. Tall for a woman, she had an athletic build that commanded attention. Beneath the hat's brim was a guileless oval face, with round cheeks and a mouth built for laughing.

Mike Jay liked what he saw. He declared her the prettiest swimmer to come out of Australia. Isabel smiled even harder. She was 19 and didn't mind a bit of flirtation.

'I guess I'm going to have a harder job of it in your waves here,' she continued. 'Our waves are long rolling combers but these are short snappy breakers.'

The taxi was pulling in, time to wrap things up.

Yes, she was headed for New York; yes, she hoped to crack into the movies; yes, she planned to stay in America at least six months.

With that, Isabel ducked into the taxi, leaving a smitten reporter in her wake.

Down at Waikiki, Duke's board would be waiting for her. He'd promised. Duke himself was away on the mainland; they'd missed each other due to rotten timing, but at least she could ride his board on the beach where he learnt to surf.

Almost four years earlier, in January 1915, Duke Kahanamoku had lifted Isabel onto his longboard at Sydney's Freshwater Beach and transformed her into a surfer. Kahanamoku was a native Hawai'ian, nine years her senior, and one of the world's top swimmers. He swam for the United States at the 1912 Olympics, winning gold in the 100 metre freestyle. In the summer spanning 1914 and 1915, Duke toured Australia to test his swimming skills against local talent, but it was his surfing prowess that really got the punters excited.

Back then, barely anyone in Sydney had encountered a surfboard. At that point, even taking a dip was a novelty; only several years earlier, public bathing was illegal. In 1915, there were only a handful of surfboards around – souvenirs from Hawai'i, where the sport was invented. Most beachgoers, Isabel included, entertained themselves with surf shooting (later known as body surfing) – the fine art of throwing their bodies into the waves. Every summer, she'd spend long days at Freshwater Beach, down the road from her family home.

When Duke plucked her out of the beachside crowd, and she surfed in his muscled arms before hundreds of spectators, Isabel was hailed the 'Freshwater mermaid'. The pair were a sensation. Overnight, she went from ordinary schoolgirl to 'surf queen'. She got used to reporters' questions and the flash of cameras. That's when Isabel acquired a taste for celebrity. That's when she got serious about saving for America.

Down at Waikiki, Duke's board was there as promised, but there were no decent waves to be seen. The water was flat as a pancake. Isabel paddled out and waited, hoping the breakers would pick up.

Hours later, when she finally paddled back in, defeated by the calm swell, there was a familiar figure on the shore.

It was that reporter again, Mike Jay from the *Honolulu Star-Bulletin*. This time he'd brought a photographer to snap a few pics for the paper.

She posed standing in front of the board, still in her bathers and swimming cap, squinting into the sun, with Duke's name emblazoned on the wood above her head.

Jay peppered her with questions, trying to prolong their encounter. What did she think of Honolulu? Why had she come to America?

'If Honolulu is a sample of America, I am going to like America. My, I do admire the Americans,' Isabel said agreeably.

'While we Australians talk and talk and talk about what we are going to do, you Americans talk and do things. That's what I love about the Americans.'

Ever since that Freshwater summer with Duke, Isabel knew America was the place for her. The Hawai'ian didn't inspire her American dreams – Hollywood had already done that – but meeting real Americans made the dream seem possible. Now, she was determined to make a go of life across the Pacific. Even though the *Niagara* was still days away from the mainland, she was already considering US citizenship.

'You know you Americans are awful boasters,' Isabel continued. 'You boast you can do the impossible, and then you go out and do it. That's what makes you such wonderful people.'

By now Isabel and Jay were getting along famously. She sparkled with energy, and he couldn't take his eyes off what he called her 'pretty face' and 'well proportioned' figure. Her ship was leaving that same day, but could he write to her? Why, sure, Isabel replied, thinking nothing of it. The day was getting away, and she still needed to visit Diamond Head (or Lēʻahi) and the Nuʻuanu Pali lookout. It was only later, when Jay's epistles kept finding her, that she realised he was serious. But Isabel wasn't interested; she had bigger fish to fry.

In her interview with Mike Jay, Isabel recognised something important: Hawaiʻi was part of the United States. She was still in the Pacific, 2500 miles from California, but in one sense she'd already reached her destination.

Hawaiʻi did not become the 50th state of the union until 1959, but the islands had been annexed by the United States in 1898. The former Polynesian Kingdom was now a US territory, a westward extension of the American colonial state. By 1918, when Isabel passed through, locals were US citizens and conducted commerce with dollar bills. US immigration monitored arrivals. For all intents and purposes, Waikiki was American soil.

Yet it also remained part of the Pacific, home to a large Polynesian and Asian population. In the 1910s, the islands were being developed into a modern tourist playground for affluent white travellers. Hawaiʻi was styled as an archetypal Pacific paradise, rich in swaying palm trees, inviting beaches and tropical flowers. When steamers like the *Niagara* came into port, native Hawai'ians were rolled out to titillate the passengers by handing out leis and singing welcome songs in grass skirts. It was Polynesia served up as primitive spectacle, submitting itself to the white gaze, a ritual that allowed travellers like Isabel to re-enact European imperial conquest of the Pacific.

Hawai'i hence had a dual identity: it was part of the 'primitive' Pacific and also belonged to the modern 'white man's country' of the United States. This hybridity was unsettling. Given its geographic location, Hawai'i typically represented Australians' first encounter with the United States, but it also challenged much of what they'd been taught about America. Americans were imagined as white settlers like themselves; how could a native Hawai'ian or Japanese businessman claim this identity? And if America was populated by people of colour, did this mean that the United States was not kin to White Australia after all?

After her day in Waikiki, Isabel returned to her first-class cabin on the *Niagara*, the 'queen of the Pacific'. Although war was still raging in Europe, the steamer was packed, with 559 passengers on board. They did lifeboat drills each day and kept the lights off at night. Several days later, the *Niagara* docked in British Columbia. Isabel travelled south to San Francisco, then boarded a train to visit a former teacher now living in New York City. Upon arrival, Isabel took a taxi to the exclusive Vanderbilt Hotel. No frugal boarding house for her; she was already acting like the movie star she planned to be.

For the next few months, Isabel partied hard. By day, she did good works. Much like Rose Cumming, the swimmer did her bit for the war effort, volunteering with the Red Cross. The nights were reserved for pleasure. In November, the city celebrated the end of the Great War. At a Manhattan nightclub, Isabel toasted peace in Europe with a crowd of Russian nobles who'd escaped the Bolsheviks. The men kissed her hands; the women wore fur stoles. One lent her a sable throw. It was heady stuff. Only months earlier she'd been kicking a football with local boys on the sands of Freshwater, now here she was living it up at the Waldorf Astoria.

Hanging out with Russian aristocrats in New York was an expensive pastime, and the young Australian soon blew through her savings. When the well ran dry, she left the Vanderbilt and moved into cheap digs on 118th Street. More than once, she cabled home for extra money. Yet she refused to stop enjoying herself. Isabel was living for the moment, spending like a rich kid born into a luxury dacha.

At 19, Isabel had not yet reached her majority, but already knew her own mind. Even before her encounter with Kahanamoku, she'd set her sights on an American career, later recalling, 'when I was 14 I'd made up my mind I was going to America'. Hollywood was taking off and Isabel planned to leverage her athletic skills to find work as a stunt woman. She could surf, swim and dive like a pro; surely the studios could use her.

Then as now, countless Australians dreamed of Hollywood. After an afternoon at the picture palace, it was tempting to indulge in fantasies of a glamorous career on the silver screen. Film magazines traded in stories of unknown girls who became overnight stars, a genre that fuelled the fantasy that stardom was just over the horizon. In 1919, Sydney's *Picture Palace* magazine published a photomontage titled 'Australian Girls Who Some Day May Be Stars'. A flock of posed faces covered the page, everyone one of them a putative screen heroine.

It was one thing to dream; it was quite another to get to California. Fortunately, Isabel was the kind of person who rose to a challenge. When she wanted something, she went after it, obstacles be damned. She'd already won a battle of wills against her father. William Letham was a serious Scotsman who'd initially opposed Isabel's surfing, deeming it inappropriate for a respectable young lady. But Isabel refused to be reined in. She simply kept surfing, no matter what anyone said. Faced with this rebellion, William buckled, even building her a surfboard. From that point onwards, he realised there was little point laying down the law. Within reason, Isabel was allowed to have her head.

She'd inherited this rebellious streak from her mother, Jeanie, a campaigner for women's rights and friends with Sydney feminists like Rose Scott. From an early age, Isabel was exposed to the idea that women could be more than helpmeets to men. By her teen years, she was a living embodiment of the emancipated woman. Convention did not daunt her, and independence was her middle name. 'I'd been brought up to stand on my own two feet, at a very early age,' Isabel explained. 'I never deviated from this.'

She'd need all this chutzpah to get herself to Hollywood. But if Louise Lovely and Dorothy Cumming had done it, why couldn't Isabel? They were from the same city, only a few years apart in age. Isabel had proven charisma, could do stunts, loved the camera. There seemed no reason she couldn't replicate their success.

First, Isabel had to get to California. The Lethams were comfortable but not rich. William, a builder, could afford to give his daughter a private-school education, but not to fund a harebrained scheme to crack into a new industry on the other side of the world. So Isabel went to work. She left school at 15 and became sports mistress at Kambala, a prestigious girls' school in Rose Bay. She also worked as a private swimming instructor, teaching local children. When not working, she was riding the waves at Freshwater or aquaplaning (an early form of waterskiing) in Sydney Harbour. By August 1918, she'd saved enough for a transpacific fare. She had no real plans, few contacts, little money; just a big dream and an appetite for adventure.

These days, Isabel Letham is remembered as one of the first Australian women to surf. When her name is mentioned, it's usually in reference to her famous encounter with Duke Kahanamoku in 1915. She's the girl who braved the waves at Freshwater, forebear to champions like Layne Beachley and Pam Burridge. When Burridge started her career in the 1970s, Isabel was a hero to younger women surfers, a founding patron of the Australian Women Board Riders Association. Later, she was inducted into the Australian Surfing Hall of Fame. Burridge even named her daughter after Isabel. She's the storied matriarch of women's surfing; the Freshwater girl who could.

None of this is a lie. It's all true history, an important chapter in the story of surfing on this continent. It's just that what Isabel did next – cross the ocean alone at 19 – is arguably even more remarkable, yet that part of her story gets forgotten. Her surfing was daring, to be sure, but it was engineered by a man. Kahanamoku chose her, taught her, made her famous. Going to America, by contrast – that was all Isabel. She concocted that plan; she made it happen. She chose to leave behind everything she knew, during a global war, to pursue a pipe dream, at a time when girls like her were supposed to be yearning only for babies and frocks. There were no strong arms to hold her this time; she was stepping into the unknown.

To my mind, this is the real meat of Isabel's story. Why paper over this chapter? How come we tell the story of Isabel the surfer, not Isabel the bold adventurer? It's as if, when she sailed away on the *Niagara*, she sailed out of history.

Early 1919. Isabel was in Los Angeles, knocking on Hollywood's door. A few years after May Lahey graduated from USC Law School, Isabel joined her in the boom town crowded with fortune seekers from around the globe. Like Dorothy Cumming, she was part of that great influx of young women, the first wave of Hollywood hopefuls. The next Louise Lovely, ready to be discovered.

The reality of the film industry was tough. The streets were teeming with great beauties who captivated the camera; that wasn't Isabel's style. She was more a tomboy, an athlete – 'a healthy looking kid', as she put it. As Isabel tried to crack into the industry, a fellow Australian gave her a leg-up. The Hollywood actor Billy Bevan, formerly of Orange, New South Wales, and now working at Mack Sennett Studios, helped Isabel score a few jobs. There were some crowd scenes for Paramount, bit parts in animal pictures. Not enough to hold body and soul together, that's for sure. But enough to say she'd really done it; she'd worked in Hollywood.

Yet the truth was, she didn't love movie work. 'It wasn't my cup of tea,' Isabel confessed. She did enjoy living in California however. The climate was warm and sunny, much like Sydney, with beaches aplenty. It was easy to find like-minded companions amid the waves of new arrivals. Everyone was young and far from home, up for a good time. Movie star or not, Isabel was living her best life.

With a new band of chums, Isabel went hiking, visited the beach, toured in an automobile up and down the California coast. One winter, they stayed at a friend's cabin in the Santa Cruz mountains, dressing in men's clothes to compensate for the cold. In photographs, Isabel and her friends beam at the camera – real smiles that light up the eyes, not the strained grimace of a studio portrait. The figures lean together, relaxed and warm. They clutch each other's arms and waists. It's the body language of intimates. You suspect they were giggling only moments before. There are no men in this universe; the energy is mildly sapphic. Isabel is the one with muscular thighs and wide mouth, stockier than the rest. She sometimes appears in pants and tie, smiling against a woman called Bernice. It was worth leaving Sydney for this.

The only question was: how to pay the bills? There were a few odd jobs, but nothing stuck. By mid-1919, her parents were growing concerned. Their daughter had been abroad for almost a year and money was falling through her hands. What on earth was Isabel doing over there? Her mother decided to inspect the situation.

Jeanie Letham arrived on the *Ventura* in May 1919, and stayed in California six months. Her purpose was to deliver an ultimatum: there would be no more money. The parental tap was turned off. If Isabel wanted to stay in America, she would have to fund it herself, every single penny. Isabel was determined to make it work. 'I wasn't coming home with my tail between my leg,' she said. She'd had her fun; now it was time to put her nose to the grindstone. Hairdressing beckoned.

Hairdressing was one of the pink-collar industries that flourished around the film studios. It was a way to make money from Hollywood without being in front of a camera. Isabel completed a three-month course, then went to work. She cut hair eight hours a day, six days out of seven, and took home six dollars a week. Sixty cents was allocated for the streetcar fare, three dollars went on rent. In 1920, she lodged with a married couple in Hollywood; later, she shared a Santa Monica flat with friends. After transport and housing, there was just over two dollars for everything else. Most weeks, she didn't eat on Fridays. Plus Isabel loathed hairdressing. It was a means to an end, not a vocation.

But living hand-to-mouth was a small price to pay for a bachelorette lifestyle in the city of angels. Back in Sydney, Isabel would have remained at home until she married. It was virtually unheard of for bourgeois young women to live on their own.

Single girls remained under the parental roof, even if they stayed single and aged out of girlhood altogether. Had Isabel stayed in her family home, in her close-knit childhood suburb, she would've had to toe the line of respectable womanhood, lest word get back to her parents.

Los Angeles, by contrast, dished up the pleasures of anonymity. Isabel was one of thousands of young girls who'd blown in from everywhere. She was just another face in the crowd, a stranger without history or reputation, free to roam as she pleased. So what if she missed an occasional meal? She was 20 and kicking up her heels with the gang.

There was still the occasional movie gig, but Isabel's true stage was the ocean. In Los Angeles, Isabel continued to surf shoot and aquaplane. During the summers, she wowed the locals with her mastery of these new sports, then almost unknown in California. The local press hailed her a 'young Diana of the waves', whose skills in the surf 'exceed anything we know of in this country, man or woman'. Santa Catalina Island, a tourist resort southwest of Los Angeles, was a favourite haunt for aquaplaning. Spectators would line the shoreline to watch Isabel climb down from a launch, grasp the reins, let out a 50-foot rope, then balance on a wooden plane as the boat sped her along. She could stay upright for minutes at a time, balancing without hands, arms spread wide. It was a terrific spectacle, both a feat of athleticism and 'a pleasing picture of womanly beauty'.

By late 1921, Isabel had spent three years in the United States. Now 22, she'd matured fast, transforming from impulsive kid to street-smart woman who'd learnt to survive without a parental safety net. 'I had all the nonsense knocked out of me before I was 21,' she recalled.

Now, it was time to return to Sydney. Isabel was homesick and missed her father. She'd not seen him since 1918 and now he was seriously ill. Then there was the siren call of the Australian surf. The California coast was pleasant enough, but the waves weren't a patch on Sydney's northern beaches.

Her return in October 1921 made the Sydney papers. The prodigal daughter had come home. But the city couldn't keep her for long. Having flown the nest, Isabel no longer fitted in Sydney. It was too small, too constrained, too dominated by blokes.

She was back in California in less than a year. The *Ventura* carried her northeast across the Pacific once more in September 1922. This time her destination was San Francisco. Isabel was done with Los Angeles and hairdressing and movies; she was ready for something new.

For her second tilt at America, Isabel had a fresh plan: she would lean into her swimming skills. She was a natural in the water, more fish than woman, acclaimed across two continents. Why not turn this into a career?

4
DECORATOR TO THE STARS
THE DECORATOR, NEW YORK CITY, 1923

After six years in New York, it had become Rose's habit to travel abroad each summer. In her view, it was an 'absolute necessity' for any interior decorator worth her salt to spend at least two months in Europe. As summer unfurled, Rose would decamp to France or England or Italy, before returning to New York in mid-August, laden with new treasures to display in her Madison Avenue boutique. With her bowerbird sensibility, Rose was forever finding new items to covet. Perhaps there were rolls of antique Chinese wallpaper or a smoked mirror or an Italian altar candlestick. Or even a crystal glass chandelier from the 1800s. Rose had a penchant for chandeliers and built up quite a collection. She showcased them in her boutique by directing an electric fan towards the ceiling. All day long, the chandeliers' glass pieces tinkled in the fan's breeze.

When she disembarked from the *Berengaria* on 10 August 1923, Rose's luggage would have included an abundance of hat boxes. Even though her focus was more furniture than fashion, Rose could never resist a good hat. Her preference was for broad-brimmed creations, theatrical ensembles that matched the drama of her interiors. At a 1923 society wedding at which the 'statuesque beauty' was maid of honour, Rose was 'resplendent' in an autumnal outfit of yellow velvet and brown lace, topped by a wide brown velvet hat.

At the time, Rose had good reason to look and feel resplendent. After two years in her own boutique, momentum was building around her practice. Rose Cumming was becoming the decorator *de jour*, the must-have designer of fabulous interiors for the rich and famous.

The previous spring, Rose had been showcased in a *Boston Globe* feature about the rise of interior decoration. American women finally had the vote, and were looking to make their own money. Interior decoration was a chic avenue for young ladies to craft themselves into modern career women. More glamorous than the traditional 'women's work' of nursing or teaching, yet still feminine enough to avoid stepping on male toes, interior decoration offered women a chance to express themselves while bringing home cold hard cash. As a rising star of this new profession, youngsters with their eye on a decorating career pumped Rose for advice. Rose dismissed the need for formal training, stressing it was preferable to learn on the job. Contacts were essential, Rose emphasised. Big names, important people, networks of influence. An interior decorator needed clients, and clients were best obtained through 'influential acquaintances'.

Rose was speaking from experience. The Australian had panache as a decorator but was equally talented in the fine art of networking. Once the *Vanity Fair* editor Frank Crowninshield had given her an initial leg-up, she'd kept cultivating friends in high places, diffusing her charms with strategic aim. Business and pleasure were mixed together. Rose loved to entertain and would often invite guests back to her Park Avenue apartment for supper after an evening at the theatre. Her specialities were curried oysters and devilled salmon served in patty shells. Was she enjoying an evening with friends or seducing potential clients? Both, always. Rose and her work were near impossible to separate.

Dorothy was an equally skilled networker, and her movie contacts were vital to Rose's decorating business. 'I always felt Dorothy was whispering in Rose's ear,' one friend noted. Thanks to Dorothy, Mary Pickford was a client. So too were fellow screen icons Marlene Dietrich, Norma Shearer and Gloria Swanson. With a client list that boasted some of Hollywood's biggest names, Rose Cumming was fast becoming a brand synonymous with celebrity and glamour.

Now, her other sister was about to aid Rose's prospects. In August 1923, *Vogue* announced that Eileen Cumming was engaged to marry Dr Russell LaFayette Cecil, a celebrated rheumatologist. A graduate of Princeton, Russell had served with the US military during the war and was now a faculty member of New York City's Cornell Medical School. Within a few years, Russell became a household name as editor of the *Cecil Textbook of Medicine*, a textbook first published in 1927 that, in its 26th edition, is still used today.

It was a society pairing. *Vogue*'s social pages announced the Cecil–Cumming engagement just above news that a Vanderbilt was getting hitched. The wedding, on 26 September 1923, was held at St Thomas Church on Fifth Avenue, and attracted press photographers. Eileen was 'radiant' in a simple white gown topped with a veil. Her father, Victor, was on hand to give her away, looking dapper in a top hat.

The evolution of Miss Eileen Cumming into Mrs Russell Cecil cemented Rose's place at the centre of things. If there'd been any question that the antipodean Cumming girls truly belonged in New York society, the marriage put those doubts to rest. Rose was now sibling to a society matron, with serious establishment credentials working in her favour. As the 'sister of Mrs Russell L Cecil', Rose's every move was deemed worthy of reporting in the social pages of the *New York Times*. Hosting a party? Going abroad? Rose could be sure it would make the 'newspaper of record'.

Best of all, Rose was tasked with decorating the Cecil marital home, a commission that offered a high-profile canvas to advertise her talents. Located at 153 and 155 East 61st Street, the Cecil residence was a duplex that featured its very own ballroom. Oscar Hammerstein and his Australian-born wife Dorothy moved in next door. Later, in the early 1940s, art collector Peggy Guggenheim rented two floors of the Cecil duplex, and commissioned abstract expressionist Jackson Pollock to paint a mural in the entrance hall.

Rose gave the home her signature luxe finish. Each room was alive with colour and reflective surfaces, creating the giddy feel of a carnival funhouse. In the entrance hall, visitors were greeted by a stupendous antique chandelier. Then, passing into the drawing room, they'd find a mirror-topped coffee table set before a vast wall mirror that reflected an antique Chinese screen. An aubergine carpet, green chartreuse drapes and gold cornices completed the scene. Across the hall, in the dining room, every wall reflected the light, thanks to the thin sheets of foil that served as wallpaper. Glazed to a periwinkle blue, the foil-covered walls matched chairs upholstered in silvery-blue leather. The overall effect was dazzling, a mix of 'Venetian opulence' and 'continuous melodic movement', with the 'heady effect of a garden border'.

As Rose's profile increased, her entertaining grew as lavish as her interiors. Guests at her Park Avenue apartment included the Duke and Duchess of Richmond and Princess Nina Georgievna of Russia, a great-granddaughter of Tsar Nicholas I. In July 1926, during Rose's annual summer trip to Europe, she hosted a sumptuous bacchanal on Paris's Champs Élysées. After booking out the Restaurant Laurent, a famous establishment that dated back to the 1800s, Rose invited no less than 200 of the 'Paris smart set' to a dance and supper party. The guest list included Mary Pickford and her actor husband Douglas Fairbanks, Condé Nast, composer Igor Stravinsky and F Scott Fitzgerald. Alongside these heavy hitters of the transatlantic cultural elite, Rose also welcomed a duchess, three princesses and a prince, a baron and several counts. Together, they ate supper in the garden, Rose presiding in an 'effective green gown'. It was, the *Herald Tribune* reported, a fitting climax to the hostess's 'meteoric' rise in high society. Rose had come a long way from garden parties and amateur theatricals in decorous Goulburn.

Dorothy was also hitting high notes in her career. In 1926, she clinched her biggest film role to date: the part of the Virgin Mary in Cecil B DeMille's *King of Kings*, a biblical epic that portrayed the life of Christ. The film's production coincided with the December 1926 death of Victor Cumming, the sisters' father, who had been visiting Dorothy in Los Angeles. According to *Variety*, Dorothy's grief fuelled her depiction of the stricken mother of the crucified Christ. Although the actress wanted a break from filming after Victor died, DeMille insisted they shoot the crucifixion scene that very morning, eager to channel her raw emotion into an unforgettable performance. 'Get in a taxi', the auteur demanded. So she did.

Released in May 1927, *King of Kings* was described by the *New York Times* as 'the most impressive of all motion pictures'. Yet the film that elevated Dorothy to a new level of celebrity came at a significant cost. Not only was she forced to mine her grief for cinema, but the actress lost autonomy over her off-screen existence. To secure the part, DeMille insisted Dorothy sign a contract that demanded 'strict Christian conduct and behaviour' in her private life for seven years following the film's release. Specifically, she was prohibited from acting the part of a sex worker or divorcing her husband. To maximise box office takings, DeMille was determined his Madonna would be as unimpeachable off screen as she was in the Christian imagination. In the end, however, DeMille failed to bend Dorothy to his will. In 1927, she challenged the contract and sued her actor husband Frank Elliott for divorce. After a lengthy court battle, the marriage was dissolved in 1929.

Back in New York, Rose was also failing to observe 'strict Christian conduct'. The man in question was Colonel Georges Philippoff, a former officer of the Russian Imperial Army who served as chief of staff of the Persian Cossack Division after the 1917 Revolution. He migrated to the United States in 1920 and thereafter resided in New York. Philippoff, known as 'Poffy', was a serious man conspicuous for his 'ever-present military bearing'. Lithe and impeccably groomed, Poffy had a dark moustache, gentle eyes and a chest full of medals. He was the yin to Rose's yang, the perfect foil to her theatrical persona. The couple, both born in 1884, were lovers for a decade across the 1920s and 1930s. Their liaison probably began around 1926, when Colonel Philippoff attended one of Rose's dinner parties. Certainly, by the decade's end, the two were an established item, photographed together in a domestic scene with Rose's family.

In the photograph, probably taken at Southampton in 1930, Rose is perched alongside her mother, Sarah, on a garden bench, pale limbs spilling out of a sleeveless sundress. With one arm extended, she reaches out to poke an unidentified man standing to her right. Beneath her signature broad-brimmed hat, Rose's animated face is caught in a moment of unfettered *joie de vivre*. Standing behind the two women, a moustachioed Poffy squints into the sun with a wry half-smile, his summer tan a deep mahogany against pale slacks and starched white shirt. At the centre is the matronly Sarah, smiling in pearls and a patterned summer frock, her arms around Rose's nephew Russell, a cherubic child of three or four. The adults, one suspects, had already enjoyed a cocktail or two, all the better to float into this languorous summer afternoon.

Whatever the precise occasion, this photograph is a remarkable portrait of a woman breaking the rules and getting away with it. Here Rose is with her lover and her family, unashamed and joyful, mixing the sensual and the domestic, bringing her whole self to a tableau in which she literally and metaphorically takes up space without the merest hint of apology. If there was ever a woman with main-character energy, it was Rose S Cumming.

Even though Poffy was a good time, Rose didn't let him distract her from the main game: making beautiful spaces. Specifically, her own home. When she and Poffy first met, Rose was still renting on East 55th Street, near the St Regis Hotel, but she soon relocated to her own property. She'd been looking to purchase a home near her Madison Avenue boutique, but nothing satisfied Rose's four key prerequisites: big rooms, parquet floors, open fireplaces and high ceilings. Of these, the latter was the most essential. A high ceiling, Rose believed, 'makes every woman look beautiful when she enters the room'. By contrast, 'if a low ceiling practically scalps her, she comes into the room looking like a pigmy'.

Eventually Rose settled on a brownstone at 36 West 53rd Street. Purchased in 1927 or 1928, at the fever pitch of the Roaring Twenties, Rose's new home was just a five-minute stroll from her shop at 515 Madison Avenue. The address was also directly opposite the Museum of Modern Art, which opened in 1929. Today, Rose's home is long gone, replaced by a Starbucks that caters to MoMA's tourist hordes. But back in the late 1920s, it was a 'narrow old brownstone' that boasted 16-foot ceilings and no less than 18 fireplaces. Despite its good bones, the building was in a state of 'fearful dilapidation' – the perfect excuse for Rose to give her new home a complete makeover.

Over a few months, Rose made this home into a living manifesto of her design philosophy. With no client to appease, she could give free rein to the most idiosyncratic of her tastes. As she told *Arts & Decoration* magazine, 'I have been able to indulge many little eccentricities that I have to suppress in business.' The finished residence, where she lived for over 30 years, would become a key part of the Rose Cumming mythology.

The key influence was the 18th century, Rose's favoured period for design. In keeping with that epoch, she shunned electric lighting, and illuminated the house via candles. At night, visitors arrived to a gloomy dwelling, the windows dark and forbidding. From the street, the building looked abandoned. This unconventional welcome was just one of the reasons that Rose Cumming was said to resemble Miss Havisham, the eccentric spinster of Charles Dickens's *Great Expectations*.

Inside the brownstone, every surface shone. The paint was a high-gloss enamel; the parquet floors were polished 'within an inch of their lives'; mirrors and crystal could be found in every room. English antiques predominated, but sat alongside items from China, France, Spain and the United States. Rose didn't want to be tied to any one period or aesthetic. 'I love everything that is beautiful, no matter whether it is fish or fowl,' she explained. In the dining room, she displayed an Austrian child's sleigh and a model crystal ship floating on a Venetian canal. Even more outlandish was her boudoir, Rose's 'little dream world, a kingdom of unreality'. Her bed was finished in silver leaf, with mirror bandings across the rails and footboard, topped by a silver satin bedspread. On the wall above was a painted mural, a 'mandarin's dream' of swooping birds and lush botanicals. In the adjacent dressing room, black walls were speckled with gold stars and signs of the Zodiac, beneath a gold ceiling.

This dream cave of a home defined Rose as an artist as brilliant as she was bizarre. Her reputation was enhanced by the stories that emerged from her boutique, tales of a capricious diva more interested in showmanship than customer service or sales. There was the time a customer asked to see a fabric in daylight and Rose insisted on unrolling the whole bolt of cloth across Madison Avenue – only to refuse the sale. The day a couple insisted they were 'just browsing', and Rose snorted that 'cows browse'. Then there was the wealthy woman who Rose fired after she exposed herself as a miser. When the client spent $40000 on a single room, but refused to reimburse Rose's chauffeur's 75-cent lunch, the decorator decided to wash her hands of this parsimonious individual.

By end of the decade, Rose was an established authority in interior decoration whose work featured in the pages of *Vogue*, *Harper's Bazaar*, the *New Yorker*, *House & Garden* and *House Beautiful*. As part of her stature, Rose was called upon to define the decorating profession. In a *New York Herald Tribune* article from 31 March 1929, Rose explained that interior decoration was an essential foil to architecture, a more established and masculine line of work. Only if architect and decorator worked together would a home achieve 'dignity, repose and artistic unity', she claimed. Otherwise, all sorts of aesthetic horrors may proliferate. Without designers on hand, a house was liable to be marred by 'beautiful doors swinging obstinately in the wrong direction' or even – *quelle horreur* – 'misplaced, self-assertive radiators'.

Radiators aside, this was a feminist manifesto of sorts. On close reading, Rose was not just fussing over 'the proper adjustment of curtains'; she was making a case for a feminised profession. For Rose, interior decoration was an essential counterpart to the 'great profession of Architects'. She insisted that women's work designing houses was equal to that undertaken by men. To wit, Rose explained that decoration was much more than the placement of furniture; it required an aesthetic 'sixth sense', 'a kind of artistic alchemy' that generates 'that illusive quality of aliveness which transforms houses into homes'.

Artistic alchemy, a sixth sense? This sounded suspiciously like an artist channelling their muse. It sounded like the kind of creation reserved for men. How dare a mere woman stake a claim to this tradition of romantic genius. But having already relocated across the world, helped define a new profession, built up a thriving business, shunned matrimony and motherhood, and taken lovers into her bed, Rose's life already better approximated a bachelor existence than the tightly corseted days of her female contemporaries. In New York, city of reinvention and bohemia, so far from the watchful eyes of Goulburn and Sydney, Rose had taught herself to breathe great lungfuls of life, with nary a whalebone in sight.

5
HERSTORY, WHOSE STORY

I am leafing through a family photograph album, squinting at the black-and-white portraits carefully pasted onto each page. I am seven, maybe eight, a watchful child who is drawn to adults and everything that is old. The album is an ugly thing, really. Brown checks with orange highlights, an unlovely artefact of 1970s design. It smells musty and its spine creaks with age. But for me it has the same soothing effect as a favourite blankie or soft toy. Instead of sucking my thumb, I open the album and disappear into photographs of the Olden Days. Aided by the handwritten captions, I make a map of the lives that came before my own.

There is my mother, a bolshie Women's Libber clad in overalls, sunning herself in bare feet outside a Newtown share house. There is my aunt, wearing a flowered hippie dress that accentuates her dark-haired beauty. My grandmother, snapped by a street photographer while courting the man who would become my grandfather. Her face is pale, uncertain.

I study them all with the intense scrutiny of an anthropologist doing fieldwork, or an alien newly arrived on planet Earth. My brow furrows; the darkening afternoon falls away. I want the images to tell me something, to reveal some secret. To answer a question that I don't yet know how to ask. It has something to do with being a girl. With growing into a woman. At the far reaches of my mind, there is a word emerging from the haze. *How.* How to be, how to live. How is it done.

When I started thinking about Australian women in the United States, I did so from a position of identification. They were women; I was a woman. Like them, I was a white Australian with the privilege and appetite to orient my life around travel and education and career. They felt, in many ways, like a version of me born a century earlier. Same same, not actually that different. They were my forebears, direct ancestors in a lineage of feminine resistance to being put in small boxes, women who could model how to navigate womanhood in a world that still – even in the 'post-feminist' 2010s – positioned men as the default human subject. Through them, I might finally learn how to be.

Historians, who are trained to be dispassionate and objective, aren't supposed to admit this kind of emotional entanglement with their subjects. We aren't supposed to have this kind of entanglement in the first place. Even though we know – thanks to feminist and postcolonial theory – that academic knowledge is never neutral and objective, even though we accept that the illusion of objectivity is itself an artefact of white colonial patriarchy, historians still operate in a professional culture that disciplines us into performing a coolly detached relationship to the people and stories that populate our work.

We are scholars, we are experts, we are brains on a stick. Our work is the work of knowledge and ideas. To admit we have strong feelings about our subjects – even worse, that we *identify* with them – would surely undermine our authority. How anachronistic, how very ahistorical (not to mention egocentric), for a historian to presume they could reach across the decades and discover themselves via a long-dead individual who lived in an entirely different world. What kind of intellectual would make such a rookie error?

I have always been good at following the rules. Too good, some might say. I learnt the unspoken rules of my profession and proceeded to execute them assiduously, which meant I tucked away these feelings of identification into a hidden recess of my brain. They felt too distasteful to admit, even to myself.

(Internalised misogyny alert. See me play the old game: disavow 'feminine' emotion, inhabit 'male' reason. The ideal scholar is he (still he) who can best conceal their own passions behind a wall of aloof prose.)

But all the while, the feelings raged. All the while, I was running towards Mary Cecil Allen and Isabel Letham and May Lahey and all the others like an orphaned puppy looking for a mother, a hot mess of confusion and gaping need. *How do I do this strange thing called womanhood? What does it look like to be a woman and stay sovereign over yourself? If I study you hard enough, if I join all the dots of your big and rebellious lives, will I finally crack the code?*

Teach me, show me the way. Solve my gender trouble, oh ye fellow white ladies who went before.

You can probably guess how this story ends.

Spoiler alert: when womanhood feels like a puzzle with a missing rulebook, or a role you never signed up to play, or a scratchy jumper a few sizes too small, you might not actually be a woman at all.

After I finally realised I was trans, once I understood that I wasn't, and never had been, a woman, I didn't know how to think about women in the past. Were they still my forebears? Was their history still my history?

If I wanted to feel connected to a historical lineage, something larger than myself, surely I should switch to trans history. There were plenty of genderqueer folk bobbing around the periphery of our historical imagination, just ripe for reclamation. These could be my true forebears. Or maybe I should learn to be a 'proper' historian and stop projecting my own psychodramas onto unsuspecting people from the past.

Later, I began to wonder whether women's history and trans history could be so neatly separated. If I had spent 30 years going along with my assigned role of woman, if it taken a 'trans tipping point' to prompt me to comprehend my own gender differently, who was to say how female-assigned people from history may have understood their gender assignment if they'd had concepts like *nonbinary* and *genderqueer* at their disposal? The possibilities of self-definition are always shaped by historical context. With a different context, with different ideas and words floating around, the same person might think about themselves in an entirely new light.

I had already met countless older women who told me, somewhat wistfully, that they would call themselves nonbinary or trans if only they were 30 or 40 years younger. *You still can*, I would say. *It's not too late!* But for them, it was. Had they encountered this idea in their youth, their lives might have looked very different.

How many other people, now dead and buried, might have thought the same way? Mary Cecil Allen preferred pants and came to be known by her masculine middle name. May Lahey never married and characterised single career women such as herself as a kind of 'third sex'. Cynthia Reed, a nurse we'll meet shortly, was known by the androgynous nickname Bob and had surgery to reduce her breasts. The writer Dorothy Cottrell, another character coming up, wrote an unpublished autobiographical novel with a male protagonist. In that same novel, written in the mid-1920s, another character is described as having a mix of male and female energies – a gender expression we'd now call nonbinary. 'In some natures sex is definitely marked in every fibre of being,' Dorothy wrote. 'They seem to cry from every nerve and muscle and gland, from every process of thought and emotion, "I am man" or "I am woman". But in rarer cases the blending of the elements masculine and feminine seem almost equal.'

When you start looking for it, gender failure is everywhere. At least half the women in this book exhibited some form of gender deviance or ambiguity.

This is not to say that we should start retrospectively claiming historical figures as trans or nonbinary, hunting down gender rebels like a queer game of *Where's Wally*. This is not to say that every woman in history who challenged gender norms was perhaps not a woman at all.

It is simply to say that we know less than we think. We apply terms and labels to our historical figures, just as we do for people in the present, because it is an easy cognitive shorthand. But we don't ever really know for sure.

For me, trans history is not about finding trans people in the past and studying them separately from the cisgender men and women. It is not a new little subfield that can sit neatly adjacent to women's history. Women here, trans folk over there. Instead, trans history is a way of looking, a questioning lens that encourages us to doubt our certainties about any given person's identity. We can know the gender people were assigned at birth, we can glimpse whether they accepted or challenged that assignment, but beyond that is a whole realm of unknowability and mystery. We can only wonder and imagine.

How marvellous, how beautiful.

How refreshing, to throw off the conceits of Western colonial knowledge, which controls and dominates through claiming to comprehend all, and admit how much we do not and cannot understand.

6

GETTING MODERN WITH NATATION

THE SWIMMER, SAN FRANCISCO, 1923

Isabel's new hat was wet. Not wet, sodden. Ruined beyond repair. She'd been caught in a downpour on the walk across campus and was soaked to the skin. As she perched in the waiting room, water dripped from the hat's rim, forming a puddle on the floor. The dye had run, leaving dark streaks on her face and hair.

This interview was not getting off to a promising start.

The hat had cost $20, a whole week's salary, far more than she could afford. Isabel had seen it in a shop window one evening. She'd recently found digs in Sutter Street, in Lower Nob Hill, just near the commercial hub of downtown. Each day she'd walk past elegant boutiques that catered to San Francisco's elite. The shop windows were a glittering jewel box of hats and gloves and perfumes. Normally she could restrain herself, but hats were her weakness. Her whole life, she'd bought as many as she could afford. This hat seemed the perfect thing to wear for the interview. She needed to make a good impression, after all. This job would be her ticket out of hairdressing, her excuse to stay in California. A means to capitalise on her passion for the water.

It was January, the start of a new year, and a new chapter in her life. The hat would be her lucky charm. She'd handed over the $20 and walked out with a spring in her step.

Now Isabel considered making a run for it. Amid the neoclassical grandeur of the University of California (UC) administration building, all gleaming granite and straight lines, she felt bedraggled and uncouth. Shivering in her damp clothes, she kept her eyes averted from passers-by. Isabel had rarely felt more out of place. She'd never attended a university; what made her think she could work at one? She was just a kid from Sydney, a rough-and-tumble builder's daughter, no matter what finery she wore. Even on a good day, she didn't belong here. Isabel eyed the exit, tempted to scuttle out of sight.

But then she remembered how hard she'd hustled to get this interview. How she had shamelessly badgered the university's Dean of Women, turning up at her office three times until the polite snubs turned into reluctant agreement to set up a meeting with Dean Hart. Walter Morris Hart, dean of the university, the man who pulled the reins. If anyone could give her a job, it was him. *I'll stick it out*, Isabel told herself. At least give Hart the chance to make up his own mind.

The door to the inner sanctum opened. A giant of a man loomed in the doorway, white hair framing a kindly face. He issued a gentle smile and ushered Isabel into the office, oblivious to the water that dripped from her frame. Isabel disappeared behind the closed door, leaving a puddle behind. She'd made a mess, as she so often did. But perhaps it was only appropriate that the swimmer arrived with water trailing in her wake.

Four months earlier, in late 1922, Isabel had landed in San Francisco for her second tilt at the United States. Hollywood had not worked out, but neither had a return to Sydney. She needed to find a way to pay the bills in California. She had no passion for hairdressing and it paid only a pittance. There had to be something better, something that used her talents.

In California, Isabel got wind of universities getting serious about swimming. It was the 20th century, the machine age, the age of reason and efficiency, and everything that had once been ad hoc and haphazard was coming under scientific scrutiny – with swimming no exception. The universities had reimagined swimming as a science, part of the new field of physical culture, something that could be studied and taught with methodical rigour rather than a mere survival skill or form of recreation. Natation, it was called. The art of swimming. Natation – a lofty word, a word that demanded you pay attention. A word that suggested the mere act of moving a body through water could have its own philosophy, its own textbooks and bodies of knowledge. Natation was plain old swimming remade for the modern age.

Natation sounded like Isabel's cup of tea. She was determined to get her foot in the door, so she set her sights on picking up work at Berkeley – the University of California campus just across the San Francisco Bay. She may not have any formal qualifications, but she did boast glowing references. Her employers from Sydney deemed her a 'very capable teacher' with 'a pleasant personality' that made her 'very attractive to young people'. Her tuition had led children to become 'fearless' in the water. Surely these testimonials would get her over the line.

Isabel could also count on the Annette Kellerman effect to work in her favour. Kellerman was a fellow Australian who in 1905, aged 18, swam over 13 miles down London's River Thames, and thereafter became the most famous woman swimmer in the world. For the next few decades, Kellerman toured the United States, Britain and Europe as an international celebrity. She was renowned for her public performances, film appearances and 1918 book *How to Swim*. More than anyone, Kellerman popularised women's swimming. As historian Angela Woollacott has shown, her celebrity built a strong association between Australian womanhood and aquatic aptitude. Isabel had no documented connection to Kellerman but was riding on her coattails. Kellerman's fame gave an unknown Australian swimmer like Isabel an edge over the competition.

In his office, Dean Hart let her down gently. He listened to Isabel's prepared speech then revealed she was too late.

'I'm very sorry, Miss Letham,' he said. 'We've already made our arrangements for this year's summer session. Would you be interested in next year?'

'Oh yes,' Isabel answered, painting on a big smile. But inside, her heart was sinking. Summer 1924 – that was 18 months away, a veritable lifetime. Far too long to wait. On the ferry home, watching Berkeley recede into the distance, she was despondent. *You're done now, Isabel*, she muttered, fingering the ruined hat. Perhaps she'd have to retreat to Sydney after all, with her tail firmly between her legs.

The winter dragged on. January spooled out in a series of chilly days. There was an earthquake in Hawai'i; Prince Albert was engaged to marry. France occupied the Ruhr Valley after Germany defaulted on its reparation payments. For a while, Europe once again seemed close to war. Out on her walks, Isabel averted her eyes from the window displays. She couldn't afford to burn any more cash on fripperies.

February arrived and still the cold continued. This was Isabel's second winter in a row, after a southern hemisphere winter back home. As she shivered inside her coat, Isabel must have pictured how friends in Sydney would be spending their February days. Summer afternoons at Freshwater, crashing through the white foam. Weekends on the harbour, cavorting on the aquaplane, one eye out for sharks. Isabel had no idea when or if she could expect to taste those pleasures again. She was marking time, waiting for the next chapter to begin.

One afternoon, six weeks after the disastrous job interview, Isabel trudged home up the hill and there it was. A letter addressed to Miss Letham, carrying the letterhead of UC Berkeley. Inside was a note from Dean Hart. There'd been a change of plans. He could now offer her the position of Swimming Assistant for this summer. Six weeks of work, from late June through early August. It paid a pittance, only $65 for the whole season, but it was a foot in the door. An opportunity to learn the art of natation. The hat had been a lucky charm, after all.

That summer at Berkeley, Isabel found the education she had been seeking. As assistant instructor, she taught hundreds of women in the Strawberry Canyon pool, a heated freshwater facility on the edge of Berkeley's campus. Isabel was deputy to Lyba Sheffield Mackie, a 1915 UC graduate who'd majored in the new discipline of physical education. Mackie had literally written the book on natation. *Swimming Simplified*, published in 1920, was an illustrated textbook that promised to 'simplify the learning and teaching of swimming from a scientific point of view'. Under Mackie's tutelage, the swim students started on land, with an analysis of each stroke. Then they practised with land drills, followed by water drills. Only when they'd mastered a particular stroke would they enter the swimming pool, often accompanied by rhythmic music. It was all very orderly, an aquatic version of Frederick Taylor's scientific management.

The climax of the summer was the Pageant of Mermaids, a swim meet in late July. On a sweltering day, the hottest of the season, 400 women costumed as 'Neptune's daughters' moved in formation before an enthusiastic crowd. After an opening parade, they demonstrated land drills and stroke technique followed by races. The 'goodnight race' required participants to swim in nightwear and hold aloft a lit candle; the 'bookworm race' asked swimmers to carry an umbrella and book above the water. The pageant also included an early form of synchronised swimming, with groups making shapes in the water to musical accompaniment.

All day, Isabel's students showcased their newfound aquatic skills. This was the athletic female body as public spectacle, a far cry from the modesty and frailty demanded of women only a few decades earlier. No longer were respectable white women expected to hide themselves away from the world's gaze; they could now be vigorous and strong in public. They could bare their limbs and cavort in the water and be applauded to boot. Of course, these female athletes were expected to remain appropriately feminine, and were celebrated more for their girlish charms than hard-won skills. They were still more decorative object than independent subject. But even these limited freedoms marked a radical departure from the literal and metaphorical corsets of the 19th century. In teaching women to exert their bodies in public, Isabel was on the front line of a revolution in gender norms.

She was also on the front line of modern living. Isabel's neighbourhood of Lower Nob Hill was a residential district packed with high-rises that had sprung up since the devastating 1906 earthquake. The residents lived cheek-by-jowl in apartment buildings that lined the hilly streets, drawn by the promise of freedom and anonymity amid the cosmopolitan crowds. There were always new faces on the street and in the hallways; even during the midnight hours, it was never completely quiet. From her roof, Isabel could spy the skyscrapers that clustered in San

Francisco's downtown – a man-made forest, trees of concrete and steel reaching towards the sky.

There was nothing like this in Sydney, that's for sure. Back home, there were only a handful of modern apartment buildings, and no neighbourhoods where residential high-rises were the norm. Apartment living was viewed with suspicion, associated with urban overcrowding and moral degeneracy. Behind the locked door of her private digs, a single young woman like Isabel could engage in all sorts of scandalous behaviour, with no one the wiser. Forget a room of one's own; Isabel had a whole apartment in which to do whatever she pleased.

That first teaching gig at Berkeley soon led to another. From the summer of 1923, Isabel picked up work as a swim instructor for the City of San Francisco. She was employed by the City's Playground Commission, a branch of municipal government that offered free swimming lessons to local children. There was an open-air pool in the Italian Quarter near Fisherman's Wharf and another in the Mission, the city's Latino district. After acting as assistant instructor in 1923, Isabel was promoted to chief girls' instructor in 1924. Over the next few years, she taught hundreds of children to swim. Working six days a week, she applied the scientific principles of natation to the city's youth. Everyone aged 6 to 16 was eligible, and around 300 turned up each day.

Isabel taught in sun visor and bathers, her shoulders covered with an oversized shirt, her muscled legs exposed to the sun. All day she strode the pool deck, megaphone in hand, a giant among the scores of skinny youngsters in woollen bathers and swimming caps. '[Isabel] herself is an example of what swimming does for the human form,' gushed the local press. 'She stands erect and lightly poised. When she walks she simply glides along ... Her body seems under her complete control, and she moves with the lightness of a deer.' The students squinted up at her, eyes crinkled against the sun, as Isabel ran drills and races. Soon, some began to swim competitively.

The Australian taught swimming but in return received a valuable lesson of her own. As a free service open to all, her classes were a cross-section of the city's migrant communities. Italian, Polish, Greek, Chinese, Russian: each of these languages was spoken in her pool. This was the first time Isabel had encountered such human diversity. Back in Sydney, her world was dominated by white Britons like her parents. Even at Berkeley, the students were mostly WASPs. Aside from her surfing exploits with Duke Kahanamoku, and her brief stopover in Honolulu, never before had Isabel spent so much time in the company of people not understood as white.

It was a transformative experience. For the rest of her life, Isabel would cite her time at the Playground Commission as the moment she learnt not to judge people by 'class, colour or creed'. Prior to that job, she'd accepted without question the logic of White Australia; afterwards, she would be an advocate for racial equality. In her mind, San Francisco was a paradise in large part because it fostered the co-existence of many different peoples and nationalities. It was the proverbial human melting pot.

Of course, this was not the whole story. San Francisco was heavily stratified along class and race lines, with the Chinese and Latino communities facing virulent racism. California was indeed more diverse than Sydney, yet white people ruled the roost. As a white woman, it was easy for Isabel to view her diverse student body with rose-tinted glasses. She saw evidence of successful intermixing, while remaining oblivious to the structural inequities and power dynamics at play. Her pool was open to students of many backgrounds, but some experienced more drag than others.

Within a few years, Isabel had put down roots in San Francisco. After the first few uncertain months, the city had given her a career and a community. Now aged 26, Isabel remained single, but continued to revel in her posse of female friends. On special occasions, they splurged on a restaurant meal, decked out in drop-waisted dresses and pearls, their hair cropped and shingled. It was time to commit to her Californian life. In July 1925, Isabel took out American citizenship. Like May Lahey before her, Isabel had decided she was here for good. The following month, Isabel's mother arrived in San Francisco. Back in Sydney, her father, William, had died, and now his widow, Jeanie, migrated across the Pacific to reunite with her only child. Around this time, Isabel moved to new digs in Russian Hill – a more affluent area, high up in the vertiginous hills where the city's wealthy lived. The Bay views were sometimes blanketed by white fog, thick like whipped cream, but on clear days you could see all the way to Marin, on the other side of the Golden Gate. Isabel had heard talk that a bridge was coming, but for the time being there was nothing but open water.

By 1926, Isabel was 'one of the foremost swimming instructors in the city'. No longer the job-seeking supplicant, she was a local personality, beloved for teaching the local youth to swim. She could pick and choose where she worked. The Playground Commission were keen to retain her services, but Isabel had her eye on a new pool under construction. A pool that promised to be the finest the city had ever seen.

Down on Post Street, the Women's City Club of San Francisco – a grand title that befitted this ambitious new institution – was about to open. The club was the brainchild of women engaged in the National League for Women's Service during World War I. When peace came in 1918, they were eager to maintain their camaraderie and good works, and landed on the idea of a club for community-minded women. Men had long gathered in clubs, to relax and scheme with like-minded folk; why shouldn't women do the same? Women had proven their capabilities with war work; they'd finally won the vote in 1920. Now fully enfranchised citizens, American women needed places to participate in public life.

After years of fundraising, construction on the Women's City Club began in December 1924. For 18 months, Isabel witnessed the building climb towards the sky. The Post Street site was in the heart of the city, next to the St Francis Hotel, just around the corner from her old Buckingham Apartments home in Sutter Street. She would have passed the construction site often, tracking its progress as 1925 turned into 1926.

Now, as another summer approached, the Women's City Club was about to open its doors. The first of its kind in the city, the club's modus operandi was to 'enable women to live more abundantly'. The building had cost over a million dollars, yet membership fees were modest, with a view to attracting women from all walks of life. Across eight storeys, the institution housed a library, music room, lounge, dining rooms, auditorium, cafeteria, shops, beauty salon, plus 92 bedrooms to rent.

Down in the basement was the jewel in the crown: a white-tiled swimming pool, 75 feet by 30 feet. The pool had Grecian architecture, private dressing rooms, hot showers, heated towels and uniformed attendants. Water was pumped from the ocean, seven miles away, then filtered and warmed for the swimmers' pleasure. The whole facility was emptied and cleaned twice a week. It was a marvel, 'the most beautiful indoor pool on the Pacific coast'.

Isabel wanted to make this pool her own.

She submitted an application, not daring to hope. But they offered her a position as Pool Director, overseeing five staff. Her dream job. She resigned from the Playground Commission and started at the Women's Club in summer 1926. The swimming pool, or 'natatorium', was open to members and guests from 9 am to 9.30 pm, six days a week. It offered private lessons, swimming classes and general swimming.

As the weather cooled, pool attendance began to fall, and Isabel's workload lightened. Exactly four years had passed since Isabel arrived in San Francisco. It was time to return to Sydney for a visit, to see old friends and surf at Freshwater. She'd skip the northern winter in favour of a southern summer. Plus, she wanted to spread the word about natation and scientific methods of swimming.

In November 1926, armed with her new American passport, Isabel boarded the *Sonoma* for the three-week journey across the Pacific. Was she going home or leaving home? After eight years spent primarily in California, and now a citizen of the United States, it was hard to know where she truly belonged.

7
A NEW COMET IN FICTION
THE WRITER, CENTRAL QUEENSLAND, 1927

The good news came by telegram. It arrived late on a Saturday, just as the sun sank towards the horizon. 'Glad to publish your novel in *Ladies' Home Journal*,' the cable read, 'and pay you 5000 dollars for all American and Canadian serial rights.' The sender, *Journal* editor Barton Currie, also offered to 'find book publisher if terms satisfactory'. Currie closed by requesting an urgent response. Dorothy Cottrell could scarce believe her eyes. Holding the flimsy slip of paper in one hand, she read the typed words several times over.

A few moments earlier, it had been an ordinary day on Ularunda Station. Sheep lolled in the sun, fences were mended, bread was baked. As usual, Dorothy had set up camp in the garden, writing under the shade of the jacaranda tree. Over the past three years, she'd penned four manuscripts from that spot. Today she'd been working on 'Wheel-Rhyme', her tale about a young boy who – like Dorothy – spent his days in a wheelchair. Soothed by the familiar hum of station life, Dorothy went deep into her imaginary world. Later, she tended her vegetable garden, watering the raised beds designed to be accessible from her wheelchair.

Now, as the shadows lengthened, came this unassuming slip of paper. Thirty-six life-changing words, all the way from Philadelphia. Dorothy had sent out her manuscript only a month before; she didn't expect to hear back so soon. And she certainly never dared hope for such an enthusiastic response – not from the *Ladies' Home Journal*, the highest-circulation magazine in the United States. The *Journal* was the pinnacle; every issue reached millions of readers. Surely there had been some mistake. Had the editor meant $50 instead of $5000? Convinced the telegram had been mis-transcribed, Dorothy wired for confirmation. Until the offer was confirmed, she refused to celebrate. Her uncle, however, had no doubts. In his view, this was simply an 'abnormally successful first effort to obtain a publisher'.

The date was 16 April 1927 and Dorothy Cottrell was a few months shy of her 25th birthday. Alongside her husband Walter, the writer was living on Ularunda, the family sheep station on Bidjara Country in southwest Queensland. It was sun-drenched mulga country, flat plains covered with sandy soil. Since 1907, Ularunda had been owned by Dorothy's maternal uncles Ernest and Erwin Fletcher. Dorothy, born in 1902, had spent the bulk of her short life on the property. The landscape inspired her writing and gave her a taste for the outdoor life.

Located around 700 kilometres due west from Brisbane, Ularunda could barely be more remote. The closest town was Morven, a dot on the map 30 miles away. The local hub was Toowoomba, 500 kilometres to the east. For weeks or months at a time, Dorothy's world was limited to the few dozen people who lived and worked on the property. But thanks to the marvels of modern technology, this aspiring author had sent a manuscript all the way to Pennsylvania and received a response within a few weeks.

Australian writers of this era generally sought publication in London, the heart of the British publishing world. According to the mind maps of colonial creatives, the approval of English gatekeepers was the apex of artistic achievement, the aspiration to strive towards. But Dorothy's husband, Walter, suggested she try something different. Unusually for the time, her mother subscribed to the *Ladies' Home Journal*. On rainy days they would leaf through back issues, perusing the short stories and colourful advertisements.

Why not send them her manuscript? Dorothy had heard rumours the American mass market could be lucrative.

Against the odds, Dorothy's gamble paid off. As Uncle Ernest suspected, the telegram was no mistake; his niece had hit the jackpot. Dorothy Cottrell, an unknown writer from the backblocks of northern Australia, had just sold her first novel for a fantastic sum, and was now poised to become a publishing sensation in America. It was every writer's fantasy, a fairytale come true. Once she accepted the news was real, Dorothy 'nearly died of joy'.

Even before this life-changing telegram, Dorothy was far from ordinary. Back in 1908, aged five, she'd contracted polio and lost the use of her legs. For several years, doctors subjected her to painful braces and experimental treatments, but eventually conceded Dorothy would never walk again. From that point onwards, she got about in a wheelchair. Although her family mourned Dorothy's paralysis, she herself refused to let this disability limit or define her. From a young age, Dorothy was an adventurous spirit who craved excitement. Relentlessly curious and cheerful, the budding writer was determined to taste life in all its flavours. So she did, wheelchair notwithstanding.

As a young girl, Dorothy loved cars and guns. Hunting was a favoured pastime, and she trained sheep and cattle dogs to pull her around Ularunda station. Later, she had automobiles altered to allow her to manipulate the controls with her arms. After a few modifications, Dorothy could operate a vehicle independently. With these hobbies she took after her father Walter Wilkinson, an early automobile enthusiast and passionate shot. Dorothy's parents separated around her fifth birthday, and she never saw Wilkinson again, but in her taste for adventure Dorothy was very much her father's daughter.

At Ularunda, Dorothy was homeschooled by her mother and aunts. In her teen years, during the Great War, she moved to Sydney to study art – a hobby she was determined to turn into a career. Over in the United States, she'd heard, it was possible to make a good living as a commercial artist. In Sydney, Dorothy was tutored by woman sculptor Theo Cowan and took lessons from Italian-born Dattilo Rubbo at the Royal Art Society. Living with her unmarried Aunt Lavinia at Parsley Bay, Dorothy developed a passion for swimming. Sydney Harbour, with its traffic of ocean liners, offered a glimpse of a bigger world. Here, on the brink of the continent, there were constant comings and goings – a daily reminder that Australians could and did set sail to any number of destinations across the globe.

Back at Ularunda, Dorothy embarked on her greatest adventure to date: a scandalous elopement to a tropical island. In early 1920, a few months after Dorothy returned from Sydney, a new bookkeeper arrived at the station. His name was Walter Cottrell, a fresh-faced 19-year-old from the Whitsundays. Station life pushed Walter and Dorothy together. There were only several dozen people on the whole property, and these two were almost the same age. Inevitably, they spent long hours in each other's company. They went for walks; they went for drives. They fell in love.

In May 1922, during a family visit to Brisbane, Walter and Dorothy went out for a walk and ducked into Ann Street Presbyterian Church. A few minutes later, they were married. Dorothy Wilkinson was now Dorothy Cottrell. It was a spontaneous decision, and the ceremony was quick and functional, completed before her family could notice anything awry. As Dorothy was still only 20, unable to wed without parental consent, she lied about her age to the minister. Afterwards, the newlyweds told no one. To all appearances, they had experienced nothing more eventful than a casual afternoon stroll.

The couple returned to Ularunda as secret husband and wife.

For over six months they kept their counsel. Then, on 25 January 1923, they dropped the bombshell via an elopement that exhibited a novelist's taste for high drama. Dorothy, the brains of the couple, planned it all with meticulous attention to detail. She waited until her uncle Ernest was away on business. When the moment was ripe, she faked a telegram from an invented friend of Walter's. The friend was passing through nearby Morven; could Walter spare the time to see him? With this excuse to leave the property, Walter and Dorothy set off in a family car. Before leaving, they cut the telephone wire that connected Ularunda to the outside world, an act of sabotage designed to foil any attempt to prevent their flight.

Once safely in Morven, the couple boarded a train heading east. Their final destination: Dunk Island, a tropical paradise in the Great Barrier Reef, a remote Whitsundays island made famous by long-time inhabitant EJ Banfield, author of *Confessions of a Beachcomber*. Upon arrival, Dorothy and Walter moved into a small shack, where they cosplayed Robinson Crusoe and lived off fresh fish and coconuts.

Dorothy's family, when they discovered the ruse, were enraged about the 'unnecessary duplicity', and condemned Dorothy's absence of 'contrition or regret'. Dorothy, for her part, was unrepentant. She treated the whole episode as a great lark, a romantic adventure that added a little spice to everyone's life. As she wrote from Dunk in July 1923, 'if they choose to make a tradgy [sic] out of a naughty prank I am not responsible'.

After six months on Dunk Island, Banfield died suddenly. With their host deceased, the Cottrells relocated to Sydney, where they struggled to survive on the meagre income provided by Dorothy selling the occasional drawing to magazines. After Dorothy's mother begged them to return home, they meandered back to Queensland in a red lorry, working as pedlars to fund the journey.

In June 1924, 18 months after their elopement, Dorothy and Walter arrived back at Ularunda. All was forgiven and Walter resumed his former job as bookkeeper. Dorothy started writing. She'd already published several articles in the Queensland press, including a 1922 diatribe against 'The Socialistic Menace' in the *Grazier's Review*. But now she turned to fiction in earnest. Writing replaced visual art as Dorothy's creative outlet and career aspiration. From her position under the jacaranda tree, she churned out four manuscripts in concurrent fashion. Her family knew about 'Dossie's book', but she showed the drafts to no one.

That is, until 1925, when a chance meeting pushed her onto the path to publication. That year, Dorothy visited Sydney with her mother and uncle for some medical appointments. The trio stayed at the St James Hotel in Elizabeth Street, where one day, in the lobby, they encountered a bespectacled grey-haired woman of around 60. It was the poet Mary Gilmore, a luminary of the Australian writing scene – one of the few women to make an impression in a literary landscape dominated by the bush poets who clustered around the blokey *Bulletin* journal.

In the Sydney hotel lobby, Gilmore and Dorothy struck up a conversation. Once Dorothy realised that this woman was the famous poetess, she worked up the courage to confess her own literary efforts. Dorothy remembered she was 'shaking with fright'. Yet she managed to overcome these nerves and ask the big question. Could Gilmore spare the time to look over some of Dorothy's jottings?

Gilmore would remember this moment as one of only two encounters with literary 'genius'. Her first 'wonderful literary find' was bush poet Henry Lawson, back in the 1890s; this 1925 meeting with Dorothy Cottrell was the second. After their meeting in the lobby, Gilmore agreed to peruse a manuscript. Barely two pages in, she declared: 'Here is genius.' She devoured the story in one sitting and returned it the next day. From that point onwards,

Gilmore would be Dorothy's mentor. She edited her manuscripts, advised on the publishing landscape, sang her praises in the press. Dorothy, for her part, cultivated this relationship. For all her introversion, the Queensland writer was an ambitious operator who, even as an unpublished novice, was determined to make a living from her pen. Although shy among strangers, she was not shy about asking Gilmore for help.

On 1 January 1927, about a year after they met, Dorothy sent Gilmore the full draft of *The Singing Gold*. The novel was an autobiographical bildungsroman, set on a fictionalised Ularunda station, that was classic bush Australiana with a female lens. *The Singing Gold* follows the adventures of Joan, a headstrong 'Australian Girl' who climbs trees and hunts kangaroos, a 'sunburnt, hoydenish' child of the colonial frontier reminiscent of Sybylla in Miles Franklin's *My Brilliant Career* (1902). As Joan comes of age, she secretly marries in Brisbane and then elopes to a tropical island, before moving to Sydney. This was Dorothy's story – without the wheelchair. Her fictional counterpart had full use of her legs.

With Gilmore's encouragement, Dorothy sent the manuscript out for publication. As the *Ladies' Home Journal* editor Barton Currie later recalled, the novel arrived 'from the back of beyond with no other foreword or introduction than a little note of apology from the author for having presumed to send it to her favorite of all magazines'. The next month, in April 1927, Currie sent Dorothy the telegram that changed everything.

From there, things moved quickly. By May, Dorothy received an offer to publish the novel from Boston outfit Houghton Mifflin. In June, she began fielding requests from Australian publications eager to serialise *The Singing Gold* at home. London publishers also expressed interest. Dorothy received the promised $5000 from the *Ladies' Home Journal* and looked to 'make a heap of money' from other sources. Newly flush, the writer purchased a six-cylinder Oaklands car. Meanwhile, the Australian press jumped on the story of Dorothy's 'sensational rise to fame'. She was touted as a 'new star' who was 'sailing like a brilliant new comet into the firmament of fiction'. As *Smith's Weekly* put it, 'fortune and fame have thus descended upon her all of a heap'.

More than just a personal victory, Dorothy's success was framed as a game changer for the nation's global reputation. For almost the first time, here was a local writer advertising 'the spirit of Australia' on the world stage. *Smith's Weekly* observed that 'until now Australia has had little space on the fiction shelves of the world. Now it seems that Dorothy Cottrell is to break that spell'. Her novel promised to sell Australia to the United States; it was a work of cultural diplomacy. 'This is Australia as we want the world to see it', explained Mary Gilmore in the *Daily Telegraph*. 'This Queensland girl's book is going to tell the Americans more about Australia than all the Year Books ever published.' At a time when Australia lacked formal diplomatic ties with the United States, *The Singing Gold* would bring the two countries closer together. 'It will "tell America" as nothing else has done,' Gilmore proclaimed.

When the Christmas 1927 edition of *Ladies' Home Journal* announced the highlights for 1928, chief among them was Dorothy Cottrell's *The Singing Gold*, to be serialised in the coming year. The novel was, the *Journal* declared, 'a work of genius' that would likely receive more 'enthusiastic praise' than any story published in recent years. '[R]arely have we risked such a sweeping statement in an editorial forecast,' the editor concluded.

As the *Ladies' Home Journal* arrived in mailboxes around the United States, Dorothy's words would be read by millions of Americans. But would the author herself cross the Pacific?

There was no requirement that she do so. According to historians David Carter and Roger Osborne, an estimated 250 Australians (women and men) published books in the United States in the first half of the 20th century, and many never left home. Yet by late 1927, Dorothy was making plans to sail to California. Why did she decide to go? The ostensible reason was to avoid 'iniquitous taxation' attached to foreign income. But Dorothy also needed little encouragement to leave. She adored travel and long had her eye on an American career. As she told Gilmore, she was 'awfully keen' to set sail. The financial rationale may have been partly an excuse to placate Dorothy's family, especially her mother, Ida, who was fiercely opposed to the writer moving abroad.

There were also solid professional reasons to head stateside. For much of the 20th century, there existed two distinct English-language publishing markets: the British and the American. Books published in Sydney or London would never appear in American bookstores unless an American publisher secured the rights to publish their own edition. To penetrate this ecosystem, it was far easier to be there in person. As one Melbourne writer explained in 1936, the 'mere fact of geographical distance militates against success'. By crossing the Pacific, Dorothy could meet editors and publishers in person; she could develop relationships and network; she could put a face to the name and give herself the best possible chance of success.

Whatever the true motivation, in January 1928 Dorothy and Walter left Ularunda for Sydney. From there, they would sail to California. But their attempts to purchase passage were foiled by an unforeseen obstacle: the United States quota restrictions. In 1921, the United States had introduced new border restrictions to limit the intake of 'undesirable' migrants. Inspired by the White Australia policy, this immigration regime was intended to protect the 'whiteness' of the United States. Yet the US state sought to dodge the diplomatic fallout of explicit racism. To this end, it designed a mechanism of exclusion that would present a veneer of even-handedness: nation-based quotas. Each sending nation was allocated an annual migration quota, calculated at 3 per cent of foreign-born from that country listed in the 1910 US Census. In practice, this formula did – as intended – drastically reduce 'undesirable' migrants from southern and eastern Europe. Yet by applying a blanket formula worldwide, the United States could maintain the pretence it was treating all foreigners the same.

The irony, however, was that white Australians were caught in the crosshairs of this American attempt to emulate the White Australia policy. Once the quota system commenced in 1921, only 279 Australians could migrate to the United States each year. From 1929, when the quotas were recalculated to reflect the 'national origins' of the US population, that number fell to only 100. The quota places were allocated monthly on a first come basis. At first, quota places were issued at the US border and then (from 1924) by US consuls in Australia. Invariably, demand far exceeded supply. As of 1928, Australian demand was twenty times the allocated figure. Once the monthly or annual quota was exhausted, Australians heading to the US could only enter on a six-month tourist visa (though there were some loopholes for students and professionals). Even though white Australians were deemed highly 'desirable' migrants, quota arithmetic meant that they now struggled to gain entry to the United States.

In 1928, Dorothy and Walter Cottrell ran headfirst into these immigration restrictions. When the couple arrived in Sydney, they discovered Australia's quota allocation had been exhausted. There was no chance of securing visas for at least three months. In June, after six months of stasis, the Cottrells relocated to Brisbane, where they hoped for better luck getting their paperwork in order. In the end, it took nine months to secure a quota spot. Finally, on 19 October 1928, Dorothy and Walter left Sydney on the *Niagara*. It was a perfect blue morning, with the harbour as still as a mirror.

Mary Gilmore and Aunt Lavinia said their goodbyes at the wharf, then Lavinia taxied down to South Head to wave towels as the *Niagara* sailed from the harbour. Eighteen months after her big break, the writer was going to California to – as Gilmore put it – 'stand up in the great world'.

But she had left someone behind. In 1927, Dorothy and Walter went on a road trip through the Northern Territory, where Dorothy was charmed by a First Nations child called May. She was a tiny thing, only six years old. Acting on impulse, Dorothy sought to take May back to Ularunda. Although the girl was in her mother's care, the Aboriginals Ordinance of 1918 gave the Protector of Aborigines guardianship over every Aboriginal child. After a brief exchange with the Protector, Dorothy's request was granted. The writer was permitted by the colonial state to assume custody over a child she'd only just met. May was a member of the Stolen Generations, and Dorothy was the thief.

Dorothy soon lost interest. Preoccupied with her writing, there was no space in her life for parenting. Before long, May was handed over to Aunt Lavinia, and her name was changed to Barbara Cherry Lee. When Dorothy sailed for the United States in October 1928, Barbara remained in Sydney. Dorothy's letters to the family make no mention of her. Stolen then abandoned, like a toy that had ceased to amuse.

Later, as an adult, May/Barbara reinvented herself as Cherie Leigh, a beauty with Spanish and Torres Strait Islander heritage. As Cherie, she worked in Europe as a fashion model, and settled in Amsterdam, where she married Dutchman Albert Klut. In early 1973, Cherie visited Australia and was profiled by the *Australian Women's Weekly*. As far as we know, however, she never reunited with her mother or Country.

8
A CITY OF DREAMS
THE ARTIST, NEW YORK CITY, 1927

It was love at first sight, a love that only deepened in the passing days. 'It is a wonderful experience to be in New York,' Mary Cecil Allen reported from her new digs on Riverside Drive. 'It is such a huge, dazzling city with its millions of inhabitants from every nation under heaven.' The artist adored it all: the lights of Broadway, reflected in the river at night. The cosmopolitan crowds on the subways, speaking languages from every corner of the world. The jaw-dropping art museums and the fall colours in Central Park.

Best of all was the pervasive atmosphere of modernity, the invigorating sense of living right on the edge of things. 'More than anywhere else in the world does one feel the insistence in New York of "Here" and "Now",' Mary observed. 'One realises that it is indeed 1927 and something had better be done about it!' For an artist interested in modern ways of living and expressing oneself, there was no better place to be. The city's 'emphasis on the present day' created an 'atmosphere stimulating to invention' that unleashed her creativity. As soon as she unpacked her bags, Mary began painting 'in real earnest'.

Like many great romances, the love affair between Mary and New York almost didn't happen. The artist had left her native Melbourne earlier in 1927 with no plans to visit America; rather, Europe was her intended destination. Mary was 33 years old, a single woman still living in the family home, with a burgeoning career as a painter and art educator. In 1926, her public lectures at the National Gallery of Victoria had attracted the attention of a visiting New Yorker named Florence Gillies. An unmarried 'society woman' in her 50s, a statuesque grande dame with a crown of wavy white hair, Florence came out to Australia in 1926. Impressed by Mary's art lectures, Florence approached the young artist with a proposition. Would Mary act as a personal guide to the art galleries of Italy and France?

The offer came at the perfect moment. Mary's father had recently died, and she was eager for a change of scene. Plus, a European sojourn would have career benefits. At the time, every Australian artist worth their salt studied in the so-called Old World; this was Mary's chance to likewise gain creative stimulus and boost her credentials.

After coming to an agreement, Mary and Florence set sail from Melbourne on 11 January 1927. They spent eight months immersing themselves in the wonders of the Louvre and Borghese Palace. In Paris, she met up with Australian friends, including her former teacher Max Meldrum. By late September, Mary was in London, poised to board a steamer back to Sydney. She'd bought a ticket to sail on P&O's *Mooltan* and her name was entered on the passenger list.

Then there was a dramatic change of plans. The Carnegie Trust invited Mary to lecture in New York. Should she stick with her scheduled return to Melbourne or head to America instead? It was a fork in the road that would reshape the rest of her life.

Deciding the New York invite was too good to refuse, Mary made an 11th-hour change to her itinerary. The *Mooltan* sailed off to Sydney without her on 23 September, her name struck from the ship's manifest. The following day, the artist boarded the *Aquitania*, embarking on the seven-day journey across the Atlantic. Mary planned to spend the next six months in the United

States and postpone her homecoming to the following year. She'd be back in Melbourne before long. Or, at least, that was the idea.

What the artist didn't predict was that she'd fall head over heels with New York, and that the city would return this affection. She'd be invited to lecture everywhere from the Metropolitan Museum to Columbia University to the People's Institute, an educational institution for workers and immigrants. Her lectures were published by WW Norton as *The Mirror of the Passing World* in 1928, a book hailed as a 'virile and compelling' work of 'brilliant criticism'. Its success paved the way for her 1929 book, *Painters of the Modern Mind* also published by Norton. She moved downtown to bohemian Greenwich Village, and started exhibiting her own work, attracting the notice of the *New York Times*. From there, she would receive more opportunities to lecture and exhibit and curate and tour the country.

New York's rich cultural life would swallow her up, and six months would turn into eight years.

It is no surprise that Mary became an educator, for she was raised in an educational hothouse. Born in 1893, the second child of Harry and Ada Allen, she grew up in a redbrick professorial residence within the University of Melbourne, where her father was Dean of Medicine. Mary and her two sisters, Edith Margaret and Beatrice, received a comprehensive private education, and their mother entertained members of Melbourne's intellectual elite. In 1910 Mary qualified to begin a Bachelor of Arts at the university but decided instead to enter the National Gallery of Victoria (NGV) Art School. Aside from a stint at London's Slade School in 1912, Mary studied at the NGV until 1917.

She was a talented and vivacious student, popular among her peers. Fellow student Joan Lindsay – the author of *Picnic at Hanging*

Rock – recalled 'how we students in the lunch hour used to flock around Mary like hungry sparrows picking up the crumbs of her wit and wisdom'. Although she excelled at her studies, Mary later regretted her long association with this conservative institution. Under the tutelage of Bernard Hall and Frederick McCubbin, she was taught according to rigid academic convention, and given little scope to develop her own style. Innovation was viewed with suspicion and modernism was the enemy.

During the 1920s, Mary was a rising star of the Melbourne art world. She had solo exhibitions at the Fine Art Society Gallery in 1919, 1921 and again in 1924. She also exhibited in group shows with the Society of Women Painters and Sculptors and the Australian Art Association. Her portraits and landscapes appealed to the Melbourne intelligentsia, from whom she received numerous commissions. It no doubt helped that Mary moved in the upper echelons of Melbourne society and her father had received a knighthood in 1914.

Mary was adept with a paintbrush but also had a rare knack for talking about art. She believed art should be accessible for all, as it offered 'nourishment for the minds and hearts of all mankind without distinction of education, class or religious belief'. Fuelled by this democratic impulse, Mary shared her passion with large and diverse publics. The art historian Sir Joseph Burke later described her as 'an apostle of art', a charismatic figure able to hypnotise her audience. 'When she taught,' Burke noted, 'the class or lecture room seemed to disappear, and its place was taken by a magic casement opening onto the world of the imagination.'

These skills led Mary to develop a second career as an art educator. In 1925 she became an art critic with the *Sun*, Melbourne's popular pictorial newspaper, the first woman to hold this position. The following year, she was appointed the first female guide-lecturer at the National Gallery of Victoria. In this capacity, she gave a well-attended series of lectures that covered European works in the gallery's collection. Already, Mary was unafraid to voice strong opinions. The public learnt that Rembrandt demonstrated 'supreme mastery' as an etcher, whereas Whistler's skills were 'thin and unsatisfactory' by comparison. At a time when the nation's cultural tastemakers were almost entirely mature white men, it was rare and not a little radical for a young woman to position herself as an authority on high art.

At this point, while Mary was reaching beyond her academic training, she was not a full-blown modernist. This was hardly surprising, as modernism had yet to achieve a serious foothold in the local art world. Even in the late 1920s, a full two decades after Picasso's cubism revolutionised the possibilities of painting, Australian art was still dominated by the nationalist pastoral landscapes of Hans Heysen and Arthur Streeton. During this decade, Mary studied with Max Meldrum, a tonal Impressionist whose students Arnold Shore and Jock Frater were among the first in Melbourne to experiment with modernism. Mary, however, was not yet on board. In the *Sun* she was critical of Shore's work, and in one lecture asserted that post-Impressionists 'create nothing but monsters – they invent the abnormal'.

Truth be told, Mary could be judged a little abnormal herself. She was a modern woman who shunned conventional expectations about feminine behaviour. She showed no interest in marriage and motherhood; she was unapologetically ambitious in her career. In a studio photograph from this era, Mary cuts an androgynous figure in a turban and sleeveless shift dress. She's lithe of limb, almost boyish, with a fashionable flat chest and sharp jawline. A queer specimen, elegant and assured, her gaze refuses the viewer, instead peering off to the far horizon. Perhaps she was already looking towards the skyline of Manhattan.

New York made a modernist out of Mary. 'There is no place in the world in which it was so easy to scrap old prejudices and to acquire new sympathies,' she insisted. Mary was speaking from experience. In the city, she scrapped old prejudices with lightning speed. The artist gravitated towards the progressive Art Students League, where she befriended Hans Hofmann, a German émigré later renowned as a founding father of abstract expressionism. In *The Mirror of the Passing World*, Mary offered a sympathetic account of modernist painting. As she explained in her signature jargon-free prose, modern art prioritised 'invention' over representation; it aimed not to mimic or recreate objective reality, but rather to communicate the artist's own personal vision. 'Great art is not descriptive,' she explained. Rather, the 'ideal of to-day is that each artist should create a new art in his own image, record his own individuality in paint and stone'.

Mary developed this argument in her follow-up, *Painters of the Modern Mind*. Once again, she insisted that art should convey ideas rather than imitate nature. Modern art, she explained, 'disputes and denies the supremacy of the eye in painting', and instead conveys 'a state of mind'. Although this 'denial of optical truth' could produce distortion and the 'grotesque', these elements signified the creativity of the artist, rather than a loss of technical skill. The quality of an artwork, therefore, could no longer be judged by its similarity to visible objects, but whether it succeeded in realising the artist's vision.

Within a few years, this thinking transformed Mary's own work. Her style became more abstracted, more expressionistic, less tethered to academic convention. Her 1930 exhibition at New York's Contemporary Art Gallery contained 30 new portraits, figures and landscapes painted in 'the modern manner'. Then, in October 1931, Mary was profiled in the French modern art journal *La Revue Moderne*, which praised the artist's ability to generate 'maximum expressive power with a minimum of means'. As her star rose, Mary secured more work. In 1931 she was appointed head of the Art Department at Miss Hewitt's School, an exclusive New York girls' school – a steady job that gave her a modicum of financial security.

That same year, Mary curated the first United States exhibition of Australian art. Organised at the instigation of Herbert Brookes, Australian Commissioner-General in New York (and husband of Ivy Brookes, Mary's old friend), this exhibition was exhibited at New York's Roerich Museum in February 1931. In a sign of how far Mary had come since leaving Melbourne, critics judged her work the exception to the prevailing conservatism. For the *New York Times* art critic Edward A Jewell, the exhibition indicated that 'nothing very remarkable in the way of painting has been produced by Australian artists'. Yet amid this sea of 'derivative and academic' painting, Mary's work stood out as 'arrestingly modern', he wrote on 8 February. Later that year, Mary toured the Australian exhibition to 14 cities, acting as a de facto cultural attaché. At a moment when the two nations had yet to exchange ambassadors, Mary was – much like the novelist Dorothy Cottrell – using culture to connect Australia and the United States.

Mary's newfound modernity was not limited to her art. She also embraced a modern lifestyle, renting a studio at 225 West 13th Street, in the heart of Greenwich Village. Neighbours included the *New Yorker* critic Edmund Wilson, the offices of literary magazine *The dial* (publisher of TS Eliot's *The Waste Land*), and the New School for Social Research. In 1930, she shifted a few blocks to a light-filled studio on Christopher Street – a hub of illegal speakeasies and queer life. In this liberal neighbourhood, far from the prying eyes of family, Mary tasted new freedoms and pleasures. In the early 1930s, she had a boyfriend known as Joe, a 'strong and silent' fellow. An engineer by trade, Joe slept with steel rods beneath his bed, convinced the metal would give him strength.

From whispers and innuendo, it's probable Mary enjoyed other romances over the years. In our heteronormative world, it's easy to assume these were all with men. But might there also have been women in Mary's life? It is impossible for a historian to pin down Mary's sexuality. Not only is there a lack of evidence but it is anachronistic to project contemporary sexual identities like 'bisexual' into the past. Yet there are persistent hints of queerness in Mary's American life. First is her long association with established queer neighbourhoods: in Greenwich Village and later Provincetown, Massachusetts, where Mary settled in middle age. Since the early 20th century, Provincetown has been an artist's colony renowned as an epicentre of queer America. When she moved there in the early 1950s, Mary would have known she was decamping to a rare haven for same-sex couples. Was she just drawn to the town for its rich artistic life, or did she feel at home for other reasons as well?

Second, Mary was close friends with known queer women. These included the Australian journalist Pat Jarrett and artist Maie Casey, both of whom lived stateside between 1940 and 1942 while Maie's husband, Richard Casey, served as Australia's inaugural Minister to the United States. Jarrett was Richard Casey's secretary. During those years, the three women regularly socialised in New York, painting together in Mary's studio at 903 Madison Avenue, a short stroll from Rose Cumming's boutique. Pat and Maie were both women who loved women; this was an open secret among their social networks. Later, Mary became close friends with Australian artist Frances Burke, also well known as a queer woman. Is it possible that Mary connected with these women over shared proclivities?

Third, as mentioned, Mary had an androgynous gender expression that only grew more butch during her New York years. Back in Melbourne, she'd been known as 'Mary Allen' but in New York adopted the more masculine 'Mary Cecil Allen'. Often, she was known as 'M Cecil Allen' or just 'Cecil Allen'. By the time she moved to Provincetown, Mary was universally known as Cecil. Although ostensibly for professional reasons, this change of name corresponded with a broader refusal of conventional white femininity. Mary wore her hair cropped, and favoured pants over skirts. Of course, gender expression is not the same as sexuality, but the masculine woman has long been associated with same-sex attraction. In the interwar decades, gender non-conformity and homosexuality were typically conflated, with the former regarded as evidence of the latter.

For all these reasons, it's credible Mary was queer in both senses of the word: both an unconventional freethinker, someone a bit different from the norm, and a person whose desires existed outside the heterosexual matrix. Whatever the truth of the matter, it's clear she was a rebel, a woman who followed the beat of her own drum in both work and life. As one friend recalled, Mary settled abroad 'because she felt restricted in the circle of her family'. By choosing the anonymous life of the expatriate, in the most permissive neighbourhood of the world's most modern city, Mary was able to unfurl her wings and experiment to a degree unthinkable in Melbourne.

This freedom and independence came at a cost. As an artist reliant on a fluctuating income during the Depression years, Mary often experienced financial hardship. Her unconventional life choices also fuelled conflict with her mother, who was displeased with her daughter's New York life. When Lady Allen died in December 1933, while Mary was still in New York, the artist was effectively disinherited.

Without family support, she would have to eke out a living in New York via her wits. It was worth the challenge, for she deemed it a 'city of dreams come true'. After eight years in Manhattan, Mary believed there was 'no other place in the world where it is possible to live so complete a life'. Yet the wolf was never far from the door. Now almost 40, and lacking the safety net of parents or husband, she had to hustle to survive. As Mary later noted: 'the life of a single woman earning her living in New York is a very strenuous one'.

9

WE DO NOT TEACH LADIES

THE SWIMMER, SYDNEY, 1927

Even near the water, the temperature was almost 40 degrees in the shade. The punters lining the sands at Bondi sweltered in the late summer heatwave, no doubt wishing they could plunge into the ocean. But they were there to watch rather than swim. It was the annual North Bondi Surf Life Saving carnival, an occasion for the city's best lifesavers to strut their stuff. There was an open surf race, followed by junior events, and a boat race. In a dramatic finish, Manly's boat *Sawfish* beat North Cronulla by barely a length. Finally, a swimmer feigned distress and three bronzed lifesavers from the local club demonstrated their rescue skills. Moving in tight formation, their muscled arms carried the limp body to shore while onlookers gawked.

It was a remarkable spectacle, but one member of the crowd had good reason to be unimpressed. Isabel Letham was back in Sydney that February, and likely came along to this surf carnival, an extravaganza that featured her old chums from the northern beaches. A surf community getting together on a scorching Saturday was a perfect day out to cap off a summer at home. But despite the merriment, Isabel must have been frustrated – even angry. Why? Because she couldn't participate. No matter her skills and strength, as a woman, she could never claim the title of lifesaver. She could only look and admire. This exclusion from the Bondi carnival was a painful reminder that her homecoming had not gone to plan.

When she landed in Sydney three months earlier, on 23 November 1926, Isabel was greeted by reporters at the dock. Her name was in all the Sydney papers. After four years in San Francisco, teaching swimming in the city's top pools, Isabel had arrived in Sydney as a confident professional, an expert with things to say. This was a different Isabel from the smiling girl surfer who'd won over the local public ten years before. That old Isabel was the kind of girl Sydney could get behind: pretty, eager to please, with just the right amount of pluck. Charming yet fundamentally unthreatening. But the girl had grown into a woman, a worldly adult who smiled less and spoke more. She had opinions and was not afraid to voice them. The trouble was her hometown did not take kindly to women with strong opinions. In many ways, it did not take kindly to women full stop.

From those first interviews, the returning swimmer made her intentions clear: Isabel was back in Australia as an unofficial ambassador for the swimming community, an emissary determined to build bridges across the Pacific. She sought to bring her two homes into dialogue about their shared love of water sports. California had the edge in terms of swimming facilities and pedagogy. Indeed, Isabel told the *Sunday Times*, compared to the situation in San Francisco, Australian children were being taught to swim in 'a very haphazard manner'. In a letter to the editor on 9 March 1926, she proclaimed that there was 'no really constructive work' being done. Australia would therefore do well to emulate America's 'wonderful system of scientific training of the athlete'. Yet Australia also had things to offer. The nation was a pioneer of lifesaving, a world first that had saved countless lives since the original club was founded in Bondi in 1907. Both countries therefore could learn from each other. With a foot in both camps, Isabel was determined to foster an exchange of ideas.

In particular, she wanted to export Sydney surf lifesaving across the Pacific, where nothing comparable existed. In her adopted home of San Francisco, drownings were so commonplace that ocean bathing was discouraged altogether. To address this high casualty rate, Isabel hoped to import Australian techniques into her adopted city. This plan already had the backing of big names in California, including the Executive Secretary of the San Francisco Playground Commission.

But the mooted exchange was stonewalled by the Sydney lifesaving community. Why? Because Isabel was a woman. 'We do not teach ladies the work', explained CD Paterson, president of the Surf Life Saving Association of Australia. In the 1920s, and way up until 1981, women were deemed too weak to qualify for membership of surf lifesaving clubs. No matter her athletic prowess, Isabel couldn't join this literal boys' club. Her membership application for Manly Surf Club was refused. Without official membership, she had no authority or credentials to export lifesaving techniques to the United States. Even when offered the chance to school the Americans, the lifesaving community refused to budge on the sex ban. It was a stalemate.

Back in San Francisco, the *Daily News* reported Isabel's frustration with the headline: 'Sex Ban on Girl Life-Saver: So Australia Loses Advertisement'. The newspaper condemned the sexism that foiled a potential mutually beneficial exchange. Australia could win global recognition; American lives could be saved. But it was not to be: Australian lifesaving was cutting off its nose to spite its face. The *Daily News* was confident Isabel, given her strength as a swimmer, would pass the lifesaving association's entry requirements with 'flying colours', if only she were permitted to do so. As things stood, Isabel would return to San Francisco 'a very disgusted girl'. If nothing else, this episode confirmed something Isabel had sensed for some time: that, compared to Australia, 'opportunities were high for women' in the United States.

Back in San Francisco in early 1927, Isabel resumed her work as pool director at the Women's City Club. The club had grown into a vibrant community of 7000 members, with a waitlist of 3000. There was always something going on: lectures, parties, luncheons, concerts. When Isabel entered the club's natatorium in the early morning, the basement pool had the hush of a chapel. The Grecian columns along the water's edge were reflected in the still surface. Art deco droplights made up for the lack of natural light. Once the first swimmers arrived, all was noise and motion. Each day passed in a blur of private lessons, group lessons, children's play, pool parties, seniors' nights, diving classes, club coaching, swimming tests. The pool was open to club members, plus their children and guests; it was effectively a women-only space. Here women could learn new skills and test the limits of their bodies away from the male gaze.

As pool director, Isabel had two main objectives. The first was to bring the benefits of swimming to women unused to regular exercise. In the club magazine, swimming was promoted as part and parcel of modern womanhood. It had 'medicinal value'; it produced 'health and wealth'; it made one more 'efficient'; plus, it induced the 'boyish slimness' then in fashion. Club members were urged to maximise their potential by venturing down to the natatorium. By swimming laps, you could make a better body. A century before Silicon Valley became synonymous with wellness hacks and the optimised self, the Women's City Club was urging residents of San Francisco to exercise their way to self-actualisation.

One of Isabel's success stories was music teacher Alma C Bennett, whose nervous exhaustion and general malaise was cured after learning to swim. Despite initial misgivings, Bennett discovered a new zest for life through swimming daily laps. Her energy became boundless, her mood, joyous. Bennett was inspired to become a volunteer 'swimming hostess', urging others to join her in the club pool. For the likes of Bennett, Isabel's pool was akin to a church, a site of near-miraculous healing and redemption. If only individuals would discipline themselves to the daily prayer of swimming laps, the payoffs would be boundless. This religion found ready converts, with pool attendance rising each season. According to the club's magazine, the facility had 22 000 visitors in 1927, 25 000 the following year.

Isabel's second objective concerned the development of competitive women's sport, then in its infancy. In February 1927, she organised the club's first junior swimming meet, which featured around 50 competitors aged from 5 to 17. In April, the pool hosted the first women's meet of the year, held under the auspices of the Pacific Coast Association of the Amateur Athletic Union (AAU). The event attracted state and national champions, who put on a spectacular show for paying spectators. Under Isabel's leadership, the club pool brought institutional support and legitimacy to high-level women's sport. She also coached a team of athletes, who competed at club meets and other events around the state in uniforms decorated with the club emblem. Her top swimmer Evelyn Mefford was an AAU junior national long-distance champion.

The meets, the uniforms, the rankings, the medals: it all sent a message. Female sport deserved to be taken seriously. No matter what Australia's lifesavers might say to the contrary, Isabel was determined to prove women could be elite athletes. To that end, she barrelled ahead on the lifesaving front. Even though she'd been refused official credentials, Isabel went rogue and launched her own lifesaving classes. Gatekeepers be damned; she would do things her way.

During these years, Isabel discovered a new passion: swimming for people with disabilities. It started with a small experiment. Isabel had a friend-of-a-friend who was legally blind and worked as a secretary. If this woman could type, surely she could swim? Isabel volunteered to give her lessons. *You're mad*, she was told. *Blind people can't swim. How would that work?* Isabel had no idea, but she was eager to try. After six months or so, her friend finally agreed to set up a lesson.

It happened one evening, after the club pool had closed for the day. According to Isabel, both student and teacher were nervous yet determined. Having never visited a pool before, the woman was unnerved by the echoing noises and wet surfaces. Together, they walked around the space, getting accustomed to the new sensations. They had a shower, then entered the pool. Isabel held the woman's hand and demonstrated the basic strokes. It turned out her new student was a natural, far more adept than many sighted beginners. Before long, she could swim the length of the pool, with Isabel keeping a finger on her torso for balance. Eventually, she could swim unaided.

This encounter was a highlight of Isabel's career. Swimming 'opened a new life for this girl', she recalled, 'and that was a great, great pleasure to me'. From here, Isabel developed an interest in swimming for all sorts of disabilities. If it worked for someone who was blind, why not other groups? This was a radical stance for the 1920s, a time when people with disabilities were subject to eugenic measures (such as enforced sterilisation) designed at their eradication. Unlike most of her contemporaries, who viewed disability through a deficit lens, Isabel was interested in disabled potential. For her, this kind of work was more meaningful than coaching champion athletes. There would always be coaches lining up to train the fastest swimmers; Isabel 'wanted to take care of the people nobody bothered about'.

Fast-forward to early 1929. America was kicking up its heels and Isabel was along for the ride. She had US citizenship, a community of friends, and a rewarding career, all against the backdrop of a booming economy. Australian surf lifesaving had dealt her a bruising snub, but what did it matter? That was in the past, she was an American now. Her mother, Jeanie, her only surviving family member, was with her in San Francisco. Isabel had drawn a line under her life in Sydney. Maybe she'd never go back. Her future lay in the Golden State. Here, her talents were respected. Here, she could do good work in sport for both women and people with disabilities. She had big plans to use swimming to change lives.

One evening in late winter, Isabel was walking home from work. Up along Post Street, away from the Women's Club and the hubbub of Union Square. Past the men-only Olympic Club and Bohemian Club, past lines of parked automobiles, heading west up towards the hills where the well-heeled lived. Maybe she planned her next swim meet as she walked, or mused on a coaching strategy. Or perhaps she was thinking of a weekend jaunt down the coast. Spring was just around the corner, and it would soon be ideal weather for motoring.

Whatever the case, one minute Isabel was sauntering along; the next, the ground disappeared beneath her feet and she was falling through empty space. Falling, falling, then her body slammed into the hard earth. There was confusion and fear and hurt. Her back, it was in agony. Did she hear shouts from above, as onlookers rushed to the scene? Did she look up at the night sky and see stars? Or maybe she blacked out from the shock and the pain. Isabel was lying ten feet below the sidewalk and her life had changed forever.

Isabel had slipped on some grease and fallen into an uncovered manhole. It was a calamity straight out of the slapstick playbook, so melodramatic it would be humorous if it wasn't so devastating. She had landed alongside two men working down the hole, who got the fright of their life when a young woman dropped from the sky. These workers helped her to safety, but the accident had done terrible damage to her back. Doctors diagnosed an injury to the sacroiliac joint at the base of the spine. While her body healed, she had to wear a steel corset. There was no question she could work in this condition. Isabel's job was physical, it required her to walk and swim and move all day long. It would be a long time before she could do that again.

But if she couldn't work, how could she live? Without Isabel's salary from the Women's City Club, there was little cash to pay the bills. She had insurance, but the company was loath to pay out. And she didn't just have herself to consider; with her father gone, Isabel now supported her mother. Isabel couldn't work, they had no money coming in, and no safety net. It turned out the American Dream was reserved for the fit and well.

It was time for some hard decisions. In March 1929, a few weeks after the accident, Isabel resigned from the Women's City Club. The club accepted her resignation with 'regret', noting her 'efficient and loyal service'. Two months later, Isabel and Jeanie packed up their belongings and once again boarded a transpacific steamer. The injured swimmer was heading back to Sydney to recuperate. It was the only viable option. She still couldn't work, but at least they would save money on rent by living in the old family home in Freshwater.

It pained Isabel to leave California, but it was temporary. Just until she got well and was back on her feet. She'd be back in San Francisco soon enough, picking up where she left off.

Isabel couldn't know then that, a few months later, Wall Street would crash, and the Great Depression would begin. She couldn't know that her own personal financial crisis would slam into a global one, with repercussions that lasted for years. She couldn't know that this manhole accident was no temporary blip but a turning point that would alter her life's trajectory.

Isabel didn't know any of that, yet she immediately regretted her return to Australia. 'I felt I'd made a mistake,' she said decades later.

But it was too late. She was back in Sydney now, back in her childhood home up the hill from Freshwater Beach. Unable to work, unable to surf, unable to leave.

10

AN ATMOSPHERE FOR EXCELLENCE

THE PIANIST, CHICAGO, 1928

Vera Bradford sat down at the piano, squinting in the dim light. Inside this dark practice room, you wouldn't know it was a midsummer morning. No matter the season, Steinway Hall – home of the Chicago Musical College – remained cool and dark, an 11-storey skyscraper impervious to Illinois's dramatic seasons. Even on the brightest days, electric lights were essential to banish the gloom.

After flicking the switch, Vera returned to her seat. She took a breath, settled herself. On her tongue, she could still taste the coffee she'd drunk for breakfast – an unfamiliar bitterness that reminded her she was far from home. You couldn't get tea here. No squat teapot dressed in a knitted cosy. Only strong black coffee, which she now guzzled morning and night.

With caffeine fizzing in her veins, Vera's fingers flew over the keys, a practised dance almost as familiar as breathing. Her daily ritual for almost 20 years now, ever since she'd started piano lessons at the age of seven. Perhaps this morning she practised the Chopin 'Fantasy in F minor', one of her signature pieces. Or maybe John Alden Carpenter's concertino for piano and orchestra, a modern impressionistic piece first performed only a few years before.

Like every morning, Vera's music competed with the symphony of city life. Down on East Van Buren Street, where the air was thick and humid, double-decker buses roared past, delivering commuters to downtown offices. From the surrounding practice rooms came the noise of fellow pianists warming up for the day. Directly above, Vera could hear an organ play 'Get Out and Get Under the Moon', the hit song of the season. For weeks now, the jaunty tune had formed a backdrop to the Chicago summer, its upbeat melody capturing the guileless optimism she'd found in America. Through the open window, the familiar lyrics floated in on the morning air. 'When you're all alone, any old night /And you're feeling out of tune ...' It was hard not to start humming along.

But Vera couldn't succumb to distractions this morning. In less than a week, she would compete for a Grainger Fellowship. Percy Grainger, Australia's own world-famous musician, the eccentric maestro who'd been in the United States since 1918, was offering scholarships worth $600 to study under his supervision at the Chicago Musical College. Vera had sailed through the opening rounds of the competition. The final was coming up on Friday 22 June, only five days away. If she succeeded, Vera could stay on in Chicago for a whole year, maybe even longer, with private lessons from Grainger himself.

When she arrived in the United States a month earlier, Vera's plan had been for a brief American sojourn, before moving on to Europe. Vienna and Leipzig seemed promising – those great musical centres that had produced the likes of Bach and Wagner and Mozart. But almost immediately, Vera abandoned all thoughts of crossing the Atlantic. Chicago was then a hotbed of musical talent, home to an ever-growing array of European émigrés. Toscanini, Stravinsky, Schoenberg, Rachmaninoff – all the contemporary greats had congregated in America. Why leave the United States when there was an embarrassment of riches here? The Chicago Musical College 'spared no expense' in bringing them to teach. 'All the great people, they were all living there',

Vera recalled in a 1988 interview. You couldn't turn around without bumping into a famous face. The Chicago Symphony Orchestra was just around the corner, located on the same city block as the Chicago Musical College. Every night of the week, she could attend concerts performed by world-class musicians.

For a 20-something fresh from Melbourne's blue-collar western suburbs, this was heady stuff. 'I like Chicago better every day,' the pianist told her family. The city provided 'just the atmosphere I have wanted all my life. I really think I have come to the right place, to develop what I feel I can do.' And what was that? Vera felt she could become a world-class concert pianist. That was the vision. She would follow in Grainger's footsteps and be the next Australian to leave audiences breathless in London and New York. To get there, she would need to be surrounded by musicians no less ambitious than herself. And that was precisely what Vera found in Chicago. It was 'an experience that almost shocked me it was so wonderful'.

From a young age, Vera possessed uncommon musical ambition. Born on 5 September 1904, she was the eldest of three children. The Bradfords ran a wholesale butcher business in the Melbourne suburb of Kensington, making them a prosperous family in a working-class area. They were small-business owners with English heritage, devout Protestants who voted conservative and feared God. Music and Methodism were the twin family religions. The whole family was musical, but Vera was the star. 'As a little girl I played the piano all the time I could,' she recalled. 'I knew I was going to be a concert pianist ... there was never any question about it.' By the age of 12, Vera had made her Melbourne Town Hall debut, and began winning plaudits at local musical competitions.

In 1922, aged 17, Vera entered the Melbourne Conservatorium, funded by a full scholarship. Three years later, she graduated with first-class honours and was a rising star in the local music scene. On 4 October 1927, after a solo recital at Melbourne's Assembly Hall, Vera was hailed by the *Herald* as a 'promising young pianist' with, said *The Age* 'exceptional talents'. The next step was to study abroad. Vera hatched her travel plans. Her former Conservatorium classmate Marshall Sumner was studying with Grainger at the Chicago Musical College. Vera was keen to visit before travelling to Europe.

Britain was not on her itinerary. She made a deliberate decision to distance herself from the English school of playing that dominated Australian piano. After hearing the Russian pianist Benno Moiseiwitsch perform in Melbourne during the 1920s, Vera had been won over to the Russian weighted arm technique – a louder and more dramatic approach than the English method. 'The poetry, the interpretation, and it was all so effortless,' she recalled. From that point, Vera knew 'that this is the way I want to play, and I'll never let up, until I can have that sort of work'. There was no point going to the mother country; only the Russianists scattered around Europe and the United States could teach the arm-weight method.

Vera's departure was marked by a farewell concert at the Melbourne Town Hall on 19 April 1928, a fundraiser attended by the Lord Mayor. Vera's rendition of Chopin's 'Fantasy in F minor' received cheers and rousing applause from the crowd who braved the draughty Town Hall on a cool autumn eve. Critics noted that Vera, still so young, possessed a poise beyond her years. She was a natural performer. Now she must go abroad to acquire some metropolitan polish, as so many had done before. *The Age* predicted the next day that the pianist would 'bring honor to the Australian name'. Yet despite its enthusiasm for her 'promising future', *The Age* was unimpressed with Vera's decision to head stateside. Why had this young Australian turned her back on Mother England? 'Clearly, for music as well as for other studies, our British universities and Royal colleges should be given first preference', the broadsheet sniffed. When it came to the 'general environment' and 'artistic culture', London was 'at least as the equal of Leipzig and Chicago'.

Not everyone agreed. Although Australian musicians continued to look to Britain and Europe throughout the 20th century, transpacific mobilities like Vera's were increasingly common. By the 1930s, New York could be described in the Australian press as 'the music centre of the world', home to the star-studded Metropolitan Opera and many of the 'best teachers'. The subsequent war-induced flight of émigrés across the Atlantic, which saw top European musicians relocate to the States, only increased the relative appeal of an American career.

May 1928. A fortnight after her farewell concert, Vera departed on the *Niagara*, giddy with excitement. She immediately befriended everyone aboard. No doubts or homesickness for her. 'I am having the most wonderful time I have ever had in my life,' Vera wrote from aboard ship. 'I am the most popular girl on the boat.' By her account, she had no less than five 'special admirers'. But these flirtations were, for Vera, little more than a harmless bit of fun. She relished male attention, and was forever collecting new beaux, yet was, as her niece later recalled, 'married to her music'. Her career would always come first.

After making landfall on 25 May, Vera headed east. Her destination was the Chicago Musical College, a prestigious private institution that dated back to 1867, then located in downtown Chicago. After settling into the women's dormitory, Vera put her head down and went to work. She needed that scholarship money. Her father sent the occasional cheque, and she had the money from her benefit concert, but for a lengthy sojourn in Chicago she must convince Grainger she was worthy of a fellowship.

December 2019. On a white-hot day in early summer, I drove along a dusty road to a property on the outskirts of Melbourne. Wurundjeri Country, on the upper reaches of the Yarra. To get there, I passed through country burnt in the Black Saturday bushfires of 2009, not yet knowing that the season ahead would bring its own even more deadly conflagrations. I parked outside a brick farmhouse, a sprawling residence lovingly handcrafted over many decades. Inside, in the cool dark of the living room, a treasure was waiting for me.

Several months earlier, I was drinking tea with a new acquaintance when they asked about my research.

'I'm looking at Australian women who had careers in the United States,' I said, not expecting much in response. Like every researcher, I was used to being asked about my work, and knew the interaction rarely went beyond polite expressions of interest. Wary of boring my interlocutors, I tended to say only the bare minimum before moving the conversation along.

'America, you say? Interesting. My great-aunt did that. She was a pianist. Studied in Chicago.'

This was not the response I was expecting. Suddenly I was wide awake, my historian's radar activated.

'Really? What was her name?'

'Vera Bradford.'

At that point, I almost dropped my cup of tea.

'Vera Bradford? No way! She's in my study. I've written about her.'

'You should get in touch with my aunt Pam. She still has some of Vera's things in the back shed.'

And so here I was at Pam Usher's house, sweaty with heat and nerves, itching to get my hands on whatever Vera had left behind. This was every historian's wet dream. A private archive, never-before-seen papers, a whole goldmine sitting undisturbed in a family home for decades. After Vera died in 2004, her papers ended up with her niece Pam and Pam's husband, Jim, now energetic octogenarians. After I reached out via email, they'd invited me for lunch, so I could inspect the remnants of Vera's life.

In a series of old shoeboxes, I found bundles of yellowed paper covered in a rough scrawl. I picked them up, carefully removing rusted paperclips and ancient envelopes to peer at each fragile page. These were the letters that Vera had written from Chicago. Dozens of letters, some six or more pages in length, all mailed home to Melbourne and kept for nine decades.

Once I taught myself to read the messy script, I plunged into Vera's world. It was as though I was seeing Chicago through her eyes, reliving the thrill of travelling abroad for the first time. Through her words, I tasted the unfamiliar coffee, saw snow for the first time, experienced the accelerated intimacy of expat friendships.

What was most striking was Vera's ambition. The letters felt almost hot to touch, such was the fervour with which the pianist wrote about her music. Even as a 20-something colonial, a mere girl from the provinces, Vera knew she was good. Nothing was more important than her music and Vera was determined to be the best. She had a path to get there too. Never was she self-effacing or troubled by self-doubt. She was an artiste *en route* to fulfilling her potential.

Make no mistake: Vera was no rebel. She didn't wear pants or drink alcohol or have affairs. To all appearances, she was an exemplar of respectable white femininity – a devout churchgoer who made nice and respected her elders. She couldn't be less bohemian. Yet these external signs of conventionality concealed a ferocious appetite to succeed. Beneath her neat frocks, Vera was a self-styled Great Artist, willing to sacrifice money and romance at the altar of her art. It was invigorating – almost shocking – to encounter a woman from a century ago with such formidable self-belief.

After marvelling over the letters, I dug deeper into Vera's shoebox archive. Inside a plastic bag, the flimsy kind you might get at the supermarket, I found photographs from Chicago. Dozens upon dozens of snapshots, showing Vera at the piano, or at a fancy-dress ball, or sunbaking on the shores of Lake Michigan. Vera beamed up at the camera, offering a toothy smile from beneath a cloche hat, her open face unmarked by suffering or history. She was a petite woman with dark hair set in a permanent wave, a pint-sized dynamo. To family, she was known as 'the wombat'.

In most of the photographs, Vera is surrounded by friends. There was Mary, laughing with Vera in a snowdrift, both women dusted with soft white flakes. There was Vera perched behind two women in white dresses and hats, the trio jammed into an open-topped automobile. Together, these photographs told the story of a woman with a talent for enjoying herself. Even as she was consumed by creative ambition, Vera knew how to have fun. She was young and far from home – and having the time of her life.

That afternoon, I drove home through the golden hour with Vera's papers in the boot of my car. At the end of our day together, Pam and Jim had entrusted me with this precious archive. After years researching women like Vera, I knew how rare it was to encounter a whole cache of writing that offered access to their inner world. Most often, I had to make do with press reports and government documents that told only the bare facts of a woman's story. To find anything written in a woman's own voice was a thrill; to find years of correspondence was like winning the lottery. In return, I promised I would share Vera's story with the world.

On 26 June 1928, the Melbourne papers reported the good news. Vera Bradford had been awarded a Percy Grainger Fellowship to study at the Chicago Musical College for a whole year. 'Everyone here is quite excited about my playing,' she wrote to her family. Even in the bigger pond of the United States, Vera was – according to the Chicago *Music News* – 'swiftly becoming known as a promising artist of high musical value'.

Vera was now having twice-weekly private lessons with Grainger. 'I have improved out of all recognition since I have been under his influence,' she wrote at the end of June. 'He seems to be able to give me just what I needed.' Vera was equally enamoured of the man himself. Even though Grainger was an oddball with unusual proclivities (including a rumoured incestuous relationship with his mother), he and Vera became fast friends. Bonded by their shared love of music, the flamboyant eccentric and the upstanding churchgoer got on like a house on fire. He 'is really a dear', Vera confessed. 'He has taken quite a liking to me.'

Grainger was not Vera's only teacher. Eager to make the most of her time overseas, the pianist did not let loyalty to one master get in the way of her ambition. 'I must decide to study with the best I can,' she explained in a letter. 'When I come back I want to come fully equipped with a foundation equal to any great artist.' By November 1928, Vera had won a second scholarship from Rudolph Ganz, a Swiss pianist who had taught at the College since 1900. But while Grainger and Ganz had lessons to impart, Vera learnt the most from a third man: Alexander Raab, a Hungarian renowned for teaching the Russian arm-weight technique. After studying with Theodor Leschetizky, a pioneer of the Russian school, Raab migrated to the United States in 1915 and became Head of Piano at the Chicago Musical College. There, he was renowned for his distinctive teaching method. In March 1929, Vera secured one of Raab's scholarships. Under his instruction, she hoped to be ready for the concert stage in only a year. 'My work is coming on wonderful [sic],' she reported that summer. 'My playing has changed entirely. My technique is different. I am developing a hand as big as a foot.'

Given that Raab's approach required a reset of her technique, Vera was forbidden to perform for a full year. For someone who loved the limelight, it must have been a struggle to stay off stage for so long. Yet she stuck with him, growing ever more devout as the months passed. There were plenty of decent teachers, but only Raab could develop her technique in 'the proper modern way'. 'Mr Raab is the one teacher in the world for me so I must study with him', she declared in October 1929. Raab, in turn, believed the young Australian was destined for 'a brilliant future'.

After a year in Chicago, making progress in her work, and with no plans to return home, Vera had a glow about her. Three great teachers had singled her out for tutelage, marking her as someone special. She seemed to be that rare creature: the talented young thing who could translate potential into genius. By this point, there was a momentum to her rise that made it all seem inevitable – she had been chosen, she worked hard and she would go on to a glittering career. It was so easy to imagine it unfold. She certainly wanted it enough. 'I feel as though part of me is missing when I can't play. It is my life to want to play,' Vera wrote to her family in August 1929.

PART II
THE WORLD OF TOMORROW

11

OUR ONLY WOMAN JUDGE

THE LAWYER, LOS ANGELES, 1928

It was the best Christmas present she could ask for. A gift that far exceeded anything that might appear, wrapped in paper, in a stocking or under the tree. On 25 December 1928, her 18th Yuletide in the United States, May Lahey received a life-changing piece of news: she'd been appointed to the judiciary. After 14 years as an attorney specialising in probate law, the former Queenslander would become a judge on the Los Angeles Municipal Court. In announcing the appointment, California's Governor CC Young noted that May was held in high esteem. 'I have not found anyone who has failed to speak of her in the highest terms,' Young said. The governor was a progressive Republican who'd long aimed to appoint an 'outstanding woman' to the bench; in May, he'd found his ideal candidate. As the *Los Angeles Times* put it, this popular woman attorney was a 'credit to her sex' who 'helped considerably to allay masculine disapproval of women lawyers'.

May first got wind of the news when a reporter called for an interview. Confused, she insisted there'd been some mistake. She didn't even know she'd been nominated. The judicial appointment came out of the blue, a Christmas miracle of sorts. Her colleagues, however, were unsurprised to see May's talents recognised. 'This is probably the most generally popular appointment which has ever been made to the Bench in this country', noted the president of the LA Bar Association. As the Probate Court Referee since 1916

– a role that involved appraising the property in an estate – May was 'widely and favorably known by the entire bar of the south'.

May's new job was a step forward for women in the law. She was only the second woman in California appointed to the municipal court – joining Georgia Bullock, who'd sat on the bench since 1926. Lahey and Bullock were part of a tiny handful of women municipal judges across the United States, the first of whom – Mary O'Toole in Washington DC – had only been appointed seven years earlier. Among local feminists, May's success was evidence that women 'possess intellects of a fine caliber and no longer can be regarded as a mere toy or plaything of man'. Surely, one newspaper letter-writer mused, now women like May Lahey were entering the judiciary, the United States would have a female president before too long? A century later, we're still waiting for that particular prophecy to come true.

Most remarkably, May's ascension to the bench came 37 years before Australia could boast a woman judge. No woman penetrated the Australian judiciary until 1965 when the state of South Australia appointed Dame Roma Mitchell to its Supreme Court. But on one view, May had been there first – nearly four decades earlier, she became the first Australian-born woman to claim the title of judge. Although she was officially a US citizen and presided in a Californian courtroom, May's appointment was nonetheless celebrated as a milestone in Australia. 'Our Only Woman Judge', declared the Melbourne *Herald*. As the Adelaide *Chronicle* put it, May was 'one of few women judges in the world, and the only one Australia has produced'.

May's appointment also prompted comparisons between Australia and the United States. In the Melbourne *Age* on 27 March 1929, one letter-writer touted May's success as evidence 'our talented women are able to secure the highest positions offered in other countries'. But why, the writer continued, were the nation's women not rewarded with similar kudos at home?

If Australian women were so brilliant, how come there were not women judges and MPs and professors in Australia? Up in Sydney, a columnist for *Smith's Weekly* made a similar point a year later. 'I always thought Australia led the world in woman emancipation,' the columnist 'Kitten' noted in March 1930. But now, with news of May Lahey on the judiciary, 'I find that they go one better in America'.

Although May's achievement was celebrated at the time, her name has since been written out of Australian history. These days, Dame Roma Mitchell is – as she should be – a widely commemorated individual, with her name attached to a high school, a scholarship, and both a statue and building on Adelaide's North Terrace. May Lahey, by contrast, is absent from both our history books and our urban landscape. Her story is recorded only in a self-published history of the Lahey family. As so often happens to transnational Australians, no matter how successful, she's fallen out of the nation's historical consciousness.

7 January 1929. The first Monday of the new year. As the winter sun climbed in the sky, a crowd gathered at the Los Angeles Municipal Courts Building. Located at 330 North Broadway, the building was in the heart of Civic Center, a cluster of state and federal buildings that formed the nucleus of downtown. City Hall was just around the corner. The Tajo Building, where May had attended law school, was a block away. Across the street was the Hall of Justice, a grand Beaux Arts building that housed the County Court and Jail. It was a bustling legal district, home turf for the city's powerbrokers. Over the past two decades, these streets had been May's stomping ground. First as a law student, then as an attorney, she'd carved a groove into these sidewalks, only a few miles from her Silver Lake home.

Today all eyes were on the Municipal Courts Building. As the clock struck 10 am, two new justices were sworn in. First up was Dr Ernest J Lickley, former city prosecutor, a balding man who sported a spotted bowtie and round spectacles. Lickley was a run-of-the-mill appointment – a civil servant and churchman who'd risen through the ranks with an eye to joining the bench. Lickley was the warm-up act, a man as qualified as he was unexciting. After he was sworn in, came the real star of the show: probate attorney May D Lahey. The new lady judge, the woman of the hour.

Appellate Judge Albert Lee Stephens was on hand to do the official honours. May was sworn in to preside over Division 24 of the Municipal Court, a civil non-jury department, becoming an official Mr Justice – though unlike in Britain and Australia, a wig would not be part of her wardrobe. The US justice system prided itself on being modern and democratic, and neither judges nor attorneys wore wigs and robes.

Among the crowd in court that morning was May's mother, Emily, also known as Amelia, a tiny Irishwoman who would have struggled to see over the hatted heads. The two older Lahey sisters, however, were missing. Ida had relocated to Tucson, Arizona, after marrying mining engineer Fenwick Hamilton in 1925, while Eva had moved to Vancouver, where she'd married accountant John Wylie in 1922. May's father, meanwhile, didn't live to see her success; he died in 1925. With her two sisters elsewhere, her father dead and her brothers in Australia, only Emily remained to provide a link between May's colonial Queensland childhood and this modern downtown courtroom across the globe.

Now almost 70, Emily had lived many lives. Born in the port city of Belfast amid sectarian conflict, she was a migrant to colonial Queensland, married to a fellow Irish settler who turned out to be a drunk, mother to seven children (two of whom died in childhood), and now California resident and parent to the latest poster girl for modern womanhood. What did Emily think about

May's appointment? Mothers are supposed to be proud of their offspring, but I wonder if she felt some measure of envy or even grief. Within a generation, life for the Lahey women had changed beyond recognition. It would've been understandable for Emily to mourn the opportunities and experiences she'd missed by virtue of being born too soon. Could she have even been a judge herself, given half the chance?

With the formalities done and dusted, it was time to celebrate. The following day, Los Angeles' movers and shakers congregated to toast the new Justice May D Lahey. The party was organised by Mabel Walker Willebrandt, a living legend known as the First Lady of Law. A divorced single woman who represented sex workers and victims of family violence, Willebrandt was the US Assistant Attorney General – a post that made her the highest-ranking woman in the federal government. In that role, she attracted the moniker 'Prohibition Portia' for her fearsome pursuit of bootleggers. Lahey and Willebrandt were long-time chums, both founding members of the Los Angeles Women Lawyers' Club back in 1918. Now the First Lady of Law was throwing the new lady Justice a bash to celebrate her historic appointment to the bench.

By all reports, it was quite the party. The venue was the Chateau Marmont, a gothic edifice on Sunset Boulevard. Today, the Chateau is an iconic Hollywood hotel, famous as temporary digs to everyone from F Scott Fitzgerald to Quentin Tarantino and Courtney Love. Back in 1929, however, the venue was a brand-new apartment complex. In fact, on the date of May's party, the Chateau Marmont wasn't even finished; the building officially opened its doors on 1 February, several weeks later. Willebrandt, a business associate of the Chateau's owner Fred Horowitz, was given early access to host May's reception. The party was hence both a celebration of women's advancement in the law and a sneak preview of a much-anticipated new venue.

The afternoon was cool and clear, a perfect California winter day. Inside the Chateau, baskets of spring flowers gestured towards the warmer season to come. From 4 pm, Lahey and Willebrandt stood together at the door, welcoming their guests. The *Los Angeles Times* reported a 'never-ending line of visitors', including 'gentleman judges and their wives, women lawyers galore, college nabobs'. They kept coming and coming, for four solid hours. That whole time, May stood to receive them. In total, over 600 people walked through the doors.

The party was a who's who of Los Angeles' legal and cultural elite. Among the luminaries in the crowd was Florence Collins Porter, a journalist and grande dame of the suffrage movement; Margaret Mayer, wife of Hollywood producer Louis B Mayer; Australian nurse Sister Elizabeth Kenny, famous for revolutionising polio treatment; and Edna Plummer, a lawyer who'd go on to become the first female district attorney in the United States.

May, for her part, was reportedly overwhelmed by the attention. But given her lifelong passion for acting, I wonder if some part of her revelled in the limelight. Indeed, maybe the modesty was even a performance of its own? As a high-achieving woman, she had good reason to appear humble. Taking up space within the law was provocative enough; May couldn't afford to be visibly attention-seeking, lest she be damned as arrogant or difficult. It was strategic to remain humble, to let people think she had no desire other than to serve the public. Perhaps, on the inside, May was secretly thrilled to be centre stage, showered with praise and sudden celebrity. Did the frustrated actress within light up at the flash of cameras hungry for her portrait?

There was more attention to come. Later that month, the Deputy District Attorney Florence Woodhead held a party for May at her home in East Hollywood. Then, over coming weeks, May was guest of honour at the Women's Breakfast Club, the

Friday Morning Club, and the California Daughters of the British Empire state convention. Finally, in mid-February, the Los Angeles Women Lawyers' Club held another party in her honour, this one attended by 250 guests. At that celebration, female law students mobbed the new judge, hungry for words of wisdom. What was the secret to her success? In response, May painted a rosy portrait of women's prospects. The age of prejudice against female lawyers was over, she insisted. Discrimination had vanished; the sky was now the limit. Tomorrow's women could do whatever they wanted.

Either May's recent triumph had addled her senses, or she didn't want to frighten the horses. Because sex discrimination was still very much alive and well – as the judge herself well knew. In later life, May confessed she 'almost starved' as a fledgling attorney because men proved reluctant to pay for her services. 'When I got a male client,' she noted, 'he would always suggest he was doing me a great favor to give his business to a woman and therefore a reduction in fee of about 50 % would be appropriate.' With an insecure income, she struggled to stay afloat. The lawyer frequented a budget eatery on the corner of Second and Spring streets where she could fill up on a sandwich, pie and coffee for only 20 cents. 'Without that I really would have starved,' she recalled. Only her 'iron will and sheer strength of character' kept her from giving up.

But an income gap wasn't the only sign that inequality dogged her career. For starters, May's appointment to the municipal court was the lowest rung on the judicial ladder. If May was, as everyone said, one of the most talented attorneys in the state, a star who'd topped her year at law school, why not appoint her to a higher court? Certainly, her mentor Judge Stephens expressed regret that May would join the lowly municipal bench. But at the time, that's as far as any woman had risen. Georgia Bullock became the first woman to join a superior court in California in 1931 and not until 1977 did a woman finally sit on the state's Supreme Court.

Even May's specialisation attests to women's marginalisation within the legal profession. Probate is a low-status branch of law, concerned with the domestic humdrum of wills and estates. Had May been a man, an attorney of her abilities would surely have gone into a more prestigious and lucrative field such as commercial or criminal law.

May did not dwell on these difficulties. She was an optimist by nature, a genial charmer loath to complain or make a fuss. She excelled at respectability politics; anger or confrontation was not her style. Yet in her own way, May resisted male hegemony. From the start of her career, she conspired with other women to advance their own interests via the Women Lawyers' Club, the Professional Women's Club, and the League of Women Voters. She also taught a weekly law class for women throughout the late 1920s. The class was part of the University of California's extension division – adult education offerings available to regular citizens. As an aside, May's class was to give ordinary women the legal literacy they needed to protect themselves and their children. It wasn't about training as a lawyer; it was about learning to navigate an intimidating system designed to protect male property rights. From the extension classroom in Hill Street, in the heart of downtown, May taught marriage and divorce laws, guardianship, adoption and property law.

At a time before reliable contraception or no-fault divorce, May was giving women tools to make the best of a system stacked against them. It was feminist knowledge sharing under the guise of prim adult education. Imagine the conversations that went on in that classroom. Did the space overflow with browbeaten women, desperate to change their situation? Did they find camaraderie and hope in learning to fight their oppression in a room of fellow travellers? Perhaps the classes turned into a kind of consciousness raising, as students compared notes and realised their problems were more structural than personal.

May helped married women, but she was not one of them. There was no wedding altar, no engagement, not even a recorded romance or flirtation. The lawyer remained resolutely single. It's possible that working in women's law had been a deterrent of sorts; May clearly saw marriage could be a trap for women, so why would she want it for herself? Or perhaps her romantic inclinations lay elsewhere.

The press, however, simply couldn't fathom it. How could such a 'perfectly nice, normal young woman' shun matrimony? Faced with incessant inquiries, May defended the path she'd chosen. Contrary to prevailing wisdom, she insisted, unmarried women were not pitiable spinsters. Rather than being sad rejects or unfulfilled crones, they were essential contributors to the modern world. 'Though sometimes classed as "half a woman", the single woman holds a unique place in society,' May explained. She was the 'connecting link' between domesticated housewives and the male-dominated public sphere; as such, she had 'a definitive mission: to help the sexes understand each other'. As someone who could understand both male and female interests, the single woman was responsible for 'furnishing the links of sympathy between the two groups of society'.

Today, we might query the idea that men and women are mutually incomprehensible categories – a restrictive idea that reinforces a rigid gender binary. But beneath this now-outmoded view of gender was an idea radical in the interwar decades and still today: an uncoupled woman was not a 'failure', she was an asset. Spinsterhood was a rarefied state, a life to be proud of. Despite pressure to conform, May crafted her own narrative of the good life, subverting the cultural script that defined female worthiness as contingent upon being chosen by a man.

And her life was good indeed. May juggled an absorbing career with endless voluntary work, plus a vast network of friends, with time left over for her twin creative interests: music and poetry. At the age of 40 and now a judge, May retained a girlish freshness; photographs show a bright-eyed woman who could pass for a decade younger. Smooth skin and full lips, with plucked eyebrows worthy of a Hollywood pin-up. It doubtless helped that May lived with her mother until the latter's death in 1938. With another woman on hand to run her household, May was free to live much like a man – economically independent, focused on public work, largely unhindered by domestic obligations.

Nowhere in this full life was there space to visit Australia. Neither the lingering ties of home, nor a long separation from close family, could entice May to retrace her steps to Queensland. There was talk of a visit in the late 1930s, but the trip was stymied by the outbreak of war. Even after peace returned, the visit never happened. It wasn't for lack of money or resources; it was clearly a deliberate decision. Australia may have claimed May Lahey as its first woman judge, but the former Queenslander had turned her back on the Commonwealth. She had all the home and family she needed in California.

Fulton Street Dock, Manhattan Skyline, 1935.
The New York Public Library

Isabel Letham at Bondi Beach, 1916–17.
Northern Beaches Council Library Local Studies

Portrait of Mary Cecil Allen, 1920s.

National Library of Australia, ID: 2335953

Mariposa and Sydney Harbour Bridge, 1930s.

Graeme Andrews Working Harbour Collection, City of Sydney Archives, A-00085129

Rose Cumming photographed by Edward Steichen, c.1920s.

Rose Cumming, Russell L Cecil and affiliated families photographs and papers, PR 393. New-York Historical Society, 101310d

Rose Cumming with family, Newport, 1930.

Rose Cumming, Russell L Cecil and affiliated families photographs and papers, PR 393. New-York Historical Society, 101311d

Judge May D Lahey administering the oath of office to judge Ida May Adams, Los Angeles, 1931.
University of California, Los Angeles

Vera Bradford, playing the piano, Chicago.
Courtesy of author

Vera Bradford, playing in the snow, Chicago.
Courtesy of author

Dorothy Waugh in Temple University dental yearbook, 1932.
Temple University

Alice Caporn, 1934.
Radiant Health Publishers, Boston, USA

President John F Kennedy with Members of the Consumer Advisory Council, including Persia Campbell standing to the right of the President, White House, Washington DC, 19 July 1962.

John F. Kennedy Presidential Library and Museum, AR7366-A

Persia Campbell testifying at Monopoly Committee, Washington DC, 1939.

Courtesy of author

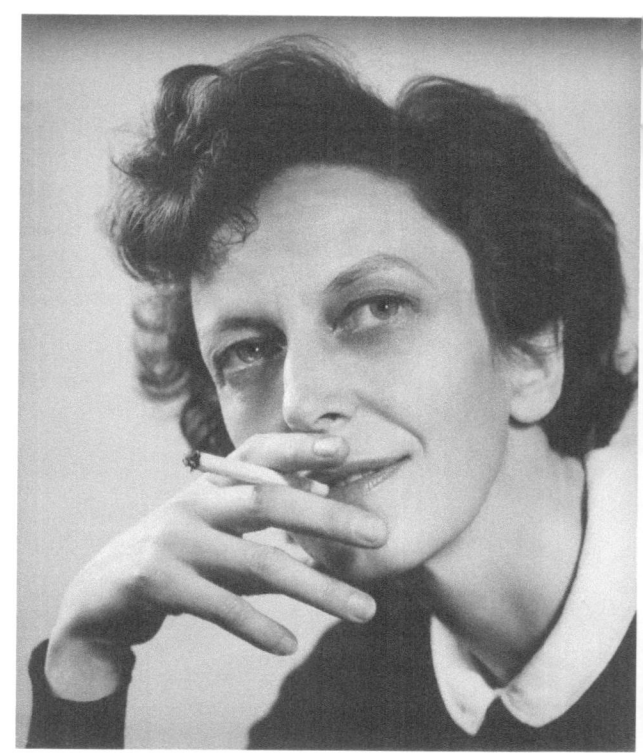

Cynthia Reed – writer 1945. Gelatin silver photograph by Margaret Michaelis.
National Gallery of Australia, IRN 48932

Dorothy Cottrell in the *Saturday Evening Post*, 10 June 1950.
Courtesy of author

12
PASSPORTS

For the first time since childhood, I don't have a valid passport.

There's been at least five over the years. First, there is baby me, an anonymous blob glowering into the camera for a relocation to Singapore that never eventuated. Next, I am eight, an anxious little face framed by a blonde mane, girding my loins to farewell the familiar for a parental sabbatical in Canada. Then, the 14-year-old, the awkward teen desperate to escape their own skin, the budding anorexic who will take pleasure in denying themselves French cheeses and pastries. Then, the undergraduate student without a driver's licence, the newly legal adult who carried their battered passport everywhere to use as ID.

When I got my most recent passport, a few weeks before jumping on a plane to San Francisco, the expiry date of 2021 sounded impossibly distant, a futuristic year invented by dystopian novelists that would surely never arrive. The world would have ended by then, or I would be dead. Or both.

As it turned out, I was essentially correct. That woman version of me had indeed evaporated by 2021. She had walked off stage some three years earlier, taking early retirement at the age of 30. The passport was for a person with long hair and red lipstick, a name that had been used by Queens, and an F listed under 'sex'. She no longer existed. (Had she ever? It was hard to say.)

The world as I knew it had also vanished. That hyper-globalised world of 2011, that playground of open borders and cheap flights and mindless mobility, evaporated overnight in March 2020. Now, we were in lockdown, and my world had shrunk to a 5-kilometre radius. I couldn't travel across the Yarra River, let alone the Pacific Ocean.

In 2021, I watched the days and weeks creep up to my passport expiration date, and then saw it disappear into my rearview mirror. I did nothing. What was the point in keeping this legal document alive? Travel was unthinkable now. Partly due to the Covid-19 pandemic. But mainly because my body, having transitioned across gender, having become visibly genderqueer, now felt like a bomb too hazardous to be admitted across borders. I couldn't travel under the old label of F, but nor could I claim M. With my newly flat chest and chin stubble and yet still girlish voice, I was visibly neither. I was the explosive device you're asked to declare at airport security.

Once domestic borders opened again and I resumed flying interstate, every encounter with airport security was a lesson in the incomprehensibility of my body.

'This way, sir. Place your bag down here.'

'Thank you.'

'Oh!' A double-take, a second glance. 'Oh, I'm sorry, I mean ma'am.'

When I enter the security scanner, the guards must set it to read me as F or M. There's always a moment of hesitation, a split-second as they struggle to pick the right box. Sometimes, they choose one; other days, the other. There's no apparent logic to the choice.

When I set off the security scanner, the guards are unsure whether the man or woman should pat me down. We three humans do an awkward shuffle beside the scanner, a mime about whether my pants contain a willy or a weapon or both, leaving us all burning with mortification.

I could order a passport with X as the gender marker. Australia has offered these since 2011. But while this kind of document will enable you to leave Australian borders, it has questionable utility in allowing you to arrive anywhere else. Only around 20 countries offer a third gender passport. The United States did not become one of them until 2022. Even in the countries where the X is recognised, it almost guarantees extra scrutiny at airports. It's akin to marking yourself as deviant. It's like putting a target on your own back. X marks the spot.

In 2023, I needed to access an archive in New York. With no passport, and a low-level terror of entering a country that had passed 86 anti-trans bills that year alone, I hired an American research assistant to visit on my behalf. When I heard the ping of the email that contained the archive documents, I saw an alternate version of me – the me who kept pretending to be a woman – striding the streets of New York City. She had blisters on her heels, a stomach full of cream-cheese bagel and an iced coffee as big as her head. Over one shoulder, she carried a tote bag from Strand Books. When she landed at LAX, the security guard had waved through this white lady who looked just like her passport photo and smiled the easy smile of someone who expected open doors.

She was over there, and I was here: spending my hours and days in the little queer bubble of Melbourne's inner north where I feel safe. The same handful of suburbs I'd barely left for the past four years.

This is all to say that opening some doors closes others. That claiming the right to cross borders of identity can make other borders harden, or even slam shut altogether. The more I move in gender, the less easily I can move in the world.

This is no accident. This is the system working as intended. Borders, and who gets to cross them, have always been about the regulation of bodies in service of the intertwined logics of capitalism, patriarchy and white supremacy. The closer a body is to the imagined ideal of a white man who is heterosexual, cisgendered and able-bodied, the more readily that body will be welcomed across the lines traced onto maps. Deviant bodies, othered bodies, those that muddy the neat categories and hierarchies that underpin oppressive systems – these bodies are met with questions and refusals and even detention centres.

The travel of Australians to the United States is part of these larger histories of borders and bodies. It was true in the 1920s, when white women from Sydney and Melbourne could treat the world as their oyster at the very moment that racialised bodies were being refused access to the 'land of liberty'. And it's still true in the 2020s, when my gender freakery has left me passport-less, but my whiteness and wealth ensure I am unlikely to encounter a cell door closing in my face.

At home, without a passport, I reflect anew about the relationship between mobility and freedom. In the Western cultural imagination, travel begets freedom; it is the ultimate route to personal liberation. From the 'Grand Tour' of the 18th century, to Jack Kerouac's *On the Road* and Elizabeth Gilbert's *Eat, Pray, Love*, moving through space to unfamiliar climes is how the individual shakes off the shackles of convention and discovers the fullest, most realised version of themselves. Those left behind are deemed less worldly. Less adventurous. Less emancipated. To be free, we must move. It is the textbook hero's journey.

Of course, this logic ignores that travel is a privilege available to the few. It costs money and requires time, not to mention the absence of caring responsibilities and the possession of a body that will be permitted to cross borders. On a global scale, how few people can satisfy all those requirements?

On one view, the travellers are not so much the rebels and adventurers of this world, but those powerful enough to have the luxury to perform rebellion.

More to the point, I wonder why we're even so sure that mobility and freedom are synonymous. In my present state of unprecedented immobility, I am the freest, the most myself, that I have ever been. Ironically, that very freedom actively inhibits my mobility. If I were to squash this messy trans self, if I were to make myself palatable, I could much more easily traipse about the globe, posting envy-inspiring pics of my culturally endorsed 'freedom' on Instagram.

In my 20s, I did just that. My then-partner and I liked to entertain ourselves by totting up all the countries we had been to. Close to 50, for him. Around 30, for me. We compiled our lists as evidence of our cosmopolitan credentials, as proof we were interesting and interested citizens of the world, more fully alive than 'ordinary' folk who stay at home. To external appearances, we were living the best possible life.

But we were children dressing up in an identity we hadn't earned. We had well-stamped passports, but we knew little about ourselves or the world. Travel, instead of making us free, left us arrogant. It made us think a plane ticket was a substitute for the work of learning to be a human among humans – work that can and does happen in the most familiar of places. Work that occurs anywhere, even on the same patch of earth where we were born.

13

THE RELIGION OF PROGRESS

THE ECONOMIST, SEATTLE, 1929

On 11 December 1929, six weeks after Wall Street crashed, the *Siberia Maru* rolled into Seattle's harbour, fresh off an 11-day crossing from Yokohama. For the past decade, this Japanese-owned steamship had plied the waters between Japan and North America, becoming a familiar sight in Seattle and San Francisco. For this crossing, most berths were occupied by Japanese delegates on their way to Britain for the 1930 London Naval Conference – staid old men and their wives, travelling on diplomatic passports. But among the crowd of mature Japanese faces was a solitary white woman. A young adult – barely 30, an observer might guess. But not a giddy ingenue or flighty flapper; no, this woman was serious and purposeful, often spotted on deck poring over some weighty tome. Apart from a family of Americans, she was the only non-Japanese person on board.

Who was she and what was her business aboard this Japanese steamship?

At the dock, when this unusual passenger emerged from the ship's hull, an immigration officer launched an interrogation. Ever since the United States rolled out immigration quotas in 1921, alien arrivals encountered a grilling at the border – and even white visitors were not immune. Men and women who arrived with insufficient funds or the wrong visa were denied entry or even detained in immigration facilities. This mysterious woman needed to be ready to prove her bona fides.

But this was not her first rodeo, and she had her answers prepared. From a distance, she could appear vulnerable – a friendless miss literally at sea – but up close, the woman held herself with a poise that belied her sex and youth. She was nothing special to look at – medium height, brown hair, an unremarkable oval face. Yet she emitted a sangfroid that stopped people in their tracks. In a soft clear voice, the kind of voice used to commanding an audience, the woman explained herself to the American authorities.

She was British, she told the official, but not from Britain. Sydney was her home. Sydney, Australia. What was her work? Government official. How much cash was she carrying? Four hundred dollars. Who paid for her passage? She did.

And her name? Miss Campbell. First name Persia, like the country. Her name was Miss Persia Gwendoline Crawford Campbell, and she had an important appointment in New York City. She had a train to catch; she was due at the Rockefeller Foundation headquarters on Broadway. Yes, those Rockefellers – owners of the Standard Oil fortune, the richest family in America.

And with that, she was gone, leaving behind the impression of someone destined for big things.

She was called Persia, a striking name that conjured orientalist fantasies of the Middle East, and which never failed to spark curiosity. For her entire life, she'd dodge questions about its origins. *Why Persia? Where did it come from?* She'd refuse to answer, a strategy that only added to the mystique. Some things were private, she'd insist, clamming up until the conversation moved on.

As for her actual backstory: that was less exotic. She was born in Nerrigundah – a small village on unceded Yuin Country on the

New South Wales south coast in 1898. It was the last gasp of the 19th century, and her parents were local schoolteachers who'd met via a newspaper matrimonial column. Her father, Randolph, was the principal of Nerrigundah Public, while her mother, Beatrice, taught sewing. Her only sibling was a younger brother called Rodney.

From a young age, Persia had a precocious intellect – too big for this small town. By her teens, she'd left Nerrigundah in the dust. She was off to Sydney for a secondary education at the academically rigorous Fort Street School followed by a Bachelor of Arts at the University of Sydney.

It was wartime, the war to end all wars, and the whole world had been upended. How to make sense of such horror? How to make sure it never happened again? Her male contemporaries were off fighting, and many never came home. 'Most of us who remained at the University were seized with a desire to "do something" to prevent a second world war,' Persia recalled. On a campus filled with empty seats once occupied by now-faraway soldiers, she applied herself to the problem of peace with all the fervour of an idealistic undergraduate.

Persia found her answer in economics. It all came down to money, she reasoned, so surely 'economic matters' must hold the key to world peace. As she watched the Paris Peace Conference, where the reparations question dominated debate, Persia concluded that international relations was a matter of dollars and cents. If only the material side of life could be properly arranged, then international conflict could be avoided. She'd found her vocation. Persia would become an economist – not because she loved numbers, or was interested in wealth, but because she believed this body of knowledge held the key to avoiding future calamity. She was a humanitarian first and an economist second; a passionate do-gooder who wanted to save the world, one piece of data at a time.

Today, when economics has become near synonymous with neoliberalism and relentless growth, this profession might seem an unlikely vocation for a great idealist. But in the 1910s, economics was a different beast. Back then, it was a young profession, barely getting started in Australia, and the top dog was none other than Persia's lecturer Robert Irvine – a Labor-aligned professor with socialist inclinations. For Irvine and his acolytes, economics was no dispassionate science, but a tool of political reform, even a kind of activism. Irvine was a creature of the progressive climate of Federation-era Australia, when the young Commonwealth led the world in pioneering 'state socialism' – compulsory wage arbitration, old age and invalid pensions, and a national minimum wage (inaugurated by the 1907 Harvester judgment). It was an exhilarating time, a moment when economic reform was making a tangible difference in people's lives. Little wonder an idealist like Persia was drawn to the discipline. Under Irvine's tutelage, she learnt that the true economist was focused on 'ethical questions' and helped 'the construction of the future'.

This was a vision Persia could get behind. She would use economics to promote justice and preserve peace. After completing her undergraduate degree in 1918, she launched straight into an MA. From there, she won a scholarship to study at the London School of Economics (LSE), where the young Australian impressed the local intelligentsia. 'I have never met anyone quite like her,' wrote suffragist Helena Swanwick. 'I wish she were not a bird of passage. I don't know that I ever met such a combination of personal charm with scientific accuracy and learning.'

Persia's LSE thesis, published as *Chinese Coolie Immigration* (1923), dared to suggest that immigration policy should consider the welfare of Chinese people. This was a scholarly book, by no means an anti-racist polemic, but it did argue for the basic humanity of people of colour. Back then, this modest departure from white supremacy was a radical idea – so controversial it almost derailed the book's publication. 'Miss Campbell reads a lot of feelings into a Chink that the Chink doesn't possess', complained LSE professor Lilian Knowles.

Still in her early 20s, Persia had proven herself in the big smoke. As one colleague put it, Persia was 'already a legend in Australia' and 'becoming a legend' in London. For most Australians of her generation, this would have been enough. They would have returned home triumphant and basked in the glow of metropolitan achievement, forever able to boast of being an LSE alumnus. But not for Persia. The mother country was only the beginning. At the height of her career, London barely rated a mention in her personal history.

The next step was Bryn Mawr. In 1922, Persia had a fellowship at the Pennsylvanian college, where she continued to study immigration. After a year, she was back in London, seeking employment at Australia House. When no job was forthcoming, she succumbed to family pressure to return to Sydney. There, Persia rejoined the cadre of reformist economists who were becoming a force to be reckoned with. They were advising governments, building university departments, lecturing to the public. Australian economics was entering its 'golden age'.

Persia, one of the only women in the profession, was soon a rising public intellectual. For her day job, she worked as an editor for the *Australian Encyclopedia*, and was later appointed a research officer at the NSW Industrial Commission – the state's wage-fixing tribunal. Alongside these commitments, she lectured at the Workers' Education Association (WEA) and flocked to the internationalist organisations that proliferated during that hopeful postwar decade. At the League of Nations Union, the Institute of Pacific Relations and the Pan Pacific Women's Organisation, Persia dared to imagine a better world. In her view, the goal was for every human on the planet to enjoy the material comforts white Australians took for granted. As she argued in one speech, 'The standards of living in the Pacific countries should be raised, and not lowered, to one level'. Indigenous peoples and people of colour enjoying the same lifestyles as whites? In 1929, this was controversial stuff. But it was just her style to push the envelope. For all her degrees, for all her erudition, a dry scholar Persia was not. Beneath the academic exterior lay an activist's spirit. By the mid-1920s, she was known as 'politically a Radical'. From this point onwards, she was a Trojan horse who used the authority of economics to promote a radical humanitarian agenda.

What about Persia the woman? In many ways, she remains as mysterious as she appeared on that 1929 steamer from Yokohama. Persia was a prolific writer and speaker, a verbose figure who left behind reams of paper that detail her views on every imaginable topic. Persia the person, however, is an elusive character. How did she cope as a rare young woman in a professional landscape dominated by male egos? What kind of life did she dream for herself?

In 2009, when I first discovered Persia's story, I found a reference to a collection of her personal papers in New York. The reference was from the 1980s, and the institution it mentioned no longer existed. When that institution dissolved, what had happened to Persia's collection? Was it still stored somewhere, or had her archive been thrown in a dumpster along with other old documents?

It took me several years to find an answer.

Eventually, a chance phone call in 2013 led me to an archivist who confirmed Persia's papers were sitting in her office. A few weeks later, I caught an early train from Manhattan's Penn Station to Westchester County, sipping coffee as we sped north along the Hudson River. Several hours later, following a hair-raising walk through a deserted industrial estate, I was shown into a windowless storage room. Entire walls were lined with archive boxes, all labelled

Persia Campbell. Dozens upon dozens of boxes, each containing hundreds of documents – all waiting to be read.

Somewhere amid this ocean of paper, I hoped to glimpse the person behind the brilliant mind. Surely there'd be a diary or reminiscences – something to colour in the woman who shone so bright. But Persia had hidden her tracks well. A fiercely private person, she'd left behind an archive that gave little away. The boxes held the minutes of virtually every meeting she'd ever attended, the transcript of every speech she'd given, yet contained almost nothing in the way of personal content.

There were only a few scraps to feed my curiosity. A couple of personal letters, some testimonials. Everyone agreed Persia was a force of nature – brilliant yet charming, with a formidable work ethic. One reporter likened her to First Lady Eleanor Roosevelt. But these were public portraits that still revealed little about the private person. In one reflection, a colleague noted her signature reserve. 'I have worked closely and affectionately with [Persia] … but she somehow kept her private life apart.' One archive box stored Persia's favourite hat. In a life that contained few indulgences, millinery was a great passion. Every photograph shows her sporting elaborate headwear, often decorated with flowers and tulle.

One handwritten letter in a box of correspondence gave rare insight into her psyche. Composed late in life, Persia, in an uncharacteristic moment of introspection, pondered 'what sort of person I am'. Her discomfort with the task is visible on the page. She prevaricated, circling around the question, speaking in generalities. After a long introduction, the economist eventually offered some reflections. She was a practical person, Persia explained, happiest when working on schemes 'projected to the future'. In her view, there were three types of people in the world: the historians focused on the past, the artists concerned with the present, and schemers oriented towards tomorrow.

Persia placed herself in the latter group. She was one of 'the utopians, the planners, believers in free will' who were 'mostly dreaming of the future'. The past held little interest. Nostalgia was foreign to her. A 'usually optimistic' character, Persia was guided by her faith in 'the capacity of man to direct or at least contrive the flow of change'. Always looking forward, always working towards the better world just over the horizon. A fully paid-up member of the modern religion of progress.

It's little surprise she found a congenial home in New York City.

After six years back in Sydney, Persia was ready to set sail again. In 1929, she was awarded a Rockefeller Foundation Fellowship to spend 15 months researching agricultural economics in the United States. The Rockefeller Foundation was one of several private philanthropic bodies that, from the 1910s, aided the expansion of American power by funding young talent from around the world to study in the United States. The model was simple: rising stars from academia and the professions were gifted an immersion in American ideas, with the expectation they would return home eager to replicate American innovations and spread goodwill towards the United States. It was a pre-emptive seduction of future leaders, who were co-opted into becoming 'instruments of US national power'. In short, it was cultural imperialism cloaked as educational philanthropy – which historian Paul Kramer describes in a 2009 article as the 'geopoliticization of international students'.

The Rockefeller Foundation and the Carnegie Corporation of New York (CCNY) were both highly active in Australia in the 1920s and 1930s, each handing out travelling fellowships to up-and-comers across a range of professions. At a time when

Australians eager to study abroad still gravitated towards Britain, these two foundations played a major role in drawing the nation's young talent into the American orbit.

It came down to money. Rockefeller and the CCNY offered generous funding; nothing comparable was forthcoming in Britain. To visit Oxford or Cambridge or the LSE, Australians generally needed to pay their own way, or win one of a few domestic scholarships. Significantly, too, American largesse extended to female talent. The few available British funding sources, such as the Rhodes Scholarship, were restricted to men until the late 20th century.

American philanthropy was a key engine of Australian women's journeys across the Pacific. Rockefeller and Carnegie poured money into female-dominated professions, such as nursing and early childhood education, and funded individual women such as Persia Campbell. Persia was one of dozens of female professionals who chose America because Rockefeller or Carnegie chose them. Who could resist a fully funded tour of world-leading educational institutions?

Before going to the United States, Persia was selected to represent Australia at the 1929 Institute of Pacific Relations (IPR) conference in Kyoto. Founded in 1925, the IPR was an NGO that applied the logic of 'Wilsonian internationalism' to the Asia–Pacific. As historian Tomoko Akami explains in *Internationalizing the Pacific*, the IPR advocated for 'an American-led regional order'. Persia was one of 11 Australian delegates. This list included two other women – welfare officer Eleanor Hinder and YWCA president (and scientist) Dr Georgina Sweet. The three women were profiled in the *Sydney Mail* under the less-than-catchy headline 'Women Who Are Doing Worth-While Jobs'. Persia, the youngest of the trio at 31, was praised for 'sacrificing her life to deal with Australia's economical problems'. The team left Melbourne on 14 September, sailing aboard the Australian Oriental Line steamer *Changte*.

After the conference, Persia travelled on to the United States to take up her Rockefeller Foundation Fellowship. She had an ambitious itinerary worked out: New York, Harvard, the Brookings Institute in Washington DC, West Virginia, Ohio. Fifteen months in the United States to study the international marketing of primary products, before returning to Australia in 1931, where perhaps she might obtain a government job or university lectureship. The universities rarely hired women, but surely the Rockefeller Foundation Fellowship would bolster her CV.

It was all planned out.

Only the logical economist didn't count on that most irrational of interruptions: love.

14

BOOM TO BUST

THE WRITER, SOUTHERN CALIFORNIA, 1929

Dorothy Cottrell's reputation preceded her. After being declared a 'genius' in the *Ladies' Home Journal*, she was a name to watch before even arriving in the United States. On the ship across the Pacific in October 1928, fellow passengers were reading the first instalment of 'The Singing Gold' in the *Journal*'s latest issue. When she disembarked in Los Angeles, the writer was inundated with invitations and speaking requests. Would she lunch with this editor or that reporter? Could she write a history of her love life? That fall, as Judge May Lahey campaigned for Republican Herbert Hoover in the presidential election, everyone wanted a piece of the wheelchair-using prodigy from Down Under.

Dorothy had different ideas. 'I hated being hawked around as exhibit A, and as a rule I declined to go,' she explained to her family. Shunning the publicity, she and her husband, Walter, headed south to find a place to call home. They were never going to live in Los Angeles. After growing up on a remote sheep station, Dorothy's nerves recoiled from the clamour of city life.

Lake Elsinore was only 70 miles from Los Angeles, but it felt like a different world. No automobiles, no blaring radios, just perfect peace. The freshwater lake was surrounded by blue hills, gentle rises blanketed with grey boulders and little streams. Everywhere were cottonwood trees that turned yellow in the fall. There was, Dorothy told the family, no 'lovelyer [sic] bit of earth' anywhere in the world – not even in her beloved Australia.

This was where Dorothy decided to build her first home. She and Walter scouted for a piece of land overlooking the lake. Prices were high, more than she could afford. But then the real estate company learnt this prospective buyer was a famous writer. Suddenly, the tables turned. A celebrity author-in-residence would put Lake Elsinore on the map and attract other buyers to the area. The estate agent started offering discounts. Then a lot at half price. In the end, they gave the Cottrells five acres for free. 'Of course they are going to get their monies worth back in advertising, I suppose, but isn't it amazing,' Dorothy wrote home. For all that she loathed the publicity circuit, the writer discovered fame could be a useful currency.

They had the land, now they needed a house. On this front, Dorothy was as ambitious as ever. She would not be content with a modest dwelling; instead, she had 'grandiose ideas' about an adobe mansion with a built-in elevator to accommodate her wheelchair. It would be expensive, but Dorothy was raking in the cash. There were book royalties, a $4000 advance on a second novel, talk of a Hollywood film adaptation. Walter secured a job with the Elsinore State Bank and started bringing in a second income. In the early months of 1929, 'the world seemed teeming with money'. They signed up to build a $30 000 residence. 'The world looked rosy,' Walter recalled, 'we thought what the heck.'

What was the worst that could happen?

In 1929, *The Singing Gold* was published by Houghton Mifflin to rave reviews. Both a critical and commercial success, it was '[o]ne of the books that has caused more comments from the press than any other in a long while'. Remarkably, one critic noted, the 'Australian background does not lessen the appeal of the novel'. The book ended up as the US top six bestseller of 1929.

The Singing Gold was also serialised in the English *Woman's Home Journal* and released by London publisher Hodder and Stoughton. In the British and colonial markets, it sold almost 25 000 copies. In Australia, the novel was serialised in the *Sydney Mail*.

With her first novel a hit, Dorothy established herself as a professional writer. First order of business: a literary agent. She signed with Eric Pinker, the son of legendary English agent James B Pinker, who started placing her short fiction in magazines. Her first published story, 'Before Bunny Came Here', was sold in 1929 to the *Ladies' Home Journal*. Thereafter, she produced a steady stream of short fiction, with other stories appearing in *Pearson's* and *Cosmopolitan*. Now she had an agent to negotiate on her behalf, Dorothy was astonished by the sums up for grabs. Back in 1927, she'd been overjoyed when the *Ladies' Home Journal* offered her $5000 for a serial; now, she discovered it was possible to earn up to $20 000 for serial rights, plus a further $70 000 in book royalties. Up ahead were veritable rivers of gold. 'There is very great wealth in American writing,' she reported home.

In 1930, Dorothy's second novel hit the shelves. *Tharlane*, published in Britain as *Earth Battle*, had a similar outback setting to *The Singing Gold*, but was darker in tone, with an older male protagonist. If her debut was a charming girl's own adventure, this follow-up was an epic drama of man battling nature. Would such sombre material win over the reading public? To boost sales, Dorothy's publisher Houghton Mifflin 'spent a staggering amount on advertising'. The novel was heralded as 'a great novel of Australian life'. The results were mixed. *Tharlane* did not sell as well as *The Singing Gold*, though the novel's critical reception was broadly positive. Reviewers praised *Tharlane*'s 'epic quality'; it was more mature than her debut, an ambitious book 'tremendous in its scope'. In December, the *Los Angeles Times* called it 'just about "the book of the year" throughout the British Empire'.

With two critically acclaimed books to her name, Dorothy had joined the ranks of 'well-known writers' in American publishing. In December 1930, the *Los Angeles Times* profiled the Australian. The paper observed that her 'two books have aroused more interest throughout the entire English-speaking world than have any other pair by one author in the last few years'. Still only in her 20s, Dorothy had a long career ahead of her. 'We ought to hear a good deal of her during the next three decades,' the *Times* concluded.

Back in Sydney, Mary Gilmore kept singing Dorothy's praises. The international publication of *The Singing Gold* was, Gilmore insisted, 'the biggest advertisement that Australia had ever had'. Other antipodean voices were less enthusiastic. Nettie Palmer, the influential literary critic, was dismissive of Dorothy's work. In her view, the Queensland writer was a commercial sell-out, a careerist who mined her 'exotic' Australian youth for easy money in the American marketplace. *The Singing Gold* received other grudging reviews in the Australian press. According to the *Australasian*, the book was 'weak in construction' and the 'critical reader may take exception to American judgement as to the book's "literary" quality'.

This Australian reception reflects the prevailing ambivalence towards United States mass culture. In a 1935 pamphlet on 'Mental Rubbish from Overseas', Australian literary tastemaker (and fascist) PR Stephensen railed against the 'dumping' of 'cheap and undesirable' American imports in the Australian market. For the likes of Stephensen, 'America' was jazz, Hollywood, commercial radio, magazines. Cheap entertainments, fresh off the factory line, the cultural equivalent of frosted icing: too sweet to be wholesome. They were made and consumed by women, so could hardly be real art. Even worse, this mass culture was infused with Black and Jewish influences; it was 'cosmopolitan' – a racist dog whistle to denote anything not quite white.

This cultural context shaped attitudes towards Dorothy's work. By going straight to a US women's magazine, she undermined her prospects of a serious literary reputation in Australia. In choosing the path of mass readership, Dorothy damned herself as popular. She was, in this sense, the Liane Moriarty of the Jazz Age. Always and forever an author of commercial 'women's fiction'.

Yet Dorothy had no regrets. She was invigorated by life in California, where the culture of entrepreneurship and ambition aligned with her personal sensibilities. Every letter home contained breathless accounts of American innovation in the realm of diet, health and technology. Fresh orange juice, oven timers, tinned food – what delights! 'This really is an amazing people,' she told her family in mid-1931. '[W]e have come to love the United States.' Like other antipodean visitors, Dorothy was also struck by the political and cultural influence of America's women – so different from blokey Australia. 'The woman's club vote is the great power of the country,' she observed. Everywhere she looked, Dorothy noted the 'compleat [sic] and abject servitude of the American man to the American woman'. As a powerful woman herself, the dominant partner in her marriage, it's no wonder Dorothy flourished in such a setting.

All in all, this expatriated Australian felt at home in the United States. Through her writing, she returned the favour, telling stories that helped Americans feel 'at home' with Australia. Via her novels of outback life, Dorothy sold Americans a romantic vision of 'Down Under' that drew upon shared settler mythologies of plucky colonists making productive use of 'vacant' space. It was a narrative that resonated with US readers because it was akin to the stories they told about themselves. As one California reviewer noted, Dorothy's work was concerned with the 'sturdy pioneer race' and 'pioneer phase of life' – a settler fantasy that thrived on both sides of the Pacific. *The Singing Gold*, the story of a gutsy white woman on the colonial frontier, bares more than a passing resemblance to Laura Ingalls Wilder's contemporaneous *Little House on the Prairie* novels. In invoking the common mythology of the 'pioneer', Dorothy's work allowed transpacific affinities to be seen and nourished.

Viewed through this lens, *The Singing Gold* and *Tharlane* were more than light entertainment. Rather, Dorothy's fictions enabled white Americans to understand themselves as kin to white Australians. Precisely because of her mass readership, Dorothy was a cultural intermediary whose work fostered an understanding that Australia and the United States were twin nations, with a shared 'pioneer' past and the potential to develop an aligned future. Her storytelling wove two societies together.

After a stellar beginning, Dorothy's career hit the skids as the Great Depression took hold. The pain started in 1931. *Tharlane* wasn't selling and it grew harder to place short fiction. Then her husband, Walter, lost his job at the local bank. There was little income coming in, and the couple still faced the construction costs of their dream home. Contracts had been signed; money promised – but there was no money left. As the months passed, the debts mounted, big numbers snapping at their heels. In early 1932, the unthinkable happened. The Cottrells lost their Lake Elsinore home. Only a few years earlier, Dorothy was so rich and famous she was given land for free. Now, she was effectively homeless.

The couple filled a car with possessions and hit the road. They had joined the ranks of wandering vagrants. At the time, they were in good company. That year, nearly a third of California's workforce was unemployed. The Dust Bowl was prompting refugees from the Great Plains and the Midwest to pour into California, an internal migration depicted in Steinbeck's *Grapes of Wrath*. But the Pacific state was no promised land. Even in this sunny state, the bread bowl of the nation, people were starving.

As luck would have it, the Cottrells found a temporary bolthole at the Mission Inn at Riverside, an artists' colony-cum-hotel 30 miles from Elsinore. Walter was given a job as a 'handyman, bell boy, and what-have you'. Dorothy would act as a companion to the elderly owner Frank Miller. In return, they received free accommodation. The Cottrells had come down in the world but at least they had a roof over their heads.

Throughout this period of poverty, Dorothy kept her family in the dark. In letters home, she depicted her itinerant existence as a jolly adventure. The Mission Inn was presented as a 'great American retreat for writers'. It was as though she was visiting an exclusive writing retreat, not seeking to ward off homelessness. Although she mentioned California's 'frightful' economic conditions, Dorothy failed to acknowledge she herself was close to destitution. Was she ashamed that her literary fairytale had come toppling down to earth?

As the months passed, and the truth grew harder to conceal, Dorothy's once frequent missives slowed to a trickle. This silence created a breach between Dorothy and her Queensland relatives. Ignorant of her bleak circumstances, they interpreted her failure to write or visit as a personal snub. The famous writer had forgotten them. Too big for her boots. Too busy gallivanting around America to think of her family. The hurt bloomed and festered. Soon, correspondence all but ceased altogether.

After the Cottrells settled into the Mission Inn, they had a stroke of luck. A cheque arrived in the mail. Two thousand dollars. Dorothy had sold four stories about 'Chut the Kangaroo', earning $500 apiece. The cash was enough to get them back on their feet. Not for the first or last time, Dorothy's pen was the decisive factor in the couple's fortunes. Theirs was a most unconventional marriage, a rare coupling in which the wife – a wheelchair user to boot – had the economic upper hand.

With this injection of cash, the Cottrells paid off debts and nabbed an old 1926 Essex car. Newly mobile, the couple headed north to Los Angeles Harbor. Down at the docks, they bought an old lifeboat for a few hundred dollars, a 27-foot vessel called *Penguin*. This would be their new home. Dorothy and Walter would live cheaply on the Cerritos Channel, a concrete-lined stretch of water behind Terminal Island, where they befriended their new neighbours: the assorted eccentrics and down-and-outers who called the waters home.

Even with a house of sorts, times were tough. Nobody had any money and folks were going hungry. It was a rough existence, like being back on Dunk Island but without the tropical beauty or abundant sea life. On Cerritos, everyone tried to fish but the fish wouldn't bite. It was as though even the waters had turned against them. One friend developed a clever lurk to get a good feed: he would take out charter boats for wealthy Hollywood types and deliberately sail into rough waters to make the passengers seasick. Once everyone was green around the gills, the catered lunch would be abandoned, and the uneaten food taken back to Cerritos to share. Whenever someone wanted to go into town, they had to pool together a few cents to buy half a gallon of gas. On one occasion, they had six cents between five people.

'That was why we were all desperately wanting to go somewhere', Walter recalled. 'Anywhere must be better.' But unless Dorothy had another windfall, how could they possibly gather the money to leave? As 1932 crept into 1933, there was no respite in sight. In the end, it would take an earthquake to shake them out of Los Angeles and back onto the road.

15

PEOPLE OVER PROFITS

THE ECONOMIST, NEW YORK CITY, 1931

Persia hurried down the dark street. It was late, a brisk October evening, and even Greenwich Village was settling down for the night. The Whitney Museum, getting ready to open next month, had turned off the lights. Over at the Cherry Lane Theatre, the latest offering – a play called *The Unknown Soldier* – was approaching final curtain. Only the poets of the Grub Street Club were still going strong, reciting their verse to an enthusiastic crowd.

On MacDougal Street, in the heart of the village, Persia stopped at number 175. It was a four-storey brick building from 1837, just north of Washington Square Park, barely two blocks from Mary Cecil Allen's studio on Christopher Street. At street level was The Brick House, a teahouse that buzzed with the chatter and debate of the neighbourhood's artists. Upstairs were two flats. Virginia Needham, the artist, rented one. The other was occupied by three women: Persia's friend Neva Deardorff and her two lodgers.

Neva would be asleep at this hour, but Persia could not wait until morning. In two days, she was due to depart New York. Her ticket was booked, bags almost packed. She'd already extended her original Rockefeller Fellowship and she hadn't seen her family in over two years. Back in Sydney, they were eagerly anticipating her return.

Only tonight, Edward had thrown a spanner in the works. Edward Rice, a handsome young Quaker from Philadelphia, an engineer and inventor who'd served in the navy and invented a device to locate submarines. They'd met on a transatlantic steamer, both returning to the States after a visit to England. A shipboard romance ensued. Once back on dry land, Edward sent Persia a bouquet of roses. Tonight, on the eve of her departure, he'd asked her to marry him. And she said yes. Yes, she would become Mrs Edward Rice. Yes, she would let the ship leave without her, and instead make a home in the United States. It was a grand romantic gesture and Persia was swept up in the moment.

But now, hours later, she was filled with anxiety. Had she made the right decision? Was it foolish to act so impulsively? She needed Neva's counsel. Neva Deardorff, her oldest American friend, a confidante since Bryn Mawr days, the closest thing to family on this continent. Neva would be the voice of reason.

Neva, fast asleep, was roused by the doorbell. To Persia's surprise, her friend supported the marriage. Neva, herself unmarried, was a fierce feminist ten years her senior who'd always prioritised independence. Wary of domestic life, Neva had previously urged Persia to shun matrimony and focus on her career. Tonight, however, Neva's objections vanished. She approved of Edward; she saw their love was real. Perhaps, more selfishly, she was pleased by the prospect of Persia staying in New York.

Together they talked logistics. Given the rush, Persia explained, she and Edward would marry at City Hall, as soon as possible. No great palaver, just the basic legalities. Edward was, after all, only newly divorced; he already had three daughters by his first wife. Persia, ever practical, had no desire for a grand wedding. Getting married was the important thing; the ceremony was just the means to an end.

City Hall – really? Neva put her foot down. If a wedding was going to happen, it needed to be done right. A church, a reception, the whole shebang. Although no churchgoer herself, Neva was determined Persia marry in a religious ceremony.

Next morning, Persia awoke to discover Neva had arranged everything. For a woman sceptical of the institution of marriage, she'd gone all out in giving Persia a 'real' wedding. As she later wrote to Persia's mother, 'I decided that it fell to me to represent Persia's family and see that it was carried through properly.'

The ceremony fell on 15 October, only a few days later. At midday, the wedding party gathered in the minister's office at First Presbyterian, a Gothic Revival church on Fifth Avenue. Autumn sunshine flooded the room. The only witnesses were Neva herself and Edward's friend Richard Whitehall. The bride was radiant. Dressed in a champagne dress, set off by brown hat and shoes, Persia's eyes shone as she recited the vows.

Then Neva had a moment of feminist panic. Would the Episcopalian ceremony ask that Persia – accomplished, brilliant Persia – promise to *obey* her husband? And if so, would Persia – quite rightly – refuse? The carefully orchestrated wedding might end in an awkward stalemate. But Neva's fears came to naught. The vows made no mention of obedience and the ceremony concluded without a hitch. It was all done with – in Neva's words – 'simplicity, dignity and general good taste'. Afterwards, the wedding party retired for a celebratory luncheon. Only then was Persia's family informed of the dramatic change of plans. A quick telegram to her mother announced the nuptials. The bride showed no outward sign of missing her Australian kin – as ever, Persia's 'British reserve' kept emotions in check. But Neva suspected the absence of family tempered the day's joy. By late afternoon, the newlyweds had departed on their honeymoon to New Hampshire's White Mountains, where they would enjoy the autumn colours at a friend's borrowed home.

Just like that, the Australian economist made the most consequential decision of her young life. It was a sliding doors moment, a choice that turned a temporary sojourn into a permanent migration. The wedding was widely reported in Australia, with

Persia quoted as saying, 'Australia will always be close to her heart'. But homesick or not, Persia was a New Yorker now.

Despite Neva's concerns, matrimony did not inhibit Persia's career. On the contrary, the decision to remain in New York during the tumultuous 1930s thrust the idealistic economist into a climate in which her talents thrived. Although Persia soon became a mother – a daughter Sydney was born in 1933, followed by a son Edward in 1935 – over the next decade her passions harmonised with the broader zeitgeist to bring fresh ideas to life. By the end of the 1930s, Persia was at the forefront of a new and radical way of thinking about 'the economy'. She was no longer just a promising young thing; she was now a major thinker in her own right.

It all started with the economic hardships of the Great Depression. This mass suffering highlighted the imperative for governments to consider ordinary citizens – or 'consumers' – alongside the interests of business, or 'producers'. At a time of widespread unemployment and deprivation, it became clear that the economic health of a society couldn't just be measured by the goods produced and profits recorded; it must also consider whether consumers had their basic needs met. In other words, a good economy must be an economy in which ordinary citizens were housed and fed.

This shift in perspective fuelled a 'consumer movement'. As President Roosevelt led the nation into the New Deal, suddenly everyone was talking about consumer rights and consumer interests. Consumer advocacy groups proliferated. In politics and the press, 'consumer consciousness' became widespread. When the National Recovery Administration was established in 1933 to stimulate business recovery, this new federal agency incorporated a Consumer Advisory Committee.

Viewed from the present, 'consumer interests' can evoke the exhaustive product reviews that fill the pages of *Choice* magazine. When I first encountered these concepts, my mind conjured up comparisons of vacuum cleaners, or efforts to help buyers seek recompense for faulty products. But these associations are misleading. Back in the 1930s, the consumer movement was much more than an effort to help people spend their money wisely. It's better understood as provocative new way of understanding economic life. 'Consumers' was a synonym for 'ordinary people'. The 'consumer movement' was an effort to reorient economic activity towards the interests of the masses. It was about prioritising ordinary people alongside big business. Such notions resonated widely, and shifted the political rhetoric. By 1941, President Roosevelt identified 'freedom from want' as one of 'four essential human freedoms'.

To be sure, this wasn't socialism. Consumerist thinking still employed the capitalist logic of consumers and consumption, alongside producers and production. But within a capitalist framework, the consumer movement was truly radical. It rested on the idea – provocative then and still today – that human wellbeing, rather than revenue and growth, should inform or even structure the organisation of a capitalist economy. In a nutshell, it was people over profits.

Persia was at the centre of the action. Since her student days, she was interested in economics as a tool to enhance human wellbeing. During her time at the NSW Industrial Commission in the 1920s, she'd compiled data on living costs to help determine minimum wages – an experience that led her to become, in her words, 'consumer-minded'. From this point onwards, her main preoccupation was the question of how to raise the living standards of regular citizens. Persia was right at home amid the burgeoning consumer movement of the New Deal. In this space, she was both a scholar and an activist, following the model of her Sydney lecturer

Robert Irvine. Between 1930 and 1970, every major US consumer organisation featured Persia in the leadership team.

In 1937 Persia helped found the Consumers National Federation (CNF), the first national consumer organisation. Persia was the executive secretary, later described as the federation's driving force. According to founding chair Helen Hall, 'it would have been impossible' without Persia's voluntary labour. During its two-year existence, the CNF organised conferences, published reports, and sent delegates to Washington DC. The overriding objective was improved living standards. In January 1938, the organisation ran a Conference on the High Cost of Living, which ended up sparking a milk boycott.

Persia also pursued consumer questions at a theoretical level by undertaking a PhD at Columbia University. Her dissertation, published as *Consumer representation in the New Deal* (1940), was an impassioned manifesto that insisted standards of living – not GDP – were the best measure of national wellbeing. In the conclusion, Persia urged government policy be directed 'towards the goal of a better living standard for all ... not only the people of this nation, but for all people'. In her view, consumer rights were central to this objective. She wrote that living standards were best raised by 'making the voice of the consumer more effective'.

During these years, Persia applied the lessons of Australia's Federation-era 'social laboratory' to the American context. Much like Isabel Letham's efforts to bring lifesaving to California, the economist invoked the Australian example for the United States to emulate. At the NSW Industrial Commission, Persia had observed the importance of the government regulating wages and living standards; she now urged similar practices in the United States. As early as 1933, when the National Industrial Recovery Act introduced minimum wage provisions, Persia suggested that 'some study of Australian experiences in wage-fixing' would be 'opportune'. Having studied and regulated 'a fair and reasonable wage' since 1907, Australian economists had much to teach their American counterparts. In this respect, the Antipodes were more 'advanced' than the metropole.

By exporting Australian innovation, Persia followed in the footsteps of an earlier generation of antipodean progressives. As historian Marilyn Lake shows in *Progressive New World*, the likes of suffragist Vida Goldstein and jurist HB Higgins (responsible for the 1907 Harvester judgment that instituted a 'living wage') also influenced their counterparts in the United States back in the first decade of the 20th century. Now, 30 years later, the economist was continuing their work. 'Australia', Persia pronounced in *Pacific Affairs* in 1939, was a 'true Commonwealth' which had 'made experiments of great worth in parliamentary democracy and social legislation in the past' and was still 'trying to maintain a high uniform standard of living'. The Australian example was 'of great practical value to the rest of the world'.

Yet Persia herself was no longer Australian. In fact, for several years, she had no citizenship at all. Due to legal irregularities at the time, British women (including Australians) who married Americans found themselves stateless. Under British law, they lost their British subjecthood, but US law stipulated that foreign wives of Americans did not automatically acquire US citizenship. Persia was one of many who fell into the cracks between these systems. When she first applied for US citizenship, she was deterred upon learning she'd be required to renounce her pacifism. At some point, however, pragmatism overrode idealism, and in 1936 Persia pledged her allegiance to the United States. She was now officially an American.

After a brief stint in New Jersey, the Rice family settled in Manhattan's upper west side. Edward worked as a steamship agent, and the family lived in a sunny two-bedroom flat opposite Morningside Park. Persia developed a close relationship with Edward's daughters from his first marriage: Eleanor (Nora),

Joan and Elizabeth (Betsy). Nora and Betsy even came to live with them, squeezing into the New York flat. In the summers, the family rented a house in Westport, Connecticut, where they enjoyed yacht races.

Life was good, full of family, meaningful work and intellectual stimulation. Only the name given to her daughter – Sydney, after Sydney, Australia – hinted at any yearning for that other home on the opposite side of the world. Persia visited Sydney with her daughter in late 1934 for two months before returning to New York to resume her busy life. In New York, Persia's name began to appear in the newspapers on a regular basis. And remarkably, her name remained Persia Campbell. Despite her marriage, she retained a strong independent identity, using her maiden name for professional purposes. If ever someone referred to her as Mrs Rice, she was quick to offer a sharp correction.

Then, in 1939, the run of good years came to an end. That year, when the outbreak of war put paid to her visions of world peace, Campbell's private life also imploded. Edward, unwell with a heart condition, had travelled to Florida to convalesce. In February, on the tiny resort island of No Name Key, he suffered a fatal heart attack. He was only 45. Persia, about to turn 41, was in New Jersey when it happened. The man she'd upended her life for was gone before she had a chance to say goodbye.

She found herself widowed with two young children and a further two stepchildren in her care. Her family was 10 000 miles away, and the money from her husband's estate soon dried up. Although Persia had plenty of work – running the Consumer National Federation, finishing a PhD – none of it paid a salary. She had no reliable income, no blood relations, no one to share to load.

The world had gone dark.

16

WHY SHOULD WE HATE EACH OTHER?

THE PIANIST, CHICAGO, 1932

A November bonfire, burning on a sandy beach. Hungry flames stretch up to the black night. Around the fire huddle a small crowd, 50 or so young adults swaddled in thick coats. Cups of coffee warm cold hands. On long sticks held out to the flames, they toast marshmallows and hotdogs. Once everyone has filled their stomachs, the singalong begins. With a banjo for accompaniment, the crowd come together in song, their voices carrying across Lake Michigan. One by one, they contribute a tune from back home. As the night deepens, and the temperature drops, they huddle closer to the flames. They can afford to stay out late, as the entire group live just a block away – at Chicago's International House, on the other side of Jackson Park.

This is a self-consciously 'American' gathering, a 'Weenie Roast' dedicated to the fine art of placing meat in bread. Yet the humans thronged around the bonfire are largely visitors from elsewhere. China, India, Japan, Bulgaria, Germany. Somewhere within the crowd, there is also a lone Australian – the pianist Vera Bradford, who'd become an inaugural resident of International House two months earlier.

As the group share music, Vera's spirits soar. Here is a cosmopolitan crowd, one that includes former wartime antagonists, coming together in the spirit of friendship. From her position on the beach, Vera feels she's witnessing something profound, as though this humble singalong might seed a new era of peace and harmony. Perhaps, with enough nights like these, this group of international students – future leaders in the making – might even change the course of history.

For Vera herself, that change had already begun. Her encounter with difference at Chicago's International House was a hurricane that blew open her heart and mind. Raised in Melbourne among a majority Anglo population, she'd not previously mixed with non-English speakers or people of colour. 'In Australia we come only in contact with English or English descent, a few Germans etc,' Vera noted, 'but on the whole we don't really know the foreigners.' Now, she was thrust into a miniature League of Nations. After forging cross-cultural friendships, she no longer believed 'the English are the greatest people on earth'. Her newfound internationalism 'helped me to better – to see a little farther,' she wrote. '[W]e mustn't think we are the only & greatest people.'

By the night of the Weenie Roast in November 1932, Vera had studied piano at the Chicago Musical College for just over four years. Under the tutelage of Alexander Raab, Vera developed her arm-weight technique and worked towards the goal of becoming a concert pianist. In May 1930 she made her debut with the Chicago Symphony Orchestra. The following June she was a soloist at the Chicago Opera House. After the latter performance, the *Chicago Music News* declared Vera Bradford was 'among the coming greats'.

During her first years in Chicago, Vera boarded with a local family she'd met through the Methodist Church. The Hubers lived in the Southside suburb of North Kenwood. With her own parents and siblings thousands of miles away in Melbourne, the

Hubers became a second family. They shared meals and outings and conversation. During the week, Vera practised on their home piano. In May 1932, however, Vera was invited to move into International House, a student residence due to open that September. It was an offer too good to refuse. For only $5 per week, plus a dollar per day for meals, she would have her own room and unfettered access to an in-house Steinway Grand Piano. Best of all, she'd be immersed in a vibrant community, living cheek-by-jowl with fellow students from around the world.

Vera was already a committed internationalist. In the wake of World War I, there'd been an explosion of organisations based around the idea that cross-cultural friendship could prevent another world war. Vera, like many idealistic youths, latched onto 'cultural internationalism' with evangelical fervour. Since 1929, she'd been a stalwart of Chicago's International Club, where she made friends from India, China, Japan, Germany and the Philippines. Together, club members debated world affairs and donned national costume for fancy dress balls. After long evenings of conversation, Vera was converted to the cause of Indian independence. Once a fervent imperialist, she now deemed Gandhi a 'great man'. As Vera told her family, the International Club was 'doing wonderful work to help bring about world peace & human understanding'. In her mind, international friendship was a prophylactic against conflict. '[W]hen we get to know these different foreign groups they are just plain human beings like ourselves – why should we hate each other,' she reflected.

Internationalism was her new religion. What, then, could be better than an International House? It promised to be a utopian community, a model of a better world. Vera moved into International House in September 1932, shortly before the official opening on 5 October. The house was a nine-storey Gothic limestone building, with a U-shaped design that separated the sexes to assuage anxieties about co-educational living. Men lived in the east wing, women in the west. The connecting section housed the common areas. Vera's room was on the fourth floor, one of 525 private bedrooms. Heliotrope wallpaper matched the sage carpet and bedspread. The French casement window looked out over lush green lawns. Every morning, a maid service tidied the room and made the bed. Out in the corridor, Vera could find communal bathrooms, electric irons and electric sewing machines. It was 'the most luxurious place' she'd ever lived.

When not sleeping or practising, Vera enjoyed the building's amenities, which included a library, cinema, lounges, dining room, cafeteria, post office and barber shop. At mealtimes, she ate alongside 'many interesting young people from all parts of the world'. Outside, fountains and gardens gave the house the feel of a summer resort. To travel into the city, where Vera taught private students, it was a quick 13-minute ride on the electric train. Altogether, International House was 'just a dream'. It was 'too wonderful to describe', a 'fairy tale' existence 'too good to be true'.

Chicago's International House was the third such institution to be developed in the United States, following New York in 1924 and Berkeley in 1930. Funded by the Rockefeller Foundation, these residences were intended to foster international friendship by bringing together domestic students with friendless foreigners from around the world. The ostensible ethos of the International House movement was 'brotherhood will prevail' – a phrase inscribed on the façade of each building. In practice, however, the residences were less concerned with building fraternity for its own sake than fostering pro-American sentiment to bolster US power. This ambition was made explicit by John D Rockefeller Jr himself in a letter to US Secretary of State Charles E Hughes. 'As these young men and women from the nations of the world are received with sympathy, interest and cordiality by the United States,' Rockefeller wrote, 'they will naturally cherish a friendly feeling for our country.'

For Vera, Chicago's International House did indeed foster 'friendly feeling' towards the United States. This luxurious residence, fitted out with the latest mod-cons, helped to make her Chicago years a peak life experience. For decades to come, she would wax lyrical about the cultural riches and astonishing modernity of the United States. 'The most fantastic six years of my life,' was how Vera later described her American sojourn.

But International House did more than make Vera a booster for the US of A. It also shifted her worldview, opening her mind to ideas and relationships that back in Melbourne would have been inconceivable. Her new friends included Mr Ahmed, a 'young Hindu student'; Dr Tashero, a Japanese dentist; Dr Hi-Shih and Dr Yen, both Chinese doctors; an architect from Chile; Dr Pareck, 'an Indian gentleman' who was a 'personal friend of Ghandi'; and a 'brilliant young Korean cellist'. These cross-cultural relationships challenged Vera's conservative politics, making her more 'broad-minded' and better able to 'see the other person's point of view'. Through living side-by-side, 'foreigners' came into focus as complex individuals. '[A]fter we get to know all the various students from different countries, we forget their color or race, and treat them just like ordinary human beings,' Vera reflected.

At International House dances, the pianist twirled and flirted with partners from India, China, Korea and the Philippines – a form of interracial mixing that would have been scandalous back home. Indeed, only a few years before, in 1928, a group of African American musicians had been driven from Vera's hometown of Melbourne following reports they'd fraternised with local white women. After a local tabloid published the headline 'White Girls with Negro Lovers', the federal government not only deported the jazz band in question but instituted a decades-long ban on 'coloured' musicians. Against this backdrop, it was no small thing for a white woman like Vera to dance cheek-to-cheek with a racialised person. Yet in the idealistic environs of International

House, the sexual 'colour line' could be largely disregarded. Vera cheerily reported her dancing partners to her family, taking pains to emphasise how open-minded she'd become. '[I] think nothing of it because I know all these people personally & find them just like ourselves,' she noted. In a subsequent letter, the pianist hinted she might marry a Chinese beau.

Class was an important factor here. The students at International House hailed, by and large, from their home country's elite. They were the children of the rich and powerful, destined to become figures of influence themselves. As Vera's letters make clear, this fact shaped the desirability and respectability of crossing the colour line at International House. For an ambitious artist like herself, the prospect of befriending future leaders – no matter their race – held considerable appeal. Her new friends' affluence and Western education also made them more proximate to whiteness – and hence, more 'suitable' associates. Could Vera's critique of racial hierarchies extend to more 'ordinary' people of colour? Certainly, she was silent on the oppression of Chicago's large Black population. Nor did she reflect on the dispossession of Indigenous peoples in the United States or Australia. For all that International House challenged racial prejudice, it was still easier to see the humanity of some racialised peoples more than others.

After a year at International House, Vera had 'friends in nearly every country in the world'. She'd developed intimate bonds with fellow students from India, China and Japan, and now hoped to visit those countries in the future. 'I have grown to like the oriental people very much,' she wrote. Much like Isabel Letham's experiences in San Francisco's public swimming pools, American life provided an eye-opening exposure to racial difference that was unimaginable in Australia. In visiting the United States, Australian women glimpsed a world beyond whiteness.

These relationships did more than enrich Vera's personal life; they also benefited her music. While at International House, Vera continued to study at the Chicago Musical College and made greater progress than ever. 'I am stimulated to do better work myself', she wrote, noting that 'my practicing has been so inspired'. Her music, always her 'first goal', was only enhanced by life in the 'miniature world' of International House, which pushed her to 'broaden my view for my own work'.

Vera described a solo recital on 26 January 1934, as her 'biggest triumph' to date. Held on a Friday evening at the International House Theater, the recital attracted a record-breaking crowd who welcomed Vera with a 'marvellous ovation'. The pianist, dressed in a turquoise chiffon gown, seduced the audience with a mix of Haydn, Schumann, Chopin, Brahms, Bartók, Ravel and Debussy. On stage, Vera entered a flow state: 'I was just being led on to play and unfold the beauties of sound.' In this reverie, she played 'as I have never played before'. Between pieces, you could hear a pin drop. After the final piece, Liszt's 'Mazeppa', the audience burst into rapturous applause. As Vera gave her bows, she was presented with great armloads of bouquets. Esther Strote, critic for the local *Musical Leader*, was confident Vera had 'big things' ahead. 'I don't know when I have enjoyed a piano recital quite as much as this one of yours,' Strote wrote. 'You have grown tremendously these past two years.'

Vera was on the verge of greatness. After six years honing her craft in Chicago, she appeared destined to become a concert pianist on the international stage. But before that glorious future could unfold, Vera needed to go home. She hadn't seen her family since 1928, and her mother was ill. In spring 1934, Vera sailed to London, and boarded the *Moreton Bay*, bound for Australia.

When Vera disembarked at Port Melbourne on 24 April, she told reporters she would stay six months. She would catch up with loved ones and perform a series of concerts. The standard homecoming tour for deracinated antipodean artists. Then, Vera would be off again, back to the northern hemisphere where – so it seemed – all the real and important things happened. Australia was to be just a stepping stone on her trajectory, a brief interlude before real life began.

Or at least, that was the plan.

17

A PHILOSOPHY OF NAKEDNESS

THE HEALTH GURU, CHESAPEAKE BAY, 1933

Mud, everywhere. Thick wet Maryland soil, gooey between the fingers. More grey than brown, a sticky and fragrant ooze. Alice Caporn dug into the rich mud and slathered another handful across her legs. Her skin, already deep brown from the sun, was darkened by wet earth. From top to toe, Alice wore a coating of soil. It was dug from the bed of a local spring-fed brook, then transported to a freshwater lake for the daily mud bath.

'The earth is full of vitamins,' Alice instructed the watching students. 'It's good for you, the next best thing after the sun.' With that, she lay down to bake. As the mud dried into a crust, Alice meditated on the goodness entering her body. 'Can you feel it?' she asked. 'Your skin is sucking in the richest element of life.'

Dirt was good; sunshine even better. Following their mud baths, Alice took her students down to the 'sun parlour' – a stretch of sand down on the shore of Chesapeake Bay. It was mid-week, so the waters were quiet. No gawking strangers in sight. To be safe, she posted a sentinel on the cliffs, to warn of any passing boats. Then her solarium was ready for business. Alice whipped off her dress and underclothes, exposing bare flesh to the light. All around, her students followed suit. Men on one side of a tree trunk, women on the other. A gaggle of nude bodies, over three dozen in total, surrendering to the July sun on a peaceful stretch of sand. Calvert Beach was today a nudist colony.

With an infectious smile, Alice told her nude flock they were 'recharging the human dynamo with electricity from the sun's rays'. Without the constraint of garments, the body's pores could breathe. Clothes kept the skin starved of air and light; outdoor undress restored lifegiving connection to the sun. By combining sunbathing with natural sleep, food and exercise, it was possible to reach total mental and physical fitness.

Alice was a walking advertisement for the nudist lifestyle. Although in her late 50s, she could pass for decades younger. Slim and deeply tanned, with an erect spine and apple cheeks, she was the picture of vitality. The health entrepreneur hustled day and night, but hadn't had a day's illness in years. Her eyes twinkled beneath dark hair, not yet faded into grey. The sun's rays had worked wonders on her.

There was just one small problem. Nudism was not respectable. Men and women together, cavorting in public with their privates on full display? The idea was scandalous. It evoked promiscuity, loose living, general debauchery. Over in Europe, they might dabble in such things, but upstanding Americans looked askance at anything that smacked of sexual deviance. Never mind that Alice was a married Christian woman with an earnest health agenda. Never mind that she urged nudists to commune with the sun rather than each other.

When word got out that Alice was leading a nudist colony on the outskirts of Washington DC, all hell broke loose.

The colony in question was at a summer camp run by the League for the Larger Life, on the ancestral lands of the Piscataway people. Founded in 1916, the league was a Christian self-help organisation, part of an American spiritual movement known as New Thought. As the name suggests, New Thought was concerned with consciousness. It emphasised the power of the human mind to influence the material world. The core idea was that our thoughts make our reality. With the mind alone, humans can cure disease and generate success. Over the decades, this logic gave rise to the prosperity doctrine, the positive thinking movement, and the law of attraction (or manifesting). If you've ever uttered an affirmation or read Rhonda Byrne's *The Secret* (2006), you've been influenced by New Thought.

Inspired by such ideas, the League for the Larger Life was established in New York City to promote 'successful living' and 'the health of the individual and the Nation'. In 1922, the league formed a Washington DC chapter. Each summer, the league's DC membership enjoyed vegetarian food and healthful exercise on the shores of Chesapeake Bay. It was an annual fiesta of self-optimisation; individual striving on steroids. A celebration of the twin American religions: individualism and Christianity.

In 1933, Alice Caporn joined as a visiting teacher. Advertised as a 'noted endocrinologist and biologist-food scientist', she stayed at the league camp for the entire summer. But then, in July, Alice made a terrible mistake. She talked to reporters. The world learnt that the esteemed food scientist was also an evangelical nudist. In a splashy feature, accompanied by a full-length photograph, the Washington DC *Evening Star* reported that Alice had brought nudism 'within the Capital's resort area'. The rhetoric conjured the spectre of menacing sinners at the gates, poised to corrupt the nation's moral backbone. Suddenly the celebrity health guru was a dangerous liability.

Predictably, there was an uproar. League members complained of being tarnished by association. JR King, a developer who owned land adjacent to the league camp, railed against 'indecent exposure'. He announced a $100 reward for information leading to the arrest and conviction of persons guilty of this crime. To save face, the League for the Larger Life went into damage control. The Washington DC leadership held an emergency board meeting, and a committee was appointed to investigate reports of nude sunbathing. The league declared itself emphatically opposed to nudism. We are 'normal people of good standing', a spokesman told the *Evening Star*. 'Faddists and extremists' had no place in the organisation, which was definitely not a 'nudist cult'. Meanwhile, camp director Milton Trenham travelled down from Washington to confront Alice in person. That same afternoon, she abruptly vacated the camp. The official story was a resignation. Alice insisted she'd been forced out.

In the aftermath, Alice was defiant. 'In every movement, there must be pioneers, and pioneers are always misunderstood', she declared. She doubled down on her 'philosophy of nakedness' and outlined plans to move her colony elsewhere. New Jersey, perhaps. Or maybe West Virginia. Eventually Americans would come to appreciate the benefits of natural living – nudism included. As for the supposed law-breaking, Alice pleaded ignorance. 'It seems some people down there consider that I have broken some "blue law",' she said. 'I am an Australian and I have never before heard of a "blue law".'

Alice Caporn's words should always be taken with a grain of salt. She was an ambitious hustler, a one-woman health empire who made questionable statements on the daily. She declared herself immune to all disease. She boasted she'd live to a hundred. She denounced potatoes as unfit for human consumption and promised to rid the world of infantile paralysis. Alice was, in other words, hardly a reliable narrator of her own existence. But amid the murk of half-truths and outright fabulation, she got one thing right: the infamous nudist Alice Caporn was indeed Australian. A child of South Australia, she was born Alice White in 1875, in the Barossa town of Angaston. Although by 1933 she'd lived over a decade in the United States, the health guru maintained her antipodean identity. She was the 'food specialist of Australia', a 50-something 'Australian girl'.

Back in Australia, Alice was no one special. For the first four decades of her existence, she'd lived a quiet and unremarkable life. Not yet a health entrepreneur, there was little to suggest that outraged headlines or notoriety lay in her future. After a Barossa childhood, she'd worked as a nurse in the Western Australian mining towns of Coolgardie and Kalgoorlie. In 1904, aged 29, Alice married Henry Caporn and soon after discovered Christian Science. Established in 1879, Christian Science was a new church founded by American woman Mary Baker Eddy. Like the larger New Thought movement, Eddy's church emphasised the power of thought and focused on spiritual and physical healing. From the 1890s, when Christian Science arrived in Australia, it won over many progressive women, including feminists Vida Goldstein and Miles Franklin.

Caporn was one of these converts. She fell hook, line and sinker. More than her husband, Christian Science was her great love. So, in 1917, she made a big decision. That winter, with World War I still raging, Caporn ditched Henry and sailed to the United States. At the age of 42, Caporn made a new home in Boston, the headquarters of the Christian Science faith. Although she arrived knowing no one, Alice immediately felt among friends. She understood the United States as a fellow bastion of the 'Anglo-Saxon race'. 'It is not difficult for me to foster affection for this great Nation, which is akin to us,' Alice wrote. 'I have a real love for Americans and have felt entirely at home here from the moment I landed.'

Once settled in Boston, Caporn worked as a nurse within the Christian Science community. She also penned *Awake! Christian Scientists*, a 1921 polemic that challenged the church's governance in the aftermath of Eddy's death in 1910. Over 250 pages, Alice warned Christian Science had been infected with 'the canker worm of Romanism, in other words, ECCLESTICAL DESPOTISM'. This diatribe was the first inkling that Alice was not afraid to question authority or disrupt the status quo. From that point onwards, she would revel in ruffling feathers. Unafraid of conflict, Alice was forever painting herself as a misunderstood prophet, a martyr ahead of her time.

She would bring that rebellious energy to her next great love: the science of nutrition. After the discovery of vitamins in 1912, the United States had become the global hub of nutrition research and a pioneer of the dietetics profession. Thanks to innovations in technology, modern dietary science was providing the tools to optimise vitality and health. Yet modernity was also a threat, with new stresses such as a sedentary lifestyle and processed foods that risked devitalising the Western world. This was the high watermark of eugenic thinking. Fears abounded that the 'white races' would soon be usurped by the 'rising tide of colour'. The imagined stakes couldn't be higher. Could correct diet protect the white population from the scourges of modern living, before it was too late?

Caporn dove headfirst into these debates, remaking herself as a proto-wellness influencer. Like health gurus before and since, she boasted her own redemption narrative. As Caporn entered midlife she'd been beset by aches and pains. Liver trouble. Heart trouble. Insomnia. Weight loss, swollen legs, fallen arches. All looked hopeless, a slow decline towards death. Then she discovered the cure: 'natural foods' and vigorous exercise. With her vitality restored, Caporn became a convert to naturopathy and 'modern food science'. In Boston and New York, she pursued qualifications with proponents of the 'nature cure', such as naturopath Benedict Lust.

Caporn developed her own system of 'Health and Beauty Exercises'. From the mid-1930s, she lectured on 'Dynamic

Health!' across the eastern seaboard. Around this time, she also began claiming a PhD from Columbia, though her name is absent from the university's list of graduates. A prolific writer, Caporn published 14 books under the Boston-based Radiant Health imprint. Her oeuvre ranged from *Sex Intelligence* and *Phosphorus Foods* to *Sunshine Treatment* and *Care of the Feet*. In these publications Caporn proclaimed herself an 'Australian author, lecturer, teacher, food scientist, endocrinologist'.

She continued to live apart from her husband, not even returning to Australia when he died in 1934. Her schemes grew more ambitious each year. After her Chesapeake solarium was thwarted by the nudism scandal, Alice moved her efforts to West Virginia. There, she became manager of Minnehaha Health Spa. Located at a mineral spring in the Allegheny mountains, the health spa offered a spring-fed pool and personalised dietary advice.

In late 1936, Caporn bought land in Belize, then known as British Honduras, believing it would offer 'the ideal climate and ideal environment to start our Modern Health Colony'. Away from the puritanical United States, Alice could put the principles of modern health science into practice. It would be her own private utopia, a place for her followers to raise children in harmony with nature. She acquired land near the Guatemalan border, then began clearing the jungle and planting banana crops.

It had all the makings of a cult. Alice as architect of a new society, hidden away in the jungle, peopled by true believers who would raise a new generation in her image. Free from scrutiny, Alice could build her heaven on earth. She would be guru-in-chief, wafting about in her signature white robe, making mystical pronouncements to be deciphered by adoring acolytes. It could have been benevolent, or it could have gone the way of so many attempted utopias: conflict, scandal, abuse. At the very least, we can assume Alice would have enforced her vision of 'Anglo-Saxons' as a master race and homosexuality as a 'pernicious perversion'. Her idea of heaven was based on a strict hierarchy of bodies.

She came so close to making it happen. She had the land, the followers, the ambition and the self-belief. After nearly a year, her funds ran out and the work stalled. She made a reluctant return to the United States, to earn some cash on the lecture circuit and advertise her colony. She just needed a bit more capital to get things going.

But then, at the crucial moment, news arrived from the Antipodes. Alice's mother was ill; she was needed at home. As so often happened to Australian women abroad, the expectation that daughters would care for ageing parents cut short an overseas adventure. The Modern Health Colony would have to wait. After 20 years abroad, it was time to return to Australia.

18

FROM COLONIAL GIRL TO FIERCE FEMINIST

THE DENTIST, MELBOURNE, 1934

As the clock approached three o'clock, a stream of women headed towards the lift, striding across the mosaic tiles of the Block Arcade. Outside, on Collins Street, it was a miserable Melbourne winter day, but inside under the electric lights and carved cornices you could imagine yourself in London or Paris. Every window drew the eyes with a tantalising display: gloves at Cameron's, cameras at Kodak, sewing machines at Singer. Yet these women took no notice of the gleaming shopfronts. One by one, they bypassed the street-level boutiques, and bustled up to the clubroom on the first floor.

There was Julia Rapke, the diminutive feminist dynamo who belonged to every organisation and committee. Amy Wheaton, not long returned from the London School of Economics, arrived with her usual cigarette in hand. Lady Peacock, wife of the late premier Sir Alexander Peacock, could be spotted in her signature furs and round glasses. These women were not here to window-shop or eat scones; they had a more serious purpose this afternoon. The Victorian Women Citizens' Movement was holding a meeting.

For 12 years, the movement had been lobbying to get women into Victorian parliament. When it started, back in 1922, women were not permitted to stand for election. They'd been able to vote in state elections since 1908 but couldn't represent their fellow citizens in parliament. That rule had been overturned in 1923, but, over a decade later, women still couldn't penetrate the state legislature.

The previous year, in 1933, Lady Peacock became the first woman elected to the Victorian parliament. But hers was a dubious victory; rather than winning on her own merits, she'd effectively inherited her husband's seat. After Sir Alexander's sudden death, Lady Peacock was elected in a by-election without giving a single speech. Elsewhere, politics remained a boys' club. The major parties would only preselect women for unwinnable seats. Women who stood as independents had next to no chance of getting the numbers. Importantly, this fight was all about *white* women's rights; First Nations women remained disenfranchised until 1962.

After years of getting nowhere, feminists were losing patience. Following the exhilarating days of the early 1900s, when white Australian women led the world in political rights, progress had slowed to a snail's pace. In the aftermath of the Great War, the bold experiment of the Federation years had faded away. As Miles Franklin wrote in 1924, 'it seems to me that Australia, which took a wonderful lurch ahead in all progressive laws and women's advancement about 20 years ago has stagnated ever since. At present it is more unintelligently conservative & conventional than England.'

In that climate, hope and energy were hard to sustain. But the Victorian Women Citizens' Movement, like similar organisations nationwide, plugged away, year after year. Meetings, delegations, paperwork – it was unglamorous, painstaking labour. Today, though, there was a buzz in the air, grim weather notwithstanding. This afternoon, they would entertain a special guest. A Melbourne woman, one of their own, from the genteel eastern suburbs, who'd just returned from a decade in North America.

Dr Waugh, was her name. The granddaughter of James Swanton Waugh, the founding president of Wesley College, the

Methodist private school on St Kilda Road. Dr Waugh, because she was that rare thing – a woman medic. A dentist, to be precise. She'd left Melbourne as Miss Dorothy Burrowes Waugh, just another young lady from Hawthorn. Now she was back as Dr Waugh, world traveller and associate professor at one of the world's top dental schools. At that time, there were only 135 women dentists in Australia – barely 4 per cent of the profession. Certainly, none of them could claim a professorship. In 1934, Dr Waugh was something special indeed.

Women clustered into the Block Arcade clubroom to hear Waugh's impressions. Back in Melbourne for only a month, Dr Dorothy Waugh had sacrificed an afternoon to tell the city's feminists all about life and work in the United States. Over the next few hours, her audience would learn they were right to feel short-changed and frustrated. They would learn their anger was justified.

Up until 1924, when she left home for the first time, Dorothy had lived in a cosseted world, neatly tucked into a few square kilometres in Melbourne's leafy eastern suburbs. Boonwurrung Country, the stretch of land east of the Yarra down to the Mornington Peninsula. The Waughs were a prominent local family, Irish Methodists who'd been in Victoria since the goldrushes. Dorothy had six siblings; her father Theo Waugh was one of ten. Home was on Glen Street, Hawthorn, a quiet street sheltered by plane trees; school was Milverton Girl's College in nearby Camberwell. Her father died in 1906, when Dorothy was 12. But unlike many women of her generation, her siblings were untouched by the Great War.

After school, Dorothy was apprenticed to a city dentist. Dr James Monahan Lewis had offices at 12 Collins Street and taught at the University of Melbourne. In the late 1920s, Lewis was president of the state Dental Board and, by 1939, president of the Australian Dental Association. When Dorothy started working for Lewis, sometime in the 1910s, dentistry was undergoing a quiet revolution. In the early 1900s dentistry, like many occupations, went from being a largely unregulated industry to a modern profession – complete with university degrees, professional associations and formal accreditation. As historian Tamson Pietsch has documented, the change was dramatic. In the 19th century, a dentist was anyone willing to extract teeth for cash, skilled or otherwise; by the 1930s, a dentist was a medical man in a white coat with a framed university degree.

Dorothy arrived at the mid-point of this transition. Everything was in flux. The old apprenticeship training model lingered on, but the universities had started to offer dental degrees. Dentists now needed to be registered with state Dental Boards. As dentistry entered the ivory tower, the professional demographics changed. Fewer women, more rich men. The number of women dentists nationwide declined 90 per cent across the 1920s – from 26 per cent of the profession in 1921 to 4.3 per cent in 1933.

Dorothy was not one of them. Under the informal tutelage of Dr Lewis, she was known as a dental technician – not a dentist proper. In keeping with the broader marginalisation of women within the profession, her training was limited to learning on the job. She did not study at the University of Melbourne, nor did she sit the Dental Board exam. Yet Dorothy hungered for more. In 1924, she left Australia to undertake advanced training at the Royal College of Dental Surgeons in Toronto, Canada. The following year, she travelled on to London, where she studied with Dr William Griswold, former dentist to the Duke of Windsor. In 1928, Dorothy was back in North America where the 34-year-old commenced a Bachelor of Dental Science at Temple University.

Temple was a public university in Philadelphia, Pennsylvania, on traditional Lenape land. Founded in 1884, the university boasted the second-oldest dental school in the United States. Dorothy was the only woman in her class of 135 students, and her arrival caused quite a stir. But she was a star student and soon disproved any misgivings about her aptitude. In the 1932 Dental Yearbook, her classmates recalled: 'Dorothy from the crack of the gun stood forth as one of the leaders of our class.' Her average mark was 100. In her final year, she took home three academic prizes, including the Alumni Award for highest average. She did all the extracurriculars: class treasurer, *Dental Review* staff, secretary to multiple societies. A classic overachiever. 'We know that nothing can stand in the way of success for our Dorothy,' the Yearbook concluded. It was a familiar story: in a male-dominated profession, the token woman had to be absolutely stellar, beyond reproach, if she had any hope of proving the naysayers wrong. Her male peers could be mediocre; Dorothy had to be remarkable.

In her graduation photo from 1932, Dorothy has a steely gaze beneath fashionably marcelled hair. Now almost 40, her thin mouth is set in a determined line. No make-up adorns her oval face. Heavy brows, high forehead, arrow-straight nose. This is a resolute woman who knows her own mind; a battle-hardened professional who can hold her own with the boys. It's a photo that makes me wonder what she'd weathered. What humiliations had she stomached as the sole woman among a crowd of young men? How had the sheltered Miss Dorothy remade herself into the formidable Dr Waugh?

Dorothy funded her own way through university. There was no family money to smooth the path. Instead, she worked and studied in harsh Pennsylvania winters all through the Depression years, a single woman reliant on herself, with family three weeks away. By 1932, we can speculate, she'd survived some tough moments. We know for certain she got homesick. 'I would very much like to see a blue Australian sky just now,' she wrote in the Melbourne *Argus* from a snowy Philadelphia in March 1928. In total, she would go 10 years before seeing that sky again. Ten years without hearing her mother's voice. No phone calls, no quick visits home. Just letters that took weeks to arrive, plus telegrams for emergencies.

But the years of struggle would be rewarded. In 1932, just after graduating, Dr Waugh was appointed to the Temple faculty. Now a member of staff, she taught prosthetic dentistry to undergraduates, who likened her to Jo March from Louisa May Alcott's *Little Women*. Like Jo, she was renowned for her exacting standards and fierce independence. At the same time, Dorothy practised as a dentist – one of only three women dentists in Philadelphia. With two jobs on the go, a 17-hour workday was not uncommon. Thanks to the American novelty of central heating, she could keep working until two or three in the morning. While busy in the lab, she listened to the radio to keep up with news and current affairs. In 1933, she won an essay prize for her research. Again, it was as though she needed to work twice as hard to prove herself.

By 1934, Dr Waugh could afford a trip back to Melbourne. Over the northern summer, Dorothy retraced her journey across the Pacific aboard the *Mariposa*. She would catch up with friends and family; she might give a public talk or two. The prodigal daughter was coming home.

Before heading overseas, Dorothy had not been politically active. As a young woman in her 20s, there's no evidence she engaged with women's clubs and associations. She did not comment about life in a male-dominated profession. Nor did she have anything to say about women's place in society. Like most of her peers, Dorothy accepted, or at least tolerated, the status quo, coasting on her proximity to power.

Ten years abroad changed much of that. For her, the United States was a site of feminist politicisation. In Pennsylvania,

Dorothy woke up to the problem of gender inequity for the first time. This was not because she'd encountered unprecedented sexism in Philadelphia; on the contrary, it was because she experienced unprecedented opportunity. Despite being the only woman among dozens of men and facing jibes about the 'weaker sex', Dorothy still found her US experience a marked improvement on conditions in Australia. After all, she'd secured a degree, established a career, won awards – all as a dentist in skirts. In her view, this was gender equity in action. This taste of how things could be exposed the dearth of possibilities in Australia. With the benefit of distance and comparison, and the tools to imagine life otherwise, Dorothy could see how grim things were back home. As happened to so many Australian women, America had made a fierce feminist out of the genteel colonial girl.

American women, however, had a different perspective. No local feminists were proclaiming the United States a woman's paradise. On the contrary, the decades between female enfranchisement in 1920 and the birth of Women's Liberation in the 1960s were understood as a period of stagnation and backlash. These were the doldrums, the era between feminist waves when change slowed or went backwards. As historian Julia Mickenberg documents in *American Girls in Red Russia*, for disheartened American feminists, it was Russian women who provided 'models of female empowerment'. While Australian women like Dorothy held up the United States as a model to emulate, their American counterparts were casting admiring glances to Soviet Russia, where, it was imagined, the communist revolution had left women 'equal partners in love and equal builders of a new world'. Everyone saw utopia somewhere else.

When Dr Waugh arrived at the Block Arcade that rainy Tuesday afternoon, she was nearing the end of her visit to Melbourne. Over the previous month, she'd been profiled in *The Age* and the *Argus*; she'd addressed the National Council of Women; she'd even visited her old school. This speech to the Victorian Women Citizens' Movement would be her last engagement before boarding the *Mariposa* on 18 August, in four days time. It was her last opportunity to exert some influence, shake things up. Who knew when, if ever, she'd be back? It was time for her mic drop moment.

Once everyone settled into the clubroom, a hush descended. President Julia Rapke welcomed the speakers. First up was Lady Peacock, who shared a few words about her new role as Member for Allandale. She spoke in predictable platitudes: fellow parliamentarians were courteous and helpful; she was proud to be continuing her husband's work. Quite possibly, it was obvious she had no real passion for the gig. Perhaps she even hinted she wouldn't contest another election.

After this warm-up act, it was time for the main event. Following some introductory comments, Dr Dorothy Waugh got down to business: the question of women in public life. Attitudes were changing fast in the United States. Even as the Depression had fuelled concern about women 'taking men's jobs', women were proving themselves more than capable. The 1933 appointment of Frances Perkins as federal Secretary of Labor had been a game changer. Perkins's appointment had initially been criticised, but she'd proven the naysayers wrong. Now a woman had achieved such a high office, things would be easier for others to come. Already, the ripple effects could be felt across American life – even in her own career, which Dorothy deemed free from sex discrimination.

In conclusion, Dorothy spoke baldly. 'The fact that I was a woman had no bearing on my appointment to a University position,' she pronounced. 'I have never once had cause to feel that I was holding a man's job. That is the attitude in the United States, and it should be the attitude here.'

It should be the attitude here. I like to imagine that last line resonated around the room, a bolt of conviction that jolted everyone awake. It was certainly deemed important enough to be quoted verbatim in the newspapers. The way Dorothy said it, it seemed so obvious. The most self-evident thing in the world. *Of course, that's how it should be*, I imagine her audience thinking. *Why don't we have that attitude here? Why isn't Australia more like America? Why are we lagging behind?*

Dorothy had given an outsider's perspective that reminded her audience that inequality was not inevitable. Things could be otherwise. Things were already different elsewhere. Australian women were getting a raw deal and should demand more. The challenge ahead was to bridge the distance between the actual and the possible.

On that rainy afternoon, Dr Waugh laid down a gauntlet. Would it be picked up? Did her words put a bit more vigour, a bit more determination into the Victorian Women Citizens' Movement? Certainly, they had a major victory just three years later. In 1937, Ivy Weber was elected state member for Nunawading – the first Victorian woman to win on her own steam. Dorothy, however, was not there to see it. Only four days after her speech, she was on a steamship, heading east across the Tasman. The northern summer was almost over; the academic year was about to begin. Over in Philadelphia, her students would be waiting. She had to get back to her own personal paradise.

19

THE YANKS ARE ON THE RIGHT TRACK

THE NURSE, CHICAGO, 1935

Inside the laboratory, 28 women were hunched over dead cats. One cat per pair. With scalpels and forceps, each duo dissected their pickled feline to test their newfound knowledge of anatomy. Organs, muscles, nerves – each was carefully found and identified. Once a key nerve was located, the women removed the surrounding tissue and followed the cord along its route. As nurses, they would need to know these things. They needed to speak the language of modern medicine.

Outside, the late summer sun baked the Chicago streets into submission. On an afternoon like this, with heat shimmering off the asphalt, there was no sign of the gangsters who'd made the midwestern city into a byword for violent crime. Yet while the city cooked, inside the laboratory the atmosphere was as cool and hushed as a church. Reverential, bent at the altar of science, the trainee nurses reined in their usual high spirits. They spoke little and were 'breathlessly attentive', each figure 'avid with curiosity and speculation'.

Here, in the United States, nursing was no longer about making beds and emptying bedpans; it was a bona fide profession that demanded real medical expertise. To that end, the trainee nurses spent two afternoons per week studying Anatomy and Physiology at DePaul University. They also learnt Ethics and

Chemistry and Bacteriology. Every day, there were new classes; each night, there was private study in the library. It was a 'rigorous apprenticeship', an endless slog that left little time for sleep. But 'they loved it, all of it'. This 'search for knowledge' was 'a dream, a fairy story'. They bent to their task, focused on the work before them.

Once the day's classes were done, the trainee nurses walked back to St Joseph's Training Hospital. Furrowed brows gave way to chatter and laughter. The youngest were fresh out of high school, girls not yet 18. Several were older, 21 or 22, full-grown women who'd already graduated college. One trainee, however, was significantly older. A tall woman not far off 30 and a foreigner, to boot. Dark-haired, with intense eyes and a melancholic face, she'd flown in from Los Angeles the day before classes began, her figure lean and androgynous from recent breast reduction surgery.

'Cynthia', she'd introduced herself, in a clear voice polished by years of elocution lessons. Cynthia Reed was from Australia; she'd sailed from Sydney only a few months before. Because she arrived without her paperwork in order, Johns Hopkins wouldn't admit Cynthia to their prestigious nursing school, nor would the New York hospitals. She'd ended up at the only place that would have her: St Josephs, the Catholic nursing school in Chicago. It was, she reported home, an 'inferior' institution. Blocks of 'dull granite' piled onto a 'grimy back street' near Lake Michigan, the interior lousy with images of the Virgin Mary and nuns in full habit.

Cynthia was no Catholic. Raised as nonconformist Anglican, she was now a free-thinker more familiar with bohemian artists than regimented nuns. Living according to strict rules was not her style. At daily mass, held at 5.30 am, she rolled her eyes and struggled to hold her tongue. 'I want to shout out bullshit and run screaming down the aisle,' Cynthia confessed to her brother.

Nor was she impressed by her classmates: 'blonde saviours' and 'spotty virgins'. They were too earnest and didn't get her jokes. Worst of all, smoking was banned on hospital grounds. She couldn't even get a decent cup of tea. Coffee and water were all the locals had to offer.

At first, Cynthia doubted she would last. '[T]he work is going to be no joke, we have a million subjects at the university,' she wrote upon arrival. 'Christ I give myself one month.' But a month came and went, and she remained. The intellectual stimulation, the prospect of helping people – it all sucked her in. 'I am intensely interested in everything & want to stay very much,' she told her brother. Back home in Australia, she'd never been one for study. Here, however, the work was endlessly absorbing. It was a different approach to education, one that prioritised curiosity above rote learning and obedience. 'I think the Yanks are on the right track', she reflected. By her first winter, Cynthia had made up her mind: she would stay in Chicago and become an American-trained nurse. She'd found her vocation.

Today, Cynthia Reed is remembered for her relationship to two men: John Reed and Sidney Nolan. John Reed, Cynthia's elder brother, was the arts patron who, alongside his wife, Sunday, established the artists' colony known as Heide, in Melbourne's northeastern suburbs. In the 1930s and 1940s, Heide gave succour to the likes of Nolan, Albert Tucker, Joy Hester, Arthur Boyd and John Perceval. It was renowned as a birthplace of Australian modernism. Cynthia had first introduced John to this artistic milieu in the early 1930s. In turn, through John, Cynthia met artist Sidney Nolan, creator of the iconic Ned Kelly series, whom she married in 1948. As Cynthia Nolan, she once again became viewed as a sidekick to an important man. First the sister, then the wife. These days, whenever Cynthia crops up in history books, it's usually in one or both of these roles. Even a 2016 biography puts the emphasis on these two relationships.

But there is another side to Cynthia's story, unrelated to Australian modernism and its founding fathers. As well as a bit player in the history of modern art, Cynthia was a nurse who headed to the United States to learn her trade. On 18 May 1935, just shy of 27, she disembarked from the *Mariposa* in Los Angeles. When she began studying nursing in Chicago in the fall of 1935, Cynthia became part of another modern history: the travel of Australian women professionals to study across the Pacific.

In the early 1900s, the United States led the professionalisation of 'women's work'. Ahead of Australia and Britain, the United States reimagined the feminised and often voluntary labour of caring for children, the sick and destitute as skilled work that required training and expertise. This process began in the 1880s and slowly took root over the next five decades. Graduate degree programs were developed; new technologies adopted; professional journals and associations established. By 1930, the battle for professional status had largely been won. The professional nurse, social worker, dietician and kindergarten teacher replaced the well-intentioned amateurs of yesteryear. The labour of care had been remade into specialised fields of knowledge that required tertiary study and professional accreditation. (Though these women's professions remained less prestigious and less remunerative than their male-dominated counterparts like medicine and law.)

By contrast, Australia lagged behind. There, the shift 'from moral to professional authority' in fields like nursing and social work only made its first steps in the 1920s and did not take hold until after World War II. As a result, Australians gravitated across the Pacific for training and experience. For women doing care work who wanted to be understood as bona fide professionals, America shone as a beacon and example. It was 'modern', 'advanced', 'up-to-date' – a font of 'new ideas' that Australia should emulate.

Nurses, in particular, flocked to the United States. As Sydney nurse Stella Pines recalled, during the 1920s 'to go to America was the goal of all those who wanted to progress'. Already, in the United States, nurses studied science and medicine in university classrooms. In Australia, which had inherited the English 'Nightingale model' of apprentice training within hospitals, this shift to the tertiary sector did not occur until the 1980s. Until that point, nurses' theoretical education was limited. As historian R Lynette Russell puts it in *From Nightingale to Now*, 'the educational needs of the trainee nurse were subservient to the service needs of the hospital'. They were there to serve rather than learn. No wonder American study appealed.

As a trainee nurse at St Joseph's, Cynthia Reed became part of this diaspora. Although only a brief chapter in her life, it was a defining experience that formed the basis of two autobiographical novels: *Lucky Alphonse* (1944) and *A Bride for St Thomas* (1970). Both novels detail the overseas nursing training of an Australian protagonist in the late 1930s. The protagonists are not Cynthia, but these fictional accounts do offer a window into her experience. Thanks to these two novels, and her surviving correspondence, we can enjoy a front row seat to Cynthia's romance with American professional education.

Nursing was not Cynthia's first choice of career. Born in 1908, and raised in an affluent Tasmanian landholding family, she'd boarded at the Hermitage School in Geelong. After leaving school in 1926, Cynthia 'came out' into society. She moved to Melbourne and commenced an affair with Bernard Heinze, conductor of the Melbourne Symphony Orchestra (who also happened to be Vera

Bradford's mentor). During 1929 and 1930, Cynthia travelled around Europe, where she worked as an *au pair*. Back in Melbourne, she launched Cynthia Reed Gallery at 52A Collins Street in June 1932. Over the next few years, Cynthia's gallery grew notorious for displaying the most radical art ever seen in Australia. Most infamous was an exhibition of Sam Atyeo abstracts in July 1933.

Despite the gallery's success, by early 1934 Cynthia had moved on to Sydney, the heart of Australia's nascent film industry. Adopting the pseudonym Liese Fels, Cynthia reinvented herself as an aspiring film star with Spanish and Norwegian heritage. As Liese, she appeared in a stage production of JB Priestley's *The Roundabout* at the Players' Club. She also had a one-line role in the Cinesound production of *Strike Me Lucky*. More serious film work was, alas, not forthcoming. With her dark and dramatic aesthetic, Cynthia could not compete with the pretty blondes then in demand on the silver screen. Hollywood was not going to come knocking anytime soon.

Cynthia did, however, make one serious US connection: an affair with a married American producer called Michael. With Michael she set sail from Sydney aboard the *Mariposa* in autumn 1935. In *Lucky Alphonse*, Cynthia describes a fictionalised Michael who was 'beautiful to look at', 'bounding with zest' and '[f]ull of naïve joy'. He drank like a fish and flirted with everything that moved. Michael was, in short, a disaster. 'I knew I shouldn't get on that boat with Michael and yet I had to do it. Ten thousand damns,' Cynthia wrote home. By the time they arrived in California, the relationship was all but over.

In Los Angeles, Cynthia licked her wounds and partied hard. Her days were spent sunbathing at the beach. Evenings were reserved for the Cotton Club, where she guzzled champagne and gyrated to jazz. There was a rebound fling with a man called Fred. But among all the drama, Cynthia turned her mind to yet another career: nursing. 'People's bodies and minds have always interested me', she wrote home, 'always I have had my eye on nursing'. She could have trained as a nurse back in Sydney or Melbourne, but she was in no rush to return home. Already, her dalliance with an American had given way to a romance with America itself. 'I have no definite plans,' Cynthia explained. 'I want to stay in America however and will try to do just that.'

Once settled in Chicago, Cynthia was won over by the rigour and promise of American professional education. The St Joseph's School of Nursing, established in 1893, was affiliated with nearby DePaul University, where trainee nurses were immersed in college-level science and medicine. For Cynthia, it was a revelation. As she wrote in *Lucky Alphonse*, the trainee nurses were left in 'open-mouthed astonishment' as 'they learned a new alphabet, a new speech, entered a different, ordered world'. The bar was high, and the trainees pushed themselves to meet it. Their whip-smart instructor Miss Toel encouraged them to 'Keep your minds open, and ask questions.' Study became its own reward.

There was only one problem: Cynthia was there on false pretences. All the time she was dissecting cats and yawning through morning mass, this trainee nurse was an illegal alien in the United States. Within months, the immigration authorities got wind of her status and opened an investigation. How had Cynthia, an affluent white woman from a reputable family, fallen foul of US immigration law? It all began with the quota system introduced in 1921. As the writer Dorothy Cottrell discovered, the United States now had strict immigration quotas for each nation. From 1929 Australia was permitted 100 quota spots per year. Even as a respectable white Australian, the 'ideal' immigrant, it was difficult to gain access to the United States.

This was the system that confronted Cynthia. Unable to gain a quota spot, she had entered on a tourist visa – a visa that lasted only six months and prohibited formal study. She could have applied for a student visa before she left Australia but neglected to do so. Once she was in the United States it was too late. St Joseph's, to her relief, was willing to turn a blind eye to this fact, and let Cynthia enrol. Then, in November, only a few months into the semester, her tourist visa expired. Cynthia now had no legal right to remain in the United States.

Cynthia knew this and did nothing. Unconcerned about breaking the law, she was happy to hoodwink the state to suit her own purposes. As she told her brother John, 'I am quite clever at cheating'. She would keep cheating as long as possible. If the authorities found out, and she was required to leave, she would be 'simply furious'. Was this entitlement a reflection of being young and rich? Or was it also related to larger questions of race and whiteness? After all, whiteness was at the heart of immigration policy in both Australia and the United States. With border policy organised in their favour, white people were used to feeling as though the world was their oyster – and now suddenly, for Cynthia, it was not.

In *Lucky Alphonse*, there is a revealing scene in which the heroine Alphonse is visited by an 'emigration official'. Alphonse, well aware 'she had not got the right visa', lies to the official's face, making vague excuses about 'papers arriving from Australia'. But despite Alphonse's blatant falsehoods, the racialised official is the villain of the piece. He is conspicuous for his 'unpleasant accent' and 'odour of garlic'. This 'surly' man intimidates Alphonse, making 'her feel that she was under suspicion'.

Racist tropes, white victimhood. The grievance leaps off the page. Reading between the lines, it's as though she's saying: *How dare they. How dare she – the white woman – be made Other in this situation.* It's a quintessential Karen moment. Almost a century before 'Karen' became a byword for entitled white women, Alphonse/Cynthia was paving the way.

However hard she tried, Cynthia could not Karen her way out of this one. In 1936, after nine months of study at St Joseph's, the US state put its foot down. Cynthia was in breach of immigration law; she must leave the country forthwith. In *Lucky Alphonse*, the protagonist receives clear instructions: 'It is incumbent upon you to take the next boat out of this country.' For Cynthia, much the same transpired. After months in limbo, she finally got her marching orders. She was not formally deported (a special dispensation that allowed for potential return), but the nurse was told in no uncertain terms to leave the country forthwith.

What next? Not Melbourne. As Cynthia wrote home, 'I know quite well Aussie is not the place I want to be.' If she couldn't stay in the United States, she'd go somewhere else. For her fictional counterpart Alphonse, 'it was better to go forward than to retrace one's steps, and [she] had already chosen England'. But even though England was a step forward, it was also a step into the past. A step back into an older, more conservative way of doing medicine. 'Would [English hospitals] have long, grey moss and barnacles on them? She imagined so,' Cynthia wrote.

All in all, it was an unhappy departure. In *Lucky Alphonse*, the protagonist sails from New York in a foul mood. Watching the coastline recede, Alphonse 'felt lonely, and miserable to be leaving this America which had been so friendly to her, and taught her so much'. She vows to one day return.

For the rest of her life, Cynthia would yearn for those halcyon days in Chicago. 'All those months in America I was living in a dream, all right,' she wrote in 1970, in her second autobiographical novel *A Bride for St Thomas*. 'How I wished that fairy story could have come true.'

For now, however, she would have to deal with London – a city that, in 'its greyness, its bloodlessness', would prove its own living nightmare.

PART III
LESSONS

20

AN UNFORTUNATE ADDICTION TO MODERNISM

THE ARTIST, MELBOURNE, 1935

The gallery was so busy you could barely see the paintings. On the afternoon of 20 August, an 'immense crowd' jammed into the Fine Art Society Gallery on Exhibition Street, all jostling to inspect what Mary Cecil Allen had brought back from New York. The room had been made festive with large bowls of white plum-blossom. Persian rugs absorbed the noise of a dozen conversations. At the door stood Mary herself, home for the first time in eight years, typically striking in a black velvet dress topped with a matching beret. But only those who'd arrived early could gain a clear view of the 40 works that lined the walls.

At the appointed hour, Ivy Brookes called for silence. It was time to open the exhibition. In her speech, Mary's long-time friend warned that the artist who'd returned from New York was not the same woman who'd left almost a decade before. Mary was now a modernist, an adherent of what local gatekeepers dismissed as 'imported and perverted art', as JS MacDonald put it in *Australian Painting Desiderata*. Conscious that this new aesthetic would ruffle feathers, Ivy urged the public to keep an open mind. The *Argus* quoted her the next day: 'Whether we do or do not agree with what Miss Allen may show us,' she said, 'we should be very grateful to her for having come back and given us this opportunity of seeing for ourselves the progress of modern art.'

As Ivy predicted, Mary's newfound modernism caused a stir. The artist's friend Frances Derham wrote in her biography of Mary that, the exhibition 'shocked Melbourne to the core'. Audiences were scandalised by artworks that were modern in both style and content: abstracted depictions of New York skyscrapers and subways. The exhibition catalogue noted that in these new works, Mary no longer sought to produce a realistic likeness of her subject; instead, she used distortion to evoke 'as accurately as possible its inner and essential quality'. As she'd written in her *Painters of the Modern Mind* (1930), the extremity of the modern world could only be captured on canvas by moving away from realism. '[T]he skyscrapers of New York affect the American expressionist,' Mary wrote. 'Distortion of some kind is a necessity if he is to express what he is thinking about when he looks at the world around him.'

This intent, however, was not appreciated by gallery visitors. Instead, they interpreted Mary's abandonment of realism as a loss of skill. More than one was heard to whisper, 'I could paint better than that myself,' noted the *Bulletin*. Indeed, '[t]he habitual expression of placidity worn by the average art show audience gave way to repressed excitement, almost hysteria'. A few loyal friends who purchased paintings later admitted they would not dare hang them at home.

For the next week, the exhibition was the talk of the town. Visitors streamed into the gallery each morning, and Mary's scandalous new aesthetic became Melbourne's 'chief topic of conversation'. In *The Age*, Stephanie Taylor, a guide-lecturer at the National Gallery of Victoria, lamented Mary's 'most unfortunate addiction to modernism'. She predicted that 'Miss Allen will be won back to academic art if she stays here'. Mary's former teacher Max Meldrum was so disapproving that he crossed the street to avoid her. Although Meldrum's tonalism was at odds with the academicism of the NGV School, he was no fan of modernism either. He now refused to greet his ex-student, as though she was 'the Devil, with Horns'.

The reviews were eviscerating. In her biography Frances recalled a 'howl of hate in the Press'. *The Age* newspaper contrasted the 'modernist' with the 'normalist', thereby assigning Mary the status of deviant. Arthur Streeton, the elder statesman of Australian landscape painting, was equally critical in the *Argus*. His review dismissed Mary's work as outdated – 'very like many canvases exhibited in London 25 years ago' – yet still 'beyond my perceptive facilities'. Harold Herbert in *The Australasian* concluded Mary's abstracts were nothing more than 'curious geometric shapes disorderly arranged'. They were mere 'patterns' that did little but 'irritate and confuse'. 'Miss Allen's work is completely detached from my sphere of art appreciation,' Herbert sniffed.

For critic Lionel Lindsay, Mary's exhibition was emblematic of everything that was wrong with modern art. As he wrote in his anti-modern polemic *Addled Art* (1942), modernism was dominated by female artists because women were 'accustomed to follow without questioning any and every mode'. Unlike men, they uncritically gravitated to whatever was declared 'advanced' and the 'thing'. In Lindsay's view, no one embodied this trend more than Mary Cecil Allen. Her 1935 show exemplified 'the superficial nature of modern painting'. It was all surface, no depth, with 'works that were lightly rooted in a dozen different sources'.

Only a tiny avant-garde of fellow modernists dared defend Mary's new style. For Arnold Shore, writing in the *Sun*, Mary had offered up an 'impressive' exhibition that was a 'living demonstration of the courage and diversity of modern practice in art'. The painter and writer Adrian Lawlor, himself no stranger to controversy, likewise dismissed attacks on Mary's aesthetic as 'very naïve'. Their solidarity, however, was drowned out by a chorus of condemnation. The overwhelming view was that Mary's art was 'bizarre and mocking'. It was as though, by departing from the lessons of her Melbourne education, she had personally insulted the city of her birth.

Faced with this backlash, a lesser woman may have fled back to Greenwich Village. But Mary was just getting started. Her solo exhibition in August 1935 was the opening sally in a year-long campaign to educate the Melbourne public about the latest thinking in modern art and life. Everything she'd learnt from eight years in New York, Mary would now do her utmost to disseminate back home.

The artist roared into town several weeks before her exhibition opening, arriving on the *Monterey* on 19 July 1935. She just missed fellow modern Cynthia Reed, who'd left for California a few months earlier. Despite her long absence, Mary had not been forgotten in Melbourne. She was welcomed with several parties, including a lavish affair attended by local high society at the Brookes's home in South Yarra. According to *The Home*, Australia's premier lifestyle magazine, Mary was the 'most vitally interesting woman who has visited Melbourne for some time'. More than just a modern artist, she personified 'all the most attractive in modern thought'.

As such, Mary was a walking provocation. In 1935, 'modern' was a hot-button word in Australian culture. Although a growing coterie of local artists were experimenting with modernism, the art-world establishment remained virulently conservative. Under the leadership of arch-conservative JS MacDonald, the National Gallery of Victoria refused to acquire post-Impressionist artworks. For the likes of MacDonald, modernism hailed from 'the dead hand of European decadence' and threatened to contaminate the 'pure' culture of white Australia. The effect of this institutional conservatism was to relegate a modernist aesthetic to 'lesser' arts such as advertising, fashion, commercial art and design. Pushed to the sidelines, modernism came to appear trivial and feminine – a state of affairs that led women to spearhead local avant-gardism but also provided further ammunition for anti-modernist discourse. These tensions, which had been brewing for years, came to a head during the mid-1930s as a new wave of militant modernists emerged in Melbourne. Under the leadership of Adrian Lawlor and Sam Atyeo (who exhibited his abstracts at Cynthia Reed's gallery), these provocateurs sought to take an axe to the academicism of the local art world.

Arriving just as these young Turks put conservatives on the defensive, Mary found herself in the firing line of a broader antimodernist backlash. She was the perfect target: a 'Yankee-trained' woman who had abandoned the British values of her establishment upbringing in favour of a feminised American modernity. The prodigal daughter was, it transpired, a traitor of sorts. Alongside the attacks on her art, she began to face attacks on her person. For the society magazine *Table Talk*, Mary had become a deviant figure. A cartoon published in August 1935 depicted the artist as grotesquely masculinised, dressed in pants and cropped hair, with severe cheek bones and a maniacal grin. 'Mary Cecil Allen ... is let loose in local society', warned the caption. After eight years in New York, Mary was imagined as no less 'distorted' than her art, transformed into a de-sexed American modern who had betrayed both her nation and her femininity.

In their efforts to discredit Mary, these critics undermined their own agenda. As her visit grew in controversy, her profile and audience expanded in step. Her evening lecture series at the NGV attracted record audiences. Each week during August 1935, up to a thousand people turned up to hear the artist speak, with latecomers forced to stand. By the third lecture, even standing room was at capacity, and many were turned away. The next day, these lectures were reproduced near verbatim in the press, giving Mary a secondary audience of newspaper readers.

In this lecture series, Mary showed off oratorical skills she'd honed in New York. In the United States, the public lecture had developed into a fine art, described by President Theodore Roosevelt as 'the most American thing in America'. Mary, already a gifted speaker, had used her American sojourn to learn from the best. She now electrified Melbourne audiences with presentations as entertaining as they were educational. As the Adelaide *Advertiser* put it on 22 August, she'd returned from a 'country of lectures as the perfect lecturer'.

Using plain language and wry humour, Mary's NGV lectures endeavoured to make modernism comprehensible to a lay audience. To do this, she addressed the elephant in the room: for many people, modern art 'appeared grotesque and without meaning'. That was because, Mary explained, this new aesthetic was akin to a foreign language; it must be learnt before it could be appreciated. Modern art, she said, should not be judged according to its optical verisimilitude but on its ability to convey some underlying truth. 'Modern drawing does not consist in making accurate copies of objects,' Mary told her captivated audience. 'The modern artist tries to draw forces. He tries to show the solidity of nature and not simply its pattern. He is searching for reality.'

To illustrate this point, Mary's lectures were accompanied by 60 slides from New York's Metropolitan Museum, including works by Picasso, Van Gogh, Cezanne, Matisse and Monet. The climax of her lecture on 'Art and Nature' was Picasso's 1905–06 portrait of Gertrude Stein, which she declared 'perhaps the finest painting of modern times'. At this time, few modern artworks had ever been exhibited in Australia. Indeed, not until 1939, when the *Herald* sponsored a controversial exhibition of contemporary European painting, did local audiences glimpse major works of modernism in the original. Prior to that point, anyone who wished to understand the fuss about Picasso or Gauguin would have to content themselves with a visit to Leonardo Art Shop on Little Collins Street. Run by Italian migrant Gino Nibbi, who imported books and posters, Leonardo Art Shop was Melbourne's 'direct link to Europe' – the only place possible to view high-quality colour reproductions of post-Impressionist art. In this context, Mary's lecture slides were a revelation, a rare chance to actually see a radical new way of depicting the world.

Alongside these NGV lectures, the artist gave innumerable private talks. Even as her ideas scandalised the Melbourne public, they couldn't get enough of her. She was, as a *Herald* columnist reported in late 1935, 'more in demand here for lectures than any woman outside America'. In the winter and spring of 1935, Mary spoke everywhere from the University of Melbourne and English-Speaking Union to the Arts and Crafts Society and Arnold Shore Studio, to the Melbourne Church of England Girls Grammar School and Scots College. During October, she gave a second lecture series at the Centenary Hall on Exhibition Street, an event heralded as the 'first time that Cubism has been explained publicly in Melbourne'.

Mary's status as a modern career woman made her a particular hit with women's organisations. She addressed the National Council of Women, the Australian Women's National Club, the Lyceum Club, the Australian Federation of University Women, the Country Women's Association and the YWCA. For her talk to the Melbourne Society of Women Painters, Mary revealed herself as a feminist thinker keenly aware of the structural forces that kept women marginalised from creative endeavour. 'It was surprising', she noted, 'to find how favourably women's painting compared with men's when [women] had sufficient independence to spend all their time on their work and were not forced to fit in between all sorts of domestic duties'.

Like the dentist Dorothy Waugh and writer Dorothy Cottrell, the artist reported that the proverbial 'American woman' was an emancipated figure, better able to contribute to public life. 'Clever women in America,' Mary told the Lyceum Club, 'are led to believe they are wonderful.' They respond to this encouragement 'by developing an array of talents which is a constant revelation of what women can do when given a fair chance in their career'. It was common, she continued, for American women to combine marriage and career. Indeed, the whole society had an 'atmosphere of generous appreciation in which feminine talents were encouraged to flower'. For the membership of the Lyceum Club, an institution for university graduates and other professional women, this must have been a tantalising picture that fuelled discontent with their more limited horizons in Australia.

In early 1936, Mary continued her educational efforts with a Summer School in Gisborne, a picturesque town in the Macedon Ranges northwest of Melbourne. Held over February weekends, this school emulated the American custom for artists to teach intensive programs over the summer. In Gisborne, the weekends were dedicated to painting outdoors under Mary's supervision. Her goal was for the students to see and paint the 'dynamic rhythm' in nature. With this initiative, Mary was credited with importing 'the American institution of the weekend sketching school'. One of her students was Frances Burke, a textile designer who became a leading proponent of modernism in Melbourne. Frances was powerfully influenced by Mary's instruction, remembering her as 'a kind of priestess' who was 'much ahead of her time'. The two women became firm friends, with Frances later visiting Mary in the United States.

In 1936, the artist was invited back to the NGV for a second lecture series. Although, as Frances Derham put it, Mary's scandalous exhibition had 'alienated the Powers that Be', her lecturing proved so popular that the gallery could not afford to dispense with her services. Beginning in May, Mary delivered another four orations about contemporary art. For the final lecture, the audience was once again 'so large that many people could not be seated'.

But even this most enthusiastic of lecturers had her limits. After almost a year of intensive teaching, Mary needed a break. In May 1936, she concluded her homecoming with a six-week tour of Central Australia. The idea was to seek artistic inspiration in the desert, so that she might foster a distinctive national art. Convinced that Australian artists were too focused on European subjects, Mary now turned to the 'magical light and colour' of the mythologised heart of the continent. Like her contemporary Margaret Preston, she sought to develop an Australian modernism grounded in the shapes and patterns of the local landscape – neglecting to realise that First Nations artists had engaged with this landscape since time immemorial. After six weeks in Alice Springs and Coober Pedy, Mary returned to Melbourne with an overflowing sketchbook, initial studies for a planned exhibition in New York.

It was time to leave. On 20 July, after exactly a year in Melbourne, Mary boarded the cargo ship *Wichita* to return to New York. On the eve of her departure, she was hailed in the Melbourne *Herald* as a 'prophet' who 'has done more than any other person to put modern art on the map of understanding here'. By refusing to be cowed by conservative backlash, and talking herself hoarse, Mary had done the unthinkable and punctured the stigma around modernism.

These efforts helped shape the seminal debates between modernists and conservatives in the years that followed. In 1937, the reactionary Australian Academy of Art was established, followed in 1939 by the *Herald* exhibition of contemporary European painting. These two events are now remembered as the climax of the long-running culture wars around modernism in Australia. By the early 1940s, the climate had shifted, and the moderns were now ascendant. Daryl Lindsay, the new head of the NGV, relaxed the prohibition on post-Impressionist art. At the same time, a new wave of modernist innovation took shape under the patronage of John and Sunday Reed.

For contemporary observers, Mary's 1935–36 visit was critical to facilitating this transition. As the art critic Basil Burdett reflected in *Art in Australia* three years later, Mary 'exercised a profound influence in favour of the new forms'. Her exhibition and lectures, Burdett believed, 'did a great deal to make modern art more generally understood by both artists and laymen'. Mary was long gone by this point, but – like the priestess she was – her influence lingered on.

21

THE PERNICIOUS VIRUS OF AMERICAN HOOEY

THE HEALTH GURU, PERTH, 1937

For a woman who worshipped the sun, it was not an auspicious homecoming. Western Australia was known for its blue skies; it was the sunniest part of a sun-drenched continent. Yet today the state was sheathed in cloud. There was no hope of 'recharging the human dynamo with electricity from the sun' on this grey Tuesday. Alice would have to save her sunbathing for another day.

Alice Caporn was about to sink her feet onto the continent known as Australia for the first time in two decades. She hadn't been home since 1917, when she joined the Christian Scientists in Boston. She'd left as a 40-something nurse, a nobody whose departure went unnoticed; she returned as a self-proclaimed 'famous American Authority on Nutritional Science'. Reporters had got wind of her arrival and waited at the dock to get a taste of her 'advanced American views'.

Alice, as ever, lapped up the publicity. Although she was not the most glamorous passenger on board the *Orcades* – that honour belonged to Princess Melikoff, a Georgian royal who was formerly Pauline Curran of Tasmania – the 60-something health guru was the most vociferous talker. Princess Melikoff may have an elegant crepe de chine frock with navy stripe, but Alice had opinions. Lots of them. She could probably out-talk Europe's entire royalty. It's not hard to imagine a reporter from the *West Australian*, notebook in hand, struggling to keep up as Alice gave an impromptu lecture that covered dietetics, exercise, American salads, her health colony in Belize and – of course – the benefits of sunbathing. If Alice couldn't obtain the sun's electricity today, she could at least talk about it.

In the United States, Alice explained, sunbathing was the latest health trend. Americans flocked to Florida or bought sunlamps to get the benefits at home. It was all done 'carefully and scientifically to avoid overburning and harmful results'. To facilitate sun exposure, swimwear was getting smaller. Men now wore basic trunks, while women preferred two-piece costumes. Alice failed to mention her penchant for shunning swimwear altogether. She didn't out herself as a nudist, or acknowledge the nudism scandal that made headlines in Washington DC several years before. Given the limited information moving between Australia and the United States, Alice could shape a narrative that suited her purposes, confident that no one in Perth would ever discover what happened on Chesapeake Bay in 1933. In the age of steam travel, there was little capacity to fact check her account, so the story she told became gospel.

As a result, sojourners like Alice had enormous power to shape popular opinion – both about their own lives abroad, but also about the world beyond Australia. If Alice said the United States was a place of sunbathing and salads, who was anyone in Perth to doubt her? She had been there, lived stateside for years. It was straight from the horse's mouth. You couldn't get better than that. Whether objectively accurate or otherwise, these kind of travel tales shaped the public imagination. Together, they built up an idea of America that was no less significant than the physical nation itself. And in 1930s Perth, Alice would do her darndest to sell a story of the United States as a world leader in 'modern food science' – a story that positioned herself as an important authority with fresh news from the front line.

Forced to abandon her Belize health colony, Alice now channelled her considerable energies into a campaign to remake the Australian diet. Her business empire began with the Ra-D-nt Helth Centre, a health food store and café in Perth's CBD. Operational headquarters were in London Court, with the shopfront around the corner on Barrack Street. There, patrons purchased nut butters and sea lettuce, or dined on 'Hollywood salads' and 'Hollywood vegetable juice cocktails'. Alice also became a well-known public commentator. She gave twice-weekly talks on radio stations 6iX and 6PR, and lectured on Monday evenings, and Tuesday and Friday afternoons.

In 1939, Alice launched her own lifestyle magazine. *Modern Living* juxtaposed recipes, advertisements and Christian hymns. In the June issue she raged against 'devitalised white flour', advocated nude sunbathing and shared recipes for Ra-D-nt Helth macaroni and oat porridge. Unafraid of provocative claims, Alice boasted that her dietary regime could eradicate infantile paralysis. Already, she claimed, it had facilitated the complete 'rejuvenation' of her octogenarian mother. Here was the classic wellness pitch: eat this way and you'll outrun age and disease.

Almond butter and green juice might be supermarket staples today, but back then Alice's regime was revolutionary. In the 1930s, when the settler population was 98 per cent 'British', the Australian diet was structured around meat, sugar, dairy and tea – staples of a cuisine inherited from the mother country. Salads were a novelty, fresh juices virtually unheard of. All in all, it was radical stuff.

And it was all depicted as distinctly 'American'. Her diet wasn't just healthful; it was 'the very latest Hollywood diet'. In her words, Americans were a 'food-conscious race', scientific eaters whose passion for fruits and vegetables both reflected and fuelled their modernity. 'Everyone who is really modern is interested in diet', Alice proclaimed. 'Americans are more advanced in the application of dietetics to everyday meals than the English.' Now she'd arrived to spread the gospel, Australians had a chance to become modern themselves, one 'Hollywood salad' at a time. The implicit flipside of these ideas was that the stodge and starch of British tradition risked degeneracy. Too much meat and milk, and white Australia might just wither on the vine.

Alice's focus on 'modern science' might seem at odds with her religious bent. She was still a passionate Christian, and fully believed in a higher power. Yet, while it's tempting to assume that faith and modernity are antithetical, the truth is more complex. As historian Frank Bongiorno reminds us, it is important to recognise the 'role played by esoteric belief and unorthodox religion in the making of Australian modernity'. New Thought and Christian Science, along with other new age beliefs, were attempts to remake religion for the modern age. For the likes of Alice, Christian Science and food science went hand in hand.

For several months, Alice basked in the glow of positive press. Her 'advanced American views' on 'Modern Food Science' set Perth abuzz. She was given endless column inches to share her views on everything from apples to elocution to men's fashion. Everyone wanted a piece of the sprightly expat who'd returned after 20 years with better health than when she left.

But then, in mid-1939, public sentiment underwent an abrupt U-turn. Suddenly Perth's new health guru was on the nose.

The problem? Alice's views on milk.

Dairy milk was little consumed in Australia prior to 1920, but its status soared in the wake of widespread pasteurisation and the development of nutritional science. Interwar medical professionals championed milk as a 'protective food' that promised to fortify young and old alike. On the same day Alice arrived on the *Orcades* in 1937, the *West Australian* published an advertisement declaring 'Milk Banishes Fatigue'. The advertisement, sponsored by the Metropolitan Milk Board, depicted an office worker clutching a phone in one hand and a glass of milk in the other. The text promised that milk 'restores energy' in the workplace, declaring 'Milk is a balanced food and makes up any deficiency in the rest of the diet'. The federal Health Department agreed. By 1939 the department advised that Australian children should drink 1.5 pints (700 millilitres) of dairy milk per day.

Alice, however, was unconvinced. In *Modern Living*, she posed the question 'Is Cow's Milk Good for Man?' The answer? An emphatic no. 'So-called civilized man is the only animal on Earth who never leaves off drinking milk, but nature makes him pay the price for this violation of her laws,' Alice thundered. In her public talks, she explained 'Why Cow's Milk Causes Mucus, Colds and Tonsillitis'. Instead of feeding dairy to children, Alice championed an almond beverage, which 'in chemical analysis is very similar to mother's milk'. Nut milk was indeed a recipe for perfect health. 'A girl brought up in that way would never know what a headache was,' she told her audience at Arundale Hall. It was an unabashed provocation, a red rag to the pro-dairy establishment.

The backlash was fierce. First off the blocks was dairy farmer WH Taylor. On 8 May, Taylor heckled Alice from the audience, challenging her to a public debate. When Alice declined the challenge, on the grounds that Taylor was not a scientist or medical professional, the irate man took to the letters page of the *West Australian* on 16 May. In a lengthy diatribe, Taylor denounced Alice's anti-milk views as ignorant and dangerous. He depicted Alice's acolytes as gullible housewives, women who needed to be protected from misinformation. '[S]ome action should be taken to combat Dr Caporn's pernicious teaching on this milk question,' he opined. Alice responded with a counter-letter on 22 May defending her credentials. But Taylor had been joined by vocal allies. 'Taylor is to be complimented on his stand', wrote SE Turner, because we 'cannot afford to have our children's health endangered by mere notions'. Another correspondent called for a citizens' meeting on the milk question, given the beverage's 'extreme importance' to the state.

But this was only the beginning. On 4 June, Commissioner of Public Health Dr Everitt Atkinson joined forces with the Perth *Sunday Times* to demolish Alice's reputation. In a feature headlined 'Dietetic Bunk Exposed' Alice was charged with spreading an 'Absurd Doctrine' that 'Misleads Mothers' and 'Flouts High Medical Opinion'. On behalf of local doctors, Commissioner Atkinson issued a 'scathing condemnation of this foolish cult'. In his view, Alice's anti-dairy views imperilled the health of children and invalids. Not satisfied with this dressing-down, the *Times* continued its attacks over the coming weeks. 'Fantastic Food Fads Further Exposed' screamed one headline. 'Public Advised Not to Listen to Mrs Caporn's Stupid Theories' ran another. In article after article, Alice was derided as a 'modern health-diet crank' who traded in the 'pernicious virus of American "hooey"'.

As the vehemence of this response suggests, more than milk was at stake. Not simply a dispute about nutritional science, this was a battle for the physical and racial future of the nation. Conventional medical opinion held that milk was 'key to proper nutrition', the building block of individual and national strength. Yet for Alice dairy was a recipe for decline. Poor diet had led to low birth rates among the white population. 'Australians are sterile,' she explained, 'because they've been eating the wrong foods.' Milk, along with sugar and white flour, was 'like a nest of vipers in the body'.

Perth's milk war was also a battle between competing forms of knowledge and expertise. On one side was Alice, a 'milk faddist' with 'Yankee Modern Health Letters after her name' and legions of credulous female fans. On the other was an all-male league of 'recognised health authorities', who condemned the United States as 'the home of superstition' and whose pro-dairy stance was endorsed by the British Advisory Council of Nutrition. The battle lines were drawn: Britain versus America, tradition versus modernity, men versus women. By challenging British norms and masculine authority with her anti-dairy claims, Alice was asking bigger questions about Australian culture. Should the nation continue in its historic emulation of Britain? Or did a better future lie in looking to the United States, where a feminised popular modernity was on the march?

By the time Alice arrived on the scene, 'America' didn't just refer to the actual nation of the United States. The term was also a metaphor for a constellation of bogeymen – unchaste women, racial intermixing, unbridled commerce, challenges to British pre-eminence. By stressing the 'Americanness' of her thinking, Alice was playing a dangerous game. The branding strategy conferred an undeniable glamour, especially among the women who formed her main audience, but it allowed Alice to be condemned by association. Gatekeepers threatened by her views or influence could easily undermine Alice via sneering references to 'Yankee' credentials and 'American hooey'. The subtext was clear: *As if some old bat from degenerate America could have something to say.*

Alice survived the milk war of 1939. The 'unrelenting waves of persecution and misrepresentation' only fuelled her righteous conviction. As she put it, the 'concerted effort of certain powerful vested interests' had done their worst, but the 'Modern Health Science Movement' lived to see another day. On Friday 7 July a notice appeared in the *West Australian*. Dr Alice Caporn would lecture that afternoon at the Cremorne Arcade ballroom. The topic? One word: 'Milk'. This was Alice giving a defiant middle finger to the Dr Atkinsons of this world. She would not be silenced on the milk question; she would 'weather the storm of abuse and opposition' like the martyr she believed herself to be.

In fact, the storm was an apparent boon for Alice's career. Following the milk controversy, speaking invitations flooded in. From the Fremantle Labor Women's Organisation to the Methodist Ladies' Society, everyone wanted to hear from the Yankee food faddist. That year Alice commenced a popular lecture series at Boans, Perth's leading department store. Together with loyal associates, she also formed the WA National Health Association to 'instruct the community in the laws of natural living'.

On the business front, Alice expanded her operations to include a solarium and naturopathic clinic in prosperous Nedlands where she began teaching, passing on American 'food science' to a new generation. Alice herself became a local identity. Neighbours would spy her enjoying a dawn skinny-dip down at the river. And all the while she kept promoting 'American' healthy eating. 'We congratulate America for its leadership in popularising salads,' Alice wrote in 1950.

22

HARD TO TAKE AFTER AMERICA

THE NURSE, LONDON, 1937

'You are not in America now, nurse.'

Almost every day, Cynthia was chided with that line. Whenever she asked a question in class, or used technical language with a patient, or appeared in public without a hat, the result was the same. 'You are not in America.'

As if Cynthia could forget. In every possible way, she experienced England as the antithesis of the United States. If the latter had been modern and fast-paced, hurtling into the future, the former felt conservative, sleepy, painfully retrograde. 'Life here seemed peaceful and stately and so old, after America,' she noted when she arrived in Cambridge, where her sister Margaret worked as a doctor. Even London, that storied metropolis, was to her eyes an insipid city, dull in colour and spirit. 'After America how small, and squat, and grey, this city was. Even in summer London never seemed to lose its greyness, its bloodlessness', she wrote.

England's shortcomings extended to nursing education. In 1936, after arriving in London, Cynthia enrolled at St Thomas', a teaching hospital in Lambeth, perched opposite the Houses of Parliament on the banks of the Thames. Boasting a history that dated to the 12th century, St Thomas' had played a key role in the development of nursing. St Thomas' Training School for Nurses had been established in 1860 by Florence Nightingale, the founder of the modern profession. From this hospital, the Nightingale model of apprentice-style training had spread across the world –

including to Australia. St Thomas' regarded itself as an exemplar of modern nursing education, an institution that churned out the world's best nurses.

Yet in the 1930s, Cynthia found no trace of modernity. In her view, St Thomas' seemed conservative and dated, its pedagogy decades behind the approach she'd experienced in Chicago. At St Thomas', nurses were trained in hierarchy and blind obedience. Matron's word was God, and cleaning was paramount. Science, by contrast, was of scant interest. 'I think the whole system is a lousy one,' Cynthia reported home. 'I get very indignant about things here often because I think all the system is wrong you see, and things like that make me tremble with indignation.'

In her autobiographical novels *Lucky Alphonse* and *A Bride for St Thomas*, Cynthia vented her frustration. In both novels, the protagonist – Alphonse in the former, Mary in the latter – enrols in the nursing course at St Thomas' after being ejected from the United States. Arriving at this London hospital, Alphonse/Mary is greeted by a matron who is quick to dismiss her prior studies in Chicago: 'Well, my child, you cannot expect me to take this American nonsense seriously, do you?' Matron declares, throwing the St Joseph's transcript in the bin. Alphonse/Mary must begin her training all over again.

This training is, however, more about military-style discipline than actual learning. The trainee nurses are taught, in painstaking detail, the correct way to sweep a floor. They make tea and scrub baths and dust furniture – all under the strict gaze of a senior nurse determined to find fault. The classes are 'simple and straightforward', taught by 'an extremely ignorant woman' unable to answer a single question beyond the rote lecture material. Whenever Alphonse/Mary seeks further information, she is told she's been overly 'Americanised'.

Reduced to a domestic drudge, Alphonse/Mary falls into a deep depression. 'How I missed, during those early days, the

America within St Joseph's Hospital's convent walls,' Mary reflects. At St Thomas', 'there seemed to be nothing but ignorance, bustle, fault-finding and humiliation'. Her training, once so joyful, had become a grind.

These fictional accounts tracked closely with Cynthia's actual experience. In her letters home, she bemoaned the shortcomings of English nursing education. There was not enough intellectual inquiry; too much 'yessir please sir and Oliver Twisting'. 'I am not a good nurse in this country and doubt if I will ever get back to being one,' she reported home. 'I miss my yank friends terribly.'

Yet Cynthia was determined to see things through. With her training interrupted once already, she was not willing to cut things short a second time. She would stick it out. Three long years at St Thomas', grinding through endless cleaning and night shifts until she finally was a certified nurse. To cope, she turned to activism. Enraged by the shortcomings of the Nightingale model, Cynthia was involved in the establishment of an English nursing union. She also escaped the 'glum' English by socialising with Australians and Americans as much as possible. But all the while Cynthia had her eye on the finish line. 'Jesus if only I was through with the certificate in my hand,' she told John.

In London, Cynthia had a quintessential Australian experience: feeling alienated from the city and culture imagined as the 'mother country'. White Australians, raised to understand themselves as British, would arrive in Britain with expectations of belonging, only to be underwhelmed by a society that felt both alien and uncongenial. They complained of stodgy food, damp bed-sits, grey skies and grim people. They felt like a fish out of water – and hence began to question whether they were, or wanted to be, real Britishers after all. They were 'Home' but had never felt less at home. As Cynthia wrote in *Lucky Alphonse*, 'Alphonse did not understand [the English]. To her they were more foreign than any other nation in the world.'

This disenchantment was often exacerbated when comparing England with the United States. Almost invariably, among those who encountered both countries, America was judged the superior society – more modern, more progressive. The future. England, by comparison, seemed stuck in the past, a dingy relic to former glory. Disenchantment with Britain grew after 1945, when the lingering hardships of World War II produced a stark gulf between living standards on opposite sides of the Atlantic. Wartime mobilisation had propelled the United States into an age of unprecedented prosperity. In Britain, six long years of war had left the nation on the verge of collapse. London was scarred by bomb damage; rationing dragged on into the 1950s; the Empire began to crumble. Britain may have defeated the Axis powers, but it was no triumphant victor.

For Australian women who sailed from New York to Southampton during the late 1940s, the 'Old Country' was old and shabby indeed. The architecture, the food, the facilities, the fashions – all seemed, in the words of Canberra playwright Theresa Moore, 'pathetic after America'. Even basic commodities like soap, tea and hot water were in short supply. Compared to the supermarkets, skyscrapers and washing machines of the United States, the once wondrous imperial metropole was a relic from a bygone era. 'At Waterloo Station we faced English Life for the first time,' wrote Theresa, who sailed to London in 1951 after 18 months in the United States. 'It's hard to take after America. The place was cold and filthy.' A few days later, Theresa reported that London 'takes some getting used to after American cities – it is so squat and dingy'.

Britain's 'backwardness' included a condescending attitude towards Australians. It was as though England never received the memo that the Australian colonies had become a nation. In English eyes, Australians would forever remain 'colonials' – brash and childlike, inherently inferior. Alphonse/Mary, Cynthia's fictional counterpart, is told her Australianness renders her a suspect figure. 'We have had Australians here before. Not very satisfactory on the whole,' the St Thomas' matron muses. '[D]ifferent, rude, always wanting a reason for everything, thinking of better ways of doing things, impudent and opinionated.'

Old ideas, faded glory, sneering remarks. All in all, it was enough to make one doubt the whole idea that London was at the centre of things. If the United States was more modern, more advanced and more congenial to Australians, why was Australia still hitching its wagon to tired old England? After three years studying in London, Alphonse was convinced that England is yesterday's superpower, a sleepy island peopled by complacent people. 'Americans and Australians always find the English singularly inefficient,' Cynthia wrote in *Lucky Alphonse*. 'As a nation these people were slipping. Living in the British Isles for any length of time one could have no doubt of that.'

With statements like these, Cynthia left her Australian readers in no doubt that Britain was a past to slough off. Her novels gave credence to suspicions that the mother country's glory days were ending and confirm that a new Anglophone superpower waited in the wings. In this way, *Lucky Alphonse* and *A Bride for St Thomas* were a form of cultural diplomacy, books that offered a new narrative about Australia's place in the world. More than just a window into Cynthia's experiences, these novels contributed to a cultural conversation about the nation's identity and its future. Britain or America? Cynthia, in her novels, gave a resounding answer to that question.

Yet London did not stop calling. Unlike the United States, it offered an open door to white Australians. England might be dowdy and backwards, but at least it was accessible. The facts were undeniable: from 1929, only 100 Australians could migrate to the United States each year. There were some loopholes for students and professionals, but this basic framework remained in place for decades. By contrast, an infinite number of Australians were welcome in Britain. This privilege was not revoked until 1962, when Britain passed the *Commonwealth Immigrants Act* to stem the flow of migrants (of colour) from the former Empire. Faced with legal barriers to US residency, Australians were funnelled back towards Britain. It was the path of least resistance. As one Sydney woman reflected in 1927, in relation to the barriers constructed by US border control, 'I was going to the United States but I went to England instead. I was told there was so much trouble.' The US migration quotas, which lasted until 1965, helped perpetuate an Australian orientation towards Britain.

In June 1939, on the eve of World War II, Cynthia dragged herself over the finish line. She passed the final examinations; she was now a fully qualified nurse. Finally, she was free to leave London. Where to from here?

First order of business: a long-overdue holiday. Cynthia was on vacation in the south of France when war broke out in September. She made her way back to Paris, where she volunteered her services as a nurse. Fittingly, Cynthia ended up at the city's American Hospital, a private hospital in Neuilly-sur-Seine, described in *Lucky Alphonse* as 'a modern building situated on a rise and surrounded by gardens, lawns, and trees'.

As war drew closer, Cynthia escaped via Italy. A psychiatric patient travelling back to the United States employed her as a private nurse. Patient and nurse boarded the *Manhattan* in Genoa on 2 June 1940, only a week before Italy entered the war, and less than a fortnight before the Germans occupied Paris. They'd made it out in the nick of time. Eight days later, the *Manhattan* docked in New York. After four long years, and a narrow escape from war, Cynthia was back in the United States.

23

MAKING AUSTRALIA MODERN

THE PIANIST, MELBOURNE, 1938

The start of the academic year was always the same. Undergraduates thronged College Crescent and South Lawn, their faces lit up with hope and anxiety. The honeyed autumn light filtered through the elm trees that lined Royal Parade. A certain mood filled the air: a thrum of anticipation, renewed energy after the summer's languor. Vera Bradford knew this season all too well. In the early 1920s, she'd lived it three years in a row as a student at the Melbourne Conservatorium. Now she was back, a lifetime later, and yet everything felt unchanged. Melba Hall still gleamed white in the sun, fenced off by iron railings, clinging to the western edge of campus like an oversized pearl. Students climbed up the same familiar steps, laden down with instruments, scurrying out of the morning glare into the cool dark that awaited across the threshold. The only difference was the construction site on the north side of the Conservatorium, in the space where there used to be trees. The Grainger Museum – a redbrick monument to Vera's former teacher – was due to open to the public in a few months.

But this year, Vera was the teacher not the student. The previous September, she'd applied to be a Chief Study Teacher at the Conservatorium, citing her six years of study in the United States. Now, Vera was about to sit down with her first students. She would teach them the method she learnt from Alexander Raab in Chicago: the arm-weight technique, the modern approach to playing that rewarded muscular relaxation with big tones. No one else in Melbourne was using this method, and the few who'd heard of it were full of suspicion. But Vera was never one to swim with the pack. To her mind, the arm-weight method was the only way to play – and hence the only thing to teach; naysayers be damned.

Of course, it wasn't meant to be like this. Teaching at her alma mater in staid Melbourne? No, that wasn't part of the plan. Vera was meant to be long gone by now, back in the United States, performing as a concert pianist to rave reviews. When she came home in April 1934, the idea was to stay six months, before picking up her glittering career where she'd left off. Yet nearly four years had passed, and she was still here. Still living in the family home in Kensington's Bayswater Road, still playing on the same small stages to the same familiar crowds.

What had gone wrong? Several times, she was on the verge of leaving. Vera would write to friends in America, tell them to expect her back in a few months, next year at the latest. Everyone in Chicago was reportedly 'longing for [her] to come back'. Raab, her old teacher, kept asking about her 'future plans'. When was his promising student going to resume her upwards trajectory?

There was no single reason Vera got stuck. As for her contemporary Isabel Letham, a constellation of factors conspired to keep her at home. The Depression was still raging, and money was tight. Her mother was sick and there were family obligations. The ABC invited Vera to do radio work, and she got swept up in the busyness of performance and touring. And, the quota restrictions inhibited her return to the United States. As a student at the Chicago Musical College, Vera had been exempt from the national quotas, able to enter on a student visa. But to return as a professional musician, she would need a quota spot, and they were as rare as hen's teeth.

By applying to join the Conservatorium staff, Vera faced up to the truth of the matter: she would not be leaving Melbourne any time soon. This was a tacit admission that the fairytale had gone skew-whiff. Despite all her promise, her hard work, her international career had not worked out as planned. It was time to pivot towards that reliable Plan B: teaching.

Vera continued to hope. In late 1938 she told the Hubers – her adoptive Chicago family – to expect her back the following year. But, in 1939, Vera faced yet another obstacle – the outbreak of war. With civilian travel across the Pacific all but suspended, the pianist would be in Australia for the duration. She would have to make the best of things.

So she continued at the Conservatorium, teaching next door to the newly constructed Grainger Museum. First conceived by Grainger himself back in 1922, the museum was opened to the public in December 1938. In retrospect, it seems a cruel irony that this autobiographical museum – a monument to the international career of Vera's teacher – opened its doors just as her own world became smaller. Every day, she would confront this building-sized reminder of the growing gulf between Percy's trajectory and her own. Did the museum trigger joyful memories of life abroad, conjuring the inspiration of Percy's classes at the Chicago Musical College? Or did it rub salt in the wound, reminding her of what she was missing?

When she joined the Conservatorium in 1938, Vera began to reshape Australian musical culture. Over the following decades, she disseminated the lessons of Alexander Raab and the Chicago Musical College throughout Melbourne. Like so many Australians who learnt new ideas in the United States, the next act of Vera's life would be dedicated to spreading those ideas back home.

In her case, it was the arm-weight technique. This approach, which Vera introduced to Australia, attracted growing interest during the war years. Word spread about Vera's teaching, and the pianist performed the technique on stage for local audiences. What was it all about? In essence, the whole weight of the body flowed through the arms into the fingertips. The result was 'complete control in piano-playing', with 'minimum movement' and 'perfect relaxation'. It was the most 'modern technique' Vera explained, but also 'the most natural method of playing'. The weight or arm-weight technique was widely accepted in Europe and catching on in the United States. In contrast, the English 'finger technique', still dominated local playing, which in Vera's mind led to a regrettable 'primness of style'. The implication was plain: Australia was stuck in an insipid musical past and needed to get with the times.

Not everyone was receptive to this message. Vera was a controversial figure in the local music scene. Her former student Ivor Morgan recalled that Vera faced 'resentment', 'hostility' and 'opposition from colleagues' at the conservatorium. This antipathy even extended to family members. When her niece Pam started school in Essendon, she found her in-house music teacher loathed Vera. Damned by association, Pam was excluded from the school choir.

Most likely, this hostility had a gendered element. As a woman of strong opinions, Vera doubtless provoked the ire of Australian men used to feminine compliance. In Chicago, her big personality had won admirers but in Melbourne it more often got her into trouble. Unwilling or unable to keep herself small, Vera was a walking provocation. She remained unmarried, continued to prioritise her music, and was unafraid to challenge the status quo. Little wonder, then, that she would be judged 'difficult'.

These dynamics also shaped Vera's repertoire. During a 1934 national tour with the ABC, the pianist was eager to perform Brahms's concertos – works she'd already performed in Chicago. But local wisdom held these pieces were too difficult for women and Vera was forbidden to play them, a prohibition that held for over a decade. When in 1946 Vera finally managed to perform the Brahms's D minor concerto at the Sydney Town Hall, she could not escape gender policing. In his review on 5 September, *Sydney Morning Herald* critic Neville Cardus castigated Vera's performance for being insufficiently feminine. Vera was, Cardus wrote, so determined to prove 'a woman really can cope with the work' that she 'neglected or did less justice to the softer sides of Brahms' nature'. She 'put forward a strength which many men might envy or fear', but the performance was all 'masculine fist' and missed 'many details of expression'. Here was a classic example of a male cultural gatekeeper shifting the goalposts to keep a woman in her place. If she was feminine, she was trivial and unserious; if she was masculine, she was a gender failure. Either way, she and/or her art would always be somehow 'wrong'.

This hostile climate did little to subdue Vera's character. She continued to speak her mind, leading to a fraught relationship with the ABC. Since returning in 1934, Vera toured under ABC auspices and made regular appearances on the national radio network. In 1941, she was a soloist for the ABC's celebrity orchestral concert series. But she had grave misgivings about the broadcaster. The problem was money: the ABC was underpaying local performers. Vera believed artists with overseas experience, like herself, deserved higher rates of pay in recognition of their extra credentials. In 1944, Vera went public, announcing she would no longer work with the ABC, as the available payment was 'ridiculous'. In response, the ABC General manager Charles Moses was defiant. Vera had 'been paid what the commission feels she is worth'.

Ostensibly about money, this fight hinged on a deeper matter: the Australian cultural cringe. By suggesting that overseas-trained artists deserved higher pay, Vera reproduced the engrained idea that everything from abroad was superior. Yet the ABC's resistance to this logic was indicative of an even deeper cringe. By refusing to remunerate overseas-trained Australians at levels akin to international artists, the broadcaster revealed an assumption that Australianness was inherently inferior, regardless of training. Vera's argument assumed an Australian musician could be 'elevated' to international levels; the ABC's position saw antipodean origins as an irredeemable taint. No matter their training, an Australian artist – except for very rare exceptions like Grainger – would always be second-rate.

In February 1950, Vera sat in the audience of the Melbourne Town Hall. Up on stage, her former student Margaret Holden made her debut as a concert pianist. No longer the promising young pianist, Vera was now the wise elder ushering youthful talent out into the world. Holden, who'd studied the 'modern method of weight technique' with Vera at the Conservatorium, had won the 1949 Maples' P and A Parade (a local musical prize) and now appeared as a soloist with the Victorian Symphony Orchestra. With her teacher's encouragement, Holden hoped to further develop her skills in the United States.

After 16 years back in Australia, Vera's work had borne fruit: she had disseminated the weight technique among a new generation. Although Vera herself never returned to the United States, her Chicago sojourn had far-reaching effects through her teaching. The pianist did not have the performance career she wanted or expected, but her pedagogical legacy was nothing to sneeze at. 'The most fantastic six years' of her life did not just change Vera herself; they changed Australian musical culture.

24

LESSONS FROM AUSTRALIA
THE ECONOMIST, WASHINGTON DC, 1939

Persia sat down at the mahogany table. She spread out her typed notes and placed her hands in her lap. As usual, the economist was dressed for business. A dark wool coat covered her slight frame, the buttons undone to reveal a white blouse. Her face was free of make-up, exposing freckles scattered across high cheekbones. No lipstick, no jewellery. At the nape of her neck, straight brown hair was disciplined into a low bun. Only her hat, a wide-brimmed affair decorated with flowers and tulle, made any concession to feminine adornment.

It was Persia's first time in the Senate Building's Caucus Room. A Beaux Arts edifice adjacent to the US Capitol, the Senate Building was erected between 1906 and 1909. Its Caucus Room was one of the grandest rooms in Washington DC, a space modelled on Versailles. Marble floors, enormous French windows, Corinthian columns along the walls. From the ornate ceiling hung sparkling chandeliers. It was here that Congress investigated the sinking of the *Titanic*.

Today, it was Persia's turn to speak in this storied room. From her chair, she faced the assembled committee. Twelve members, all men. Three senators, three congressmen and six members of the executive. The departments of Justice, Labor, Treasury and Commerce were all represented, along with the Federal Trade Commission, and Securities and Trade Commission. Behind Persia, reporters were poised to take notes. A cameraman lunged forward to take a photograph, the flash leaching the colour from her already pale face. It was an intimidating scene, but Persia betrayed no sign of tension. Neat and composed, she was ready to state her case. You'd never guess it was only three months since her husband's sudden death.

It was May 1939 and Persia had travelled to Washington DC to testify. The previous June, President Roosevelt had written to Congress to express concern about the concentration of economic power in the United States, which he believed threatened the nation's economy and even democracy itself. In response, the Temporary National Economic Committee was established to investigate the issue. The problem, as the Committee defined it, was that 'People who are able and willing to work cannot find employment. People who are hungry cannot provide themselves with food.'

Between December 1938 and April 1941, the so-called Monopoly Committee held public hearings. Designed to gather 'a dispassionate survey of economic facts', 552 witnesses testified over 193 days. The Caucus Room became a battleground to shape the present and future of the US economic life. As historian Larry Owens later wrote, it was 'a highly charged arena in which powerful figures wrestled to redefine the nation's political economy'.

Persia was among these powerful figures. At 2.40 pm on Thursday 11 May, she took the stand, testifying in her capacity as executive secretary of the Consumers National Federation. The federation was an umbrella organisation founded in 1937 that represented 30 bodies nationwide. Despite being widowed only months earlier, despite having two children under six, and despite being in the final months of her PhD, Persia had caught the train from New York to Washington DC to represent the consumer voice.

Her testimony was an exposé of industry-backed consumer testing. These were bogus outfits, she explained, akin to company dominated labour unions. 'While we recognise the right of any group to express themselves,' she said, 'we feel that the public has a right to know who is back of them financially.' That afternoon, Persia singled out the Hearst-owned *Good Housekeeping*. She accused the magazine of publishing fraudulent or misleading guarantees about products such as toothpaste and grape juice. As a result of her testimony, the Federal Trade Commission investigated the claims and ended up slapping *Good Housekeeping* with an official complaint. In response, Hearst pushed back, claiming the accusations were undermining press freedom and stemmed from communist influence. As would happen often over the coming years, the spectre of communism was invoked to cast aspersions on consumer activism.

Persia was many things, but a communist was not one of them. On the contrary, the consumer movement was predicated on a capitalist framework. It advocated for government interventions in the free market, not the overthrow of capitalism. The accusation of communism must have rankled, but in the summer of 1939 Persia had more pressing concerns on her mind – like how to keep herself and her children afloat. Newly widowed, and without a paid job, she urgently needed to finish her PhD and secure a decent salary. Apart from modest royalties from one of her late husband's patented inventions (a device to improve refrigeration), she had no regular income. Edward's death was not only an emotional blow but a financial one.

That summer, Persia reluctantly resigned from the Consumers National Federation. The organisation had been her passion project, but it operated on a shoestring budget and Persia's work went unpaid. Without her husband's salary, she could no longer afford to volunteer her time. Soon after she left, the federation collapsed. She'd been the organisation's backbone, and it couldn't survive without her. It would be almost another decade until another national consumer organisation came along to fill the vacuum – with Persia once again at the helm.

In 1940, with her doctorate complete, Persia, now Dr Campbell, was eligible for academic employment. She secured a position as Assistant Professor in Economics at Queens College in New York. Located in the immigrant borough of Queens, on Long Island, Queens College was founded in 1937 as a free college to service the local population. With a strong ethos of public service, the institution was a good fit for Persia. That summer, Persia and her two children relocated to Geranium Avenue, Flushing, close to Queens College and down the street from Kissena Park.

The next few years would be the most challenging of Persia's life. As she fought to get 'established professionally in a new field', while running a house and raising two children 'without much help', her life was characterised by the 'management of precious resources'. She was, by temperament, a leader and reformer who hungered to change the world. Instead, during those war years, every day she struggled to keep her head above water. As she later recalled, the 'pressure of circumstances' was often deeply 'frustrating'. At Queens College, she experienced 'male chauvinism' from colleagues prejudiced against women and the feminised field of consumer economics. For many years, Persia remained a lowly assistant professor, and her applications for promotion were rebuffed – a snub one friend described as a 'disgraceful situation'.

Her solution was simply to work harder. Sydney, Persia's daughter, regularly fell asleep to the sound of her mother's typewriter, hammering out letters and speeches and reports late into the night. With her husband gone, work became Persia's great love, her source of meaning and purpose and validation. For all her humanitarian principles, the economist shied away from intimacy. Work was always the top priority. Even her closest friends knew little about her inner life.

Now widowed, Persia had lost her original reason for staying in the United States. Did she consider a return to Australia? There's no evidence for this. Back in Sydney, she could have leant upon family support, but it would mean uprooting her children from the only home they'd ever known. She would also be separated from her stepdaughters and lose her position in the American consumer movement. Moreover, Persia was now a naturalised American citizen and had lived in New York for over a decade. It was her home as much as Sydney had ever been.

Persia's children Sydney and Edward (known as Ted or Boyden) were only five and three when their father died. Persia rarely spoke about her late husband, but the children were exposed to his Quaker faith. Although Persia was raised Presbyterian, she decided to educate her offspring at the George School, a Quaker boarding school in Pennsylvania. Boyden was an easy child: athletic, outgoing and academically minded. After graduating, he attended Princeton and worked for the World Bank. Sydney's path through life was more difficult. She had, in Persia's words, an 'imaginative and inquiring mind' but experienced ongoing challenges with her mental health – including at least one adult admission into psychiatric care.

Persia settled into Queens College and resumed her work as a consumer advocate. Her diary was filled with radio talks, committee meetings and further appearances before Congress. When the National Association of Consumers was founded in 1947, Persia featured among the organising committee and board of directors. This new association took up where its forerunner – the ill-fated Consumers National Federation – had left off. In its early years, it focused on combating inflation prompted by the end of wartime price controls. Other key objectives were public housing, expanded welfare programs and an increased minimum wage. By 1948, Persia was vice-president.

At the same time, Persia worked on her magnum opus. Published in 1949, *The consumer interest: a study in consumer economics* was a 650-page attempt to give scholarly legitimacy to 'consumer economics' – an embryonic subfield regularly dismissed as a feminine triviality. Persia was conscious that fellow economists still deemed her topic 'beneath their professional considerations'. In this tome she contested the notion that consumer economics had relevance only for bargain-hunting housewives. The book presented 'the consumer interest' as a lens for understanding the totality of economic life: a comprehensive framework that inverted a producer-oriented vision of the economy. Whereas producerist thinking measured economic health via national income accounting, or GDP, the consumer lens evaluated the economy 'in terms of what people finally get out of it'. The former prioritised profit and growth; the latter addressed itself to 'the problem of how "to raise the standard of living"'. Far from a marginal subfield, consumer economics was an alternative economic imaginary structured around human wellbeing.

As she evangelised consumer economics, Persia continued to draw upon the Australian example as a model for the United States. In 1938, the United States finally established a federal minimum wage – three decades after Australia. Yet in practice, the new 40-cent hourly minimum was not enough to support a family. During the 1940s, Persia backed a proposed Fair Labor Standards Act amendment to raise the hourly rate to 75 cents. She explained that the United States should emulate the Australian model of a 'minimum wage system based on needs'. A minimum wage alone was not enough; wages must support a decent standard of living. This was the logic that Australian jurist HB Higgins had adopted with the 1907 Harvester judgment, which stipulated that the minimum wage must align with the estimated cost of supporting a three-child family. In her writings and speeches, Persia insisted the 'living wage' model was sorely needed in the United States.

Persia also hatched plans to embark on a major study of the Australasian 'standard of living', a project that would involve research into Australian and New Zealand wage-fixing and government services. The desired aim was to inform American public policy. As Persia wrote, '[t]here has been a long experience in Australia and New Zealand in these fields ... from a study of which I think we can profit in the US'. The US Department of Labor was 'deeply interested' in this project. The Australian government was also cooperative. The only problem was money. Campbell applied for many funding schemes but was granted only $1000 from the US-based Social Science Research Council.

But no matter; she had more than enough on her plate. In the late 1940s, Persia resumed participation in the international sphere, where the newfound United Nations was ushering in a new era of activity. Central to this work was international development – a project in which the economics profession played a starring role. Under the leadership of Caribbean-born W Arthur Lewis, experts in 'development economics' championed industrialisation and economic growth in the newly decolonised nations of the global south, imagining social uplift as an inevitable by-product of increased GNP. Once the pie expanded, surely everyone would receive a larger slice. This view won widespread consensus and shaped UN and US policy.

Persia, however, begged to differ. In the postwar years, she sat within a small but vocal group of experts who queried the logic of growth. Alongside like-minded figures such as Swedish UN bureaucrat Alva Myrdal, Persia stressed the need to prioritise living standards and social outcomes. In her mind, economic growth was a means rather than the end of effective development. It could be beneficial but shouldn't be pursued for its own sake. Instead, she proposed that the consumer economics framework could and should be applied to the entire world. She'd already advocated for 'living standards over GNP' within the United States; now, she was taking that model global.

This effort began at the Food and Agriculture Organization (FAO), an agency of the UN. In 1948, 1949 and 1951, Persia was a US delegate to the FAO annual conference and advised on US FAO policy. By 1949, she was 'one of the leaders of FAO work in the United States'. Already, Persia was concerned that the agency's development work gave insufficient emphasis to 'raised levels of living'. These misgivings only increased over the coming years, as the FAO succumbed to political and budgetary pressures to constrain itself to the provision of expert advice. An organisation established to solve world hunger was devolving into a talk shop. In the early 1950s, Persia sought to reverse this trend and confronted FAO Director-General Norris Dodd about the organisation's failures. The battle, while hard fought, was a losing one.

In 1955, when the Governor of New York decided to appoint the nation's first Consumer Counsel, Persia was the obvious candidate for the job. The consumer movement had long advocated for consumer representation in government. Now, it was finally happening in the state of New York. In this position, created by new Democrat Governor Averell Harriman, Persia was tasked with ensuring 'the consumer point of view would be taken into account in policy-making'. She took leave from Queens College and relocated to Albany, where she reported to the governor himself. For the first time, the consumer perspective would inform all government policy. Although she still had a noticeable Australian accent, Persia now held a senior role in the US government. Over the coming years, she would develop a national profile due to her efforts to spread awareness of consumer issues.

This new role as Consumer Counsel made Persia a pioneer. A member of Harriman's administration recalled, 'She was before her time in the issues she was talking about and that she was a woman.' Sixteen years after the death of her husband, when the future seemed bleak, Persia was now a household name with the ear of senior Democrats.

Next stop: the White House.

25

ANTI-ENGLISH AND PRO-AMERICAN

THE NURSE, NEW YORK CITY, 1940

In a world gone mad, Cynthia decided to understand madness. During the summer of 1940, as the Axis powers occupied Europe, the nurse took herself to a hulking institution perched alongside New York's East River. Ten storeys of white brick on East 68th Street and York Avenue, a neo-Gothic edifice gleaming in the sun. With its arched windows and soaring walls, it could almost have been a cathedral. And in a way, it was. A cathedral to psychiatric medicine, a temple to the mysteries of the human mind. Connected by underground tunnels to surrounding buildings, the building otherwise stood alone, pristine and untouched by the busy world.

This was the Payne Whitney Clinic, the psychiatric branch of the New York Hospital–Weill Cornell Medical Center, first opened in 1932. Eight years later, Payne Whitney was renowned as New York's leading provider of psychiatric services. Conceived as a state-of-the-art facility, more akin to a genteel hotel than Bedlam-style asylum, the rich and famous came here to alleviate their psychic distress. Patients relaxed in plush lounges or played billiards in the pool room. In 1938, the novelist Mary McCarthy was committed to Payne Whitney by her husband Edmund Wilson, an experience immortalised in her 1963 bestseller *The Group*. Later, poet Robert Lowell, writer Jean Stafford and actress Marilyn Monroe would find themselves in-patients at the storied institution.

Before all that, Cynthia Reed went to Payne Whitney to learn from the best. In 1940, she enrolled in a postgraduate course in psychiatric nursing. After getting told to leave the United States in 1936, and qualifying as a nurse in London in 1939, the Australian had made a narrow escape from fascist Europe. Once safely out of a war zone, she was free to address unfinished business in the United States. For four years, since her premature departure from St Joseph's in Chicago, Cynthia had hankered for the rigour of American professional education. Now, at Payne Whitney, she could satiate that appetite to learn.

'It was satisfying to be in America again', Cynthia wrote in *Lucky Alphonse*. At Payne Whitney, her fictional counterpart Alphonse was '[w]elcomed and smiled upon, shown kindness on all sides'. The 'skilled teachers', combined with the 'general keenness and interest' of fellow nurses, sparked 'the dawning of tremendous enthusiasm, and a great thirst for further knowledge'. It was almost too good to be true. The nurses' library was 'a joy', stocked with all the latest texts. The nurses enjoyed weekly lectures, swimming, dancing, skating and bridge. Their food, meanwhile, 'could hardly be bettered'. All in all, it could not have been more different from St Thomas', where Alphonse was treated like 'an irresponsible schoolgirl' and 'sharply reprimanded at least once a day'.

In keeping with its progressive spirit, Payne Whitney rejected physical restraints. Instead, it was hospital policy to soothe agitated patients via the use of baths and 'wet packs' – a system of wrapping a patient in wet towels and sheets. It was a humane system, one that treated mental disturbance 'gently and scientifically'. And it appeared to work: 'bitterly unhappy' people were restored to health. After a few months at Payne Whitney, Alphonse deemed it beyond reproach. This American institution was the future of psychiatric medicine, a model to emulate. 'Nowhere in the world do patients get more ideal treatment from a more highly trained, skilled staff of doctors, nurses, and therapists', Alphonse concluded. Her memory did not lie. As she'd suspected in England, America really did do it better.

Lucky Alphonse concludes with Alphonse still in New York, preparing 'to play her part' in the 'new future dawning for mankind, a future full of promise'. As a nurse at Payne Whitney, she feels the 'dawning of a great content'. The novel ends with a triumphant image of modern womanhood: an independent career woman thriving in New York, fulfilled by work and learning, a self-actualised figure following her bliss. No husband, no child, no obligations beyond her own desires. In New York, the city of the future, she is carving out a new type of female existence.

Cynthia's actual story has a different ending. Despite her apparent delight at returning to the United States, within a few months, Cynthia had swapped downtown Manhattan for suburban Melbourne. By early 1941, she was back in the southern hemisphere for the first time in six years, living with her brother John and sister-in-law Sunday at Heide.

What had compelled this world traveller, this passionate Americanophile, to abruptly return home? Had US immigration authorities once again sent her packing?

Not this time. This time it was a more ordinary interruption, the oldest story in the book of women's aborted ambitions: pregnancy. Cynthia had come home to have a baby. On 6 May 1941, she gave birth to a girl called Jinx at Melbourne's Epworth Hospital.

Cynthia spun a fine story about the baby's parentage. In December 1940, when she was still in New York, she reported her marriage to Knut Hansen, a Danish pilot and intelligence officer. Cynthia returned to Melbourne as Mrs Knut Hansen, a married woman with her husband off in battle. Around that time, she spread the word that Knut had been 'shot out of the sky over Romania', leaving Cynthia a widow. At least she would have their unborn child to console her.

Wartime nuptials to a war hero. A soldier killed in combat before he could meet his daughter. A widow left pining for her slain love. It was all terribly romantic, awfully tragic and – in the chaos of wartime – perfectly credible. Only, in Cynthia's case, it wasn't true. Knut Hansen was an invented figure – a husband conjured to protect her unborn child from the stigma of illegitimacy.

Jinx's real father was the artist Sam Atyeo. Sam and Cynthia had been friends since the early 1930s, when his abstracts were exhibited at her Collins Street gallery. Both were in Europe in the late 1930s, and both escaped wartime France to the Americas in 1940. Once safely across the Atlantic, Sam and fellow artist Moya Dyring settled in the Caribbean island of Dominica, where Cynthia paid them a visit. Jinx was conceived during this visit, in summer 1940. After her Caribbean summer jaunt, Cynthia returned to New York to study at Payne Whitney. By early December, when she invented the story about a Danish husband, Cynthia was around four months pregnant – a fact that interrupted her work as a nurse and sent her home to Melbourne.

But that was not quite the end of the story. Within a few years, Cynthia's international nursing career had secured a fictional afterlife. In 1943, when Jinx was two years old, Cynthia and her daughter moved to Sydney, where they settled in the north shore suburb of Wahroonga. There, as the war continued, and her infant grew into a child, Cynthia wrote the novel that became *Lucky Alphonse*. In 1944, the book was released by Reed & Harris, the new Australian publishing house established by her brother John Reed and Adelaide poet Max Harris.

Cynthia was already a well-known figure in Australia and her debut novel was widely reviewed. More than just a work of literature, *Lucky Alphonse* was understood as a political statement on the failures of English – and, by extension, Australian – nursing. On 29 July 1945, Sydney's *Daily Telegraph* announced that Cynthia was 'crusading for a better deal for Australian nurses'. Her polemical novel was embraced by Australian nurses, who 'applauded its frankness'. Within the nursing profession, *Lucky Alphonse* was judged a 'revealing commentary on bad nursing conditions in England, many of which ... were duplicated in Australia'. Following this report, nurses wrote into the *Daily Telegraph* to share their grievances and concerns. This sparked a larger conversation about the status of nursing in Australia.

At a moment of burgeoning discontent about the Nightingale model, and just as wartime victory propelled the United States to superpower status, *Lucky Alphonse* acted as a stimulus to express discontent with the inherited English system. It was, as Cynthia admitted to John, a novel unabashedly 'anti-English and pro-American'. Although Cynthia would never again work as a nurse, *Lucky Alphonse* ensured the lessons of her overseas experience resounded loud and clear.

26

SELLING AUSTRALIA

THE DECORATOR, NEW YORK CITY, 1942

As guests trickled into the Waldorf Astoria's Grand Ballroom, the scent of wattle flooded their nostrils. The pungent blossom, native to Australia, had rendered the cavernous space awash with gold. Beneath a sparkling chandelier, the polished parquet floors were covered with round tables set for a three-course meal. Tickets were $10 a pop, and 1800 had sold. The evening of Friday 24 April was set to be an occasion to remember.

At one table, places were laid for the Baron and Baroness de Rothschild, the Jewish banker and his wife who'd made a lucky escape from fascist Europe. Elsewhere, assorted Rockefellers and Vanderbilts were milling about. Frances Alda, the operatic diva from Melbourne, could be spotted in the crowd, as could Merle Oberon, a Hollywood star who (falsely) purported to hail from Tasmania. Polar explorer Sir Hubert Wilkins looked dashing as ever, accompanied by his Australian wife, the Broadway actress Suzanne Bennett. Wendell L Willkie, the Republican lawyer who'd run against Roosevelt in the 1940 election, was sipping a glass of Australian champagne. Absolutely everyone was there. Even the famous violinist Yehudi Menuhin had made it along.

Once the crowd was seated, it was time for the honoured guests. First the British Ambassador to the United States, Lord Halifax and his wife. Then HV Evatt, Australia's Minister for External Affairs, followed by ministers from South Africa, Canada and New Zealand. Next there was a veritable army of generals, admirals and colonels, plus a commander or two. When the room was filled with enough medals to fuel a smelter, the air reverberated with the rousing tones of 'God Save the King' and the 'Star-Spangled Banner'. With the opening formalities complete, food was served. First course was mock turtle soup, followed by New Zealand rack of lamb, accompanied by a spring salad with Rotorua dressing. For dessert, there was ice-cream flavoured with Australian almonds, and plates of Kangaroons, an antipodean twist on the classic macaroon.

Rose Cumming ate at the head table, seated next to the British Ambassador. From this perch, Rose watched over her creation with the keen eye of an auteur. This evening's extravaganza, an Anzac Dinner to commemorate the 1915 landing at Gallipoli, was her finest achievement to date. As chair of the dinner's organising committee, with her sister Eileen as vice-chair, the interior decorator had brought her creative talents to the project of marking Australia's de facto national day on American soil at a pivotal moment in the two nations' history.

The previous December, the bombing of Pearl Harbor had finally propelled the United States into the war. A few weeks later, Prime Minister John Curtin had announced that Australia 'looks to America'. In February, the fall of Singapore had shocked the world, leaving Australia in fear of imminent invasion. Now in April, all eyes were on the new Australian–US alliance. Would this partnership work out? Would the United States fill the gap left by Britain dropping the ball in the Pacific? The stakes couldn't be higher.

Rose Cumming rose to the occasion. After two decades perfecting the art of making meaning with interiors, Rose curated a showstopper of an event that was essentially a public relations exercise for a nation. With this Anzac Dinner, she sold Australia to an audience of American elites. For months, the decorator planned every detail. The guest list, the decorations, the speeches, the entertainment, the publicity and the printed program were all given the Rose Cumming touch. When it came to the seating arrangements, Rose worked closely with the British Embassy to ensure questions of rank and status were strictly observed.

She convinced big business to get on board. General Electric, Shell, General Motors, Chase National Bank and Elizabeth Arden were just some of the evening's 40-plus corporate sponsors. When guests leafed through the full-colour program, decorated with koalas and kangaroos, they would find General Electric had donated a page of photographs that showed 'diggers and buddies mak[ing] friends' as US troops arrived in Australia. Here was corporate America giving its nod of approval to the transpacific alliance.

As the night wore on, the meal was punctuated by speeches broadcast around Australia, New Zealand and the United States. One by one, each nation's representative rose to deliver a paean to wartime friendship. Anzacs and Americans had fought side-by-side during World War I, and now here they were doing it again. General Douglas MacArthur, Supreme Commander of Allied Forces in the Southwest Pacific, cabled a message of support: 'From Australia I send to you the affectionate greeting of an old soldier who is a comrade in arms of yesterday, of to-day, and of to-morrow.' Later, salutations from British Prime Minister Winston Churchill and Australian Prime Minister John Curtin were read aloud to cheers from the audience.

Once the formalities were complete, British film star Gracie Fields was on hand to serenade the crowd. She'd flown out from California especially. Sister Elizabeth Kenny, Australia's world-famous polio advocate, made a surprise guest appearance. To cap off the program, documentary newsreels of Australia and New Zealand gave the crowd a glimpse into antipodean life.

By the time the stragglers stumbled into taxis in the wee hours of 25 April, Anzac Day proper, Rose's Anzac Dinner had raised $25 000 for Australian and New Zealand soldiers. Even more significantly, the evening was a public relations triumph. According to the *Coo-ee Clarion*, New York's Australian newsletter, the evening was the 'greatest tribute to Australia in all the long years devoted to making the United States "Australia-conscious"'. If 1942 marked the beginning of the transpacific partnership that ultimately became ANZUS, this Anzac Dinner was the wedding dinner at which the official ties were consummated via an outpouring of sentiment and declarations of loyalty. The event gave emotional substance to a marriage of convenience. Thanks to Rose and Eileen, American powerbrokers were whipped up into a frenzy of fellow feeling with Australia and New Zealand. And in the early months of 1942, with war on Australasia's doorstep, that was no small thing.

Unsurprisingly, the 'Australia' sold that night in New York was devoid of First Nations sovereignty or dispossession. Growing up on a property in regional New South Wales, Rose and Eileen almost certainly encountered Indigenous people, but First Peoples escaped all mention in the Anzac Dinner. Instead, that evening's imagined nation was a white Australia not long emerged from its 'pioneering days', a 'young democracy' akin to the 'free peoples' of the United States. The underlying logic was of twin 'white' nations connected by blood bonds based on a common racial heritage. It was a story of shared white supremacy.

Australians in the United States did not typically come together to fly the flag of nationhood. There was simply no need. Accepted as quasi-Americans, they had little impetus for community gathering. During the 1920s and 1930s, there was the occasional Anzac Day dinner or dance, alongside ad hoc professional and social networks, but this was more the exception than the rule.

In the words of one Melbourne-born resident of Washington DC, 'Australians don't really seek each other out here because they're happily integrated.' Rose Cumming and her sisters were a case in point. After moving to New York in the late 1910s, they moved within a cosmopolitan milieu of Americans and adoptive New Yorkers from around the world. At their parties, you were more likely to meet English aristocrats or Russian émigrés than fellow Australians. The fact of being Australian was largely irrelevant to their daily life.

If anything, being British was more salient. During the Cummings's youth, New South Wales was still a British colony. Even post-Federation, these women remained British subjects who travelled on British passports. The category of Australian citizen did not exist prior to the 1948 *Nationality and Citizenship Act*. In Washington DC, there was no embassy or consulate to host events or represent Australian interests until 1940. Before this time, the only Australian footprint on US soil was a New York–based Trade Commissioner.

The outbreak of war in Europe was a game changer. Suddenly, Australians in the United States found themselves at odds with their host country. Their home nation was at war, and most had friends or relatives in the military, but the United States remained neutral. Americans had the luxury of continuing life as usual, disconnected from the conflict. To be swept up in a world war, among people who were not, was a jarring experience that reminded stateside Australians of their foreignness. Their otherness. When push came to shove, they were not the same as Americans after all. Suddenly, the fact of being Australian mattered in a way it hadn't before.

That year, stateside Australians started gathering with unprecedented fervour. In late 1939, an Australian Society was founded in New York – the first such organisation in the city since 1901. The society's aim was to 'provide Australians in New

York with an opportunity of meeting occasionally to continue to form friendships which have as their basis a common interest in Australia'. It was framed as a social organisation, but its creation was clearly inspired by the outbreak of war. Within its first year, the Australian Society developed a fundraising wing known as the Australian War Relief Fund, which later added a Pacific branch. The society also established the *Coo-ee Clarion*, a monthly round-up of social and military news that helped build an imagined community of Australians in the United States.

Although led by male businessmen, the Australian Society was fuelled by the labour of women. Men on the throne, women carrying the load. The artist Mary Cecil Allen was a founding director. Other contributors included singers Katrina Castles, Jean Love, Dorothy D'Orn and Marjorie Lawrence; actress Lady Wilkins (formerly Suzanne Bennett), plus Rose and Eileen. Almost every month, the Australian Society held an 'Anzac' gathering at some fashionable New York hotel – and frequently, Rose or Eileen played the role of hostess. Then, in 1942, Rose and Eileen organised the memorable Anzac Dinner. The cosmopolitan duo, who had lived as citizens of the world, were now self-consciously 'Australian'.

What of their little sister, Dorothy? Like many actresses of the silent screen, her career did not survive the shift to sound. Once the talkies took over, after 1929, she drifted out of the limelight. In 1932, she married her second husband Allan McNab, a British artist who in 1945 became art director of *Life* magazine. Dorothy continued to work in the theatre, but would never again match the acclaim of starring in Cecil B DeMille's *King of Kings*. In a cruel irony, that film that caused so much heartbreak would also be her defining role. Even in death, Dorothy would be remembered as DeMille's Madonna. It was the first line of her obituary in the *New York Times*.

When not working with the Australian Society, Rose could be found at her boutique at 515 Madison Avenue. She was, by her own admission, 'a shopkeeper at heart'. The Depression years had been rough on the decorating business, and in 1932 Rose was forced to auction off most of her stock. 'The Depression almost smashed Rose up,' Eileen later said. By the 1940s, however, things had turned a corner. With the wartime economy booming, business was once again steady. Rose was doing elaborate makeovers for the Astors and Vanderbilts. The decorator began to attract acolytes eager to learn under her guidance. She apprenticed George Stacey, Tom Britt and Luke Kelly, all of whom became major decorators.

The Madison Avenue boutique was now a New York institution, a destination that attracted everyone from design aficionados to gawking tourists. Visitors were met by a gleaming shopfront, with polished full-length windows that reflected street traffic. Rose, with her passion for mirrors and light, made sure the boutique shone no less than her interiors. Beside the door, 'Rose Cumming' was stencilled in gold copperplate. Behind the glass, on black shelves, choice items lured window-shoppers inside. A Chinese vase in baby blue. A tiny sculpture of a demon creature with a pointed snout. A roll of silken blue fabric, just asking to be stroked.

Once over the threshold, visitors would tumble into a treasure trove of furniture, fabrics and fresh-cut flowers. Customers might find themselves perusing vases alongside Hollywood icon Greta Garbo or silent screen idol Norma Talmadge or even the Duke and Duchess of Windsor. They would also spy Mr Cantor, Rose's beloved Pekingese, who surveyed the boutique from his own special pillow. He was named after comedian Eddie Cantor, as the two shared distinctive 'pop eyes'. As Rose's stalwart companion, Mr Cantor became a social personage in his own right. When he finally died at the age of 17, his demise made the newspapers. The obituary reported that Rose was in deep 'mourning' for the beloved hound, who'd been 'quite a figure in New York'.

Although never constrained by convention, Rose's eccentricities blossomed as she aged. She started dying her white hair a vivid shade of blue – an ultramarine cloud that resembled cotton candy. Her wardrobe, too, became more outlandish. Rose whipped up evening gowns from old curtains; ribbons and plastic ferns adorned her hair; she pinned fabric swabs to her dresses and fashioned belts from curtain rope. At home, she swanned about in a flowing Chinese robe. Rose turned up to a 1952 party in a chateau outside Paris with lavender hair and scarlet lipstick, wearing strings of pearls above a low-cut sleeveless dress. Beneath an oversized black hat, the 68-year-old beamed for the camera with the giddy joy of a teen at her first dance.

This mature Rose was 'a live landmark on the streets of New York', one of the city's 'Great Personalities'. She could have been the inspiration for Jenny Joseph's 1961 poem 'Warning', which begins 'When I am an old woman I shall wear purple / With a red hat that doesn't go, and doesn't suit me'. On one occasion, Rose was dismissed as a 'bag lady' by a New York doorman. Refused access to a society party, the hostess had to come downstairs to vouch for Rose as a bona fide guest. Rose's appetite for men also remained undiminished. Her possible lover Otto Kahn died back in 1934, and her long-term beau Poffy died in 1946, but Rose kept seeking out male companionship – reliably flirting with the most attractive man in every room. She still loved to entertain, and her 53rd Street brownstone hosted quirky gatherings such as a 1947 'vaccination party' at which guests were given the smallpox vaccine.

Around this time, Rose leased the upper floors of her brownstone to Carl Johan Bernadotte, a former Prince of Sweden who abandoned his title to marry commoner Kerstin Wijkmark. At first, this tenancy seemed an ideal arrangement: Bernadotte secured a prime New York address, while Rose enjoyed some extra cash and indulged her predilection for European royalty. Yet things soon went south. Bernadotte had been promised a luxury home befitting his social position; in reality, the furnishings were 'old, worn and outmoded' and rats infested the kitchen. By May 1947, the Bernadottes had moved into a hotel and taken Rose to court. They wanted to void the lease and be refunded $8000 in rent.

No matter, Rose had a new strategy to bring in cash. She would open her home to visitors, exhibiting the brownstone as a museum of antiques and curiosities. She even printed a catalogue, complete with an introduction from film director Karl Freund. 'People from all over the country had frequently asked Rose Cumming, the renowned decorator, how she lived,' Freund wrote. Now, she had generously agreed to 'open her house for inspection to the public'. Tickets were one dollar a pop; a nice little earner. As ever, Rose was an entrepreneur who knew how to sell whatever she had to flog. She could sell her house, her taste, her time – and when she put her mind to it, she could even sell Australia.

27

A BETTER WORLD FOR WOMEN

THE LAWYER, LOS ANGELES, 1945

Judge May D Lahey was not here to make friends. She was older now, had grown accustomed to taking charge, and no longer possessed patience to placate the egos of foolish men. And sitting across from her in the broadcasting studio was a right piece of work. This radio announcer asked ridiculous questions, and she was fast growing exasperated.

'You agree that a woman's place is in the home, don't you Judge?' The Mutual Network announcer suggested.

May leant into the microphone. Did he really think a prominent lawyer, a woman outside the home herself, would concur with that statement? It was time to put this fool in his place.

'Aren't you being a bit trite and "pre-war"?' May replied acerbically. 'Certainly woman's place is in the home, if that is where she can best develop her mind, body and ability to the utmost and serve society best! But woman's real place is to serve where society most needs her.'

Once teased for her Australian vowels, May now passed for a native-born American. After 35 years in Los Angeles, the former Queenslander was indistinguishable from the locals.

Before the announcer could interject, May pressed on. During the current world war, with men off fighting, women were needed in industry. And after the conflict ended, and a new society emerged, women would have other important roles to play – both within and outside the home.

'[W]hen [servicemen] return, who knows in what place women may best serve? Certainly they should have a voice in the Peace Table when that comes. On the other hand, the many women who have chosen their homes as their "career" need full legal and constitutional rights just as much as their "earning" sisters!'

May was in full swing now, determined to school the interviewer on women's lives. Did he know that it was still legal for husbands to beat their wives? Was he aware that just last year an Illinois judge said if more husbands beat their wives there would be fewer divorces? The judge talked and talked, raining down facts and examples, preventing the interviewer from getting a word in edgeways.

May was in the studio to discuss the Equal Rights Amendment (ERA), a proposed amendment to the US constitution championed by feminists since 1923. The ERA was a divisive issue within the women's movement, as some feared it would disadvantage working women. But May – like most middle-class feminists – was determined to formally protect women's rights in the constitution. As a lawyer, she was conscious American women possessed limited legal protections and faced widespread discrimination. To make her case, Judge Lahey outlined the legal principles behind the constitution, explaining that US law had inherited the English principle of regarding women as their 'husband's chattel'.

When May finally paused to take breath, the announcer was quick to interject.

'If conditions are really that bad, why don't you women do something about it?'

You women. The audio was not recorded, but it's easy to imagine disdain dripping from that phrase. May, however, didn't miss a beat.

'Unfortunately, the women who are most badly in need of help, are too beaten and helpless to help themselves! That is why, as California women, as either home or working women, it is our duty to act for the less fortunate members of our sex.'

May's words went out to a national audience, broadcast by 384 affiliate radio stations around the United States. The judge's voice – insisting that American women deserved equal rights under law – poured forth from any number of the 12 million radios nationwide. Housewives peeling potatoes, munitions workers bent over assembly lines, domestic workers scrubbing floors, young girls playing dolls – all could have caught wind of May's call for feminist solidarity.

In that final year of war, with peace on the horizon, it was a moment for looking to the future. Was there a better world to come? Would all that death and sacrifice be worth something? With the new world order still a blank slate, it didn't seem so far-fetched to ask for justice and equality. The listening audience, dotted around the nation, was an army of potential changemakers, connected by invisible radio waves. Did May's rhetoric make them feel less alone, more connected to other women, part of something bigger than themselves? At the very least, I like to imagine someone gave a hearty chuckle or even emitted a cheer as the judge drilled the male announcer on the facts of women's lives.

This radio performance was all in a day's work for the 57-year-old, who was now both a senior jurist and renowned women's rights campaigner. By this point, May had been a judge for 18 years. Since 1943, she had also acted as Presiding Judge of the Los Angeles Municipal Court – the first woman to hold this post. She was unanimously elected by her fellow judges. As presiding judge,

May oversaw the work of 29 judges around the city, three of whom were women.

One of these women, Ida May Adams, was sworn in by Judge Lahey herself back in 1931 – the first occasion in which one woman judge had sworn in another. In a photograph of the ceremony, May is an imposing figure who had grown into her authority. Gone is the girlish ingenue of only a few years before. Judge Lahey is now straight-backed and serious. She wears a comfortable loose-waisted dress as was her habit – May abhorred corsetry. A dark jacket and a simple string of beads completes the outfit. This is a practical woman concerned with doing rather than pleasing. No smiles for the camera, no effort to make herself small.

In the courtroom, Judge Lahey was an intimidating presence, a brisk professional who did not suffer fools. May's mind was 'analytical, logical and inductive'; she had a 'clear, incisive intellect'. Despite the relative informality of the American courtroom, May was a stickler for good manners and polite language. On one occasion, she threw out an attorney who uttered the word 'bloody'. Mental arithmetic was her forte, and she was infamous for correcting attorneys' calculations. 'Don't you think X dollars would be closer?' she was wont to say.

From the bench, May had a ringside seat to the underbelly of a boom town undergoing what historian Carey McWilliams famously termed 'the largest internal migration in the history of the American people'. From barely 319 000 residents in 1910, the year May arrived, Los Angeles had quadrupled to over 1.2 million by 1930 – with 2.2 million across the broader LA County. Even the Great Depression barely slowed Los Angeles' rise. After hosting the Olympics in 1932, the city was firmly on the map as a major global metropolis.

With people, came conflict and crime. Judge Lahey saw it all. Marriage ceremonies, kidnapping, automobile accidents, will disputes, gangland killings, bootlegging, raids on illegal gambling rings, domestic violence, workers stiffed on their wages, impersonation of police officers – all passed through her courtroom. Hollywood personalities made a regular appearance. The minor actress charged with drunk driving; the film players evicted for trashing a rental. The screen villain Noah Beery, sued for failing to pay for his wife's new wardrobe, and sued again a few months later for assaulting a chef. Then Paul Bern, an MGM producer, died of a gunshot wound at his Beverly Hills home in September 1932, only two months after marrying Jean Harlow, a glamorous film star 20 years his junior. Bern's death was ruled a suicide, but rumours circulated about foul play. On 19 October, Harlow appeared in Judge Lahey's courtroom to assert her claim to the estate. Film fans and reporters flooded the building to catch a glimpse of the 'Blonde Bombshell', then at the height of her fame. This was Harlow's first public appearance as Bern's widow, and she played up to the occasion. Black dress, white gloves and a sable choker that set off her platinum blonde hair. After a brief session, Judge Lahey appointed Harlow the sole executor of Bern's estate.

By this point, Judge Lahey had set her sights on a promotion. Drafted onto the Superior Court for a one-year stint to assist with a backlog of probate cases, she sought to make the appointment permanent. The judicial elections were scheduled for November 1932, and Judge Lahey put herself forward as a candidate. May ran a high-profile campaign, backed by the city's professional women and many churches. She even secured the endorsement of the LA Bar Association – the first woman to do so. However, in the vote on 8 November, Judge Lahey was roundly defeated by fellow municipal judge William S Baird. Even the Bar Association's favour was not enough to get a woman across the line. Judge Lahey remained on the Municipal Court, butting her head against a glass ceiling as solid as it was invisible.

In the world of women's clubs, May faced no such constraints. In the United States, the early 20th century was the heyday of the

'Women's Club Movement' – an era of clubs and associations that brought women together and gave them platforms for political and cultural influence. At a time of male dominance in public life, these clubs were a vehicle for women to shape the world beyond the home. The clubwoman was an active citizen, an earnest (usually middle-class) woman concerned with making a difference. May was a paradigmatic example of the species. Outside work, clubs were her whole world. They provided her with many things: a social life, political clout, leadership training, professional networks, travel opportunities, intellectual stimulation and ready-made community.

Within this female-only universe, Judge Lahey emerged as a natural leader. Alongside her day job, May was an office holder at an exhausting array of organisations: the LA Women's Lawyers Club, the Business and Professional Women's Club, the Friday Morning Club, the Phi Delta Delta legal sorority. Almost every week, her name was in the newspapers. She was giving a speech or hosting a luncheon or organising a fundraiser. Of course, it helped that other women were on hand to run the Lahey household. May's mother, Emily, had died in 1938, but around that time her older sister Ida returned to California and the two sisters lived together until Ida's death in 1968. With the widowed Ida around to act as housekeeper, May was free to spend her evenings at lectures and concerts and meetings.

All this activity took a toll, however. After decades of unrelenting work, May's health began to suffer. A doctor diagnosed a heart condition and urged the judge to slow down. Towards the end of 1946, May made a difficult decision. She would leave the bench early, a 'disability retirement' necessitated by ill health. It was not an ideal way to go. Not only did May lose the status and stimulation of legal work, but a disability retirement meant she forfeited her judicial pension, a generous stipend available upon serving to age 60. At 58, it must have been galling, to have worked so hard for so long without commensurate reward.

On 27 February 1947, the Los Angeles legal world congregated to mark Judge Lahey's retirement. The usually composed judge let her mask slip. As colleagues paid tribute to her work, her eyes welled with tears. The best speech was given by Mabel Walker Willebrandt, the fellow lawyer who'd hosted May's Chateau Marmont party back in 1928. Willebrandt, who had been there at the beginning of May's judicial career, now marked its premature end. 'She represents woman in the highest embodiment of mind,' Willebrandt said of May, 'first, an admirable woman; second, a highly intelligent, strong woman, and always an understanding person.'

A few weeks later, May's replacement was sworn in. Judge Lahey's seat on the municipal bench would be occupied by Mildred L Lillie, former assistant US attorney. This was welcome news for May, who long believed women were constitutionally suited to legal work – even more so than men. 'Everybody knows that women have always been masters of words,' May said. 'Women are quick-thinking, nimble-witted, and these are characteristics valuable in the law.'

And so the story of May's career ended. Retirement beckoned, with all its endless expanses of time. She and Ida would rattle around in their Eagle Rock home, a residence abutting the San Rafael Hills on the northern edge of Los Angeles. She would 'rest and retire to regain her health ... all the while getting some real fun out of life'.

Or at least, that was the plan.

In the early 1930s, Judge Lahey had spoken at a Chicago conference on the history of women jurists. She opened by asking whether there was even a history to speak of. Surely it was a brief one. To all appearances, women were only just then clambering onto the bench. Not so, May countered. Legal advocacy was an ephemeral art, recorded only in 'mouldering law volumes'. With few available records, it was easy to assume women had no part in this story. Yet, when you looked for them, female legal minds abounded. May cited 'Deborah, who judged all over Israel'; Zenobia, Empress of Palmyra; 'the masterly self-defense conducted by Mary, Queen of Scots'; and other royal women who 'sat in the highest courts of the land during the absence of their consorts'. Among these was Eleanor, wife of Henry III, who presided on the bench in England way back in 1253.

With this speech, later published in the Phi Delta Delta magazine, Judge Lahey constructed a historical lineage for herself. She was wielding history as weapon, using historical examples to insist women were 'natural' legal authorities. Modern women lawyers were not invading a male domain; they were merely continuing a tradition that dated back millennia. Women had always been in the law; the problem was that no one had looked for them. May constructed a 'usable past', a revisionist history intended to silence any suggestion that the woman lawyer was an aberration. The irony is that Judge Lahey later fell victim to the same scourge of historical forgetting. In the 1930s and 1940s, at the height of her fame and influence, it was almost inconceivable that her name would drop out of circulation. But it has – at least in Australia. She shone bright then the flame went out; 'Our Only Woman Judge' consigned to oblivion. In the United States, she is better remembered – but there she was always a smaller fish in a bigger pond.

Judge Lahey would indeed be forgotten – but not quite yet. Her 1947 retirement was not the full stop it initially appeared.

Fast-forward to 1951. Los Angeles had a shortage of judges, and the city was looking for jurists to pick up the slack. Against the odds, May's health had dramatically improved. Could she return to the courtroom? She could. That year, after four years of retirement, May resumed her judicial post. Back on the bench for another tour of duty, now aged 63. It was an unexpected encore that ended up lasting 14 years. Judge Lahey retired for the second and final time in 1965.

The thorny issue of the judicial pension again raised its head. Technically, May was still ineligible, having forfeited her pension back in 1946. But other women lawyers refused to see this pioneer cheated of financial security. Ariel Hilton, the Deputy LA Attorney General, campaigned for a special bill to restore May's pension rights. As Judge Mildred Lillie – May's replacement from 1947 – recalled, 'Ariel felt it would be a great injustice to a fine judge if she could not receive regular retirement after all the work she had done'. They succeeded.

But while Judge Lahey received justice, equality was still a distant prospect for women in the legal profession. Four decades after her judicial appointment, there'd been little progress. In the early 1970s, only 39, or 3.5 per cent, of the 1100 California judges were women. Of these, the vast majority sat on lower courts. Only five women sat in superior courts, and only one – Mildred Lillie – sat on the Court of Appeal.

During her second act on the bench, a new figure entered May's life. Jeane W Dole was Judge Lahey's law clerk for 11 years. Later, she became a cherished companion. Dole was a Pennsylvania-born divorcee, 21 years May's junior. May gave her younger friend power of attorney and named her executor and sole beneficiary of her will. In a fiercely private life, committed to public service, this relationship is one of the judge's only recorded intimacies. '[M]y beloved friend', is how May described Dole.

The 20th century was an era defined by unprecedented expansion of women's opportunities. Nowhere was this trend more pronounced than in California, 'where women exercise unparalleled clout in both politics and culture'. According to historian Hilary A Hallett, modern Los Angeles was the global headquarters of 'women's new professional and physical mobility'. Judge May D Lahey exemplified the opportunities the city of angels had to offer. Although no movie star or even a movie fan, her rise reflected the individualistic female emancipation that Hollywood engendered within Los Angeles and represented to the world. May's story was Californian in spirit as well as geography: a narrative of youthful migration, female self-actualisation and bootstraps-fuelled rise – with just enough setbacks to keep things interesting. It could even make a satisfying film. A young Cate Blanchett would be perfect for the leading role.

This narrative arc helps explain why May has been forgotten in Australia. Her story is so American, too American for a nation allergic to tall poppies. Judge Lahey was no larrikin – neither an outlaw nor an underdog. She was a striver, an ambitious hustler who worked hard and took up space and (mostly) got what she wanted. That's not a familiar Australian story – but then, May was not an Australian for most of her life. She left Queensland at 22, was a US citizen by 25 and remained in Los Angeles until her death. Australia might seek to claim her – as it claims pavlova and Russell Crowe – but it was in California that the judge found her true spiritual home.

28

DEMOCRACY ITSELF

On the evening of 3 November 2020, we made lockdown cocktails and settled onto the couch. Recently I hadn't been drinking much, but the gravity of the occasion seemed to demand that we punch out our brains with the strongest possible booze.

Three hours later, I was in tears.

'That's it, democracy is over. He's going to win again, and America will go full fascist. It's all over.'

On 7 November, after four days gripped to CNN, we finally dared to exhale. He hadn't won, just barely. I'd been living on US time, toggling between three different screens and developing a PhD-level knowledge of Arizona's electoral districts. I couldn't walk away, couldn't leave the house. Instead, I beat the treadmill into submission with Anderson Cooper staring down at me. Now, after Pennsylvania saved the day at 3 am, I walked into the spring sunshine to meet a friend's new puppy, feeling as though the whole world had been granted a last-minute reprieve from death row. I celebrated with a mushroom toastie and iced latte, and a meal had never tasted so good.

But then it was January, and there were angry men with exposed six-packs, antlers and guns inside the Capitol. We'd let ourselves think it was over. It wasn't. Would it ever be?

(When had it begun – in 2016? Or 1776 or 1492?)

Now, it's 2024, and the impossible has happened: he's back, the presumptive Republican nominee. This November looks to be a rematch between the same two old white men. Only this time, it's hard for anyone to get excited about the Democrat incumbent, whose government is supporting what the International Court of Justice has called a 'plausible' genocide in Gaza.

On the radio, driving to work, I hear US expert Emma Shortis warn that the man charged with 91 felonies, who sought to 'bring down American democracy' and now 'uses brazenly fascist language', has a real chance of returning to the White House. 'Democracy itself [hangs in the balance],' Shortis concludes.

A few weeks later, nonbinary teen Nex Benedict dies in Oklahoma after a school bathroom beating, a tragedy widely linked to the anti-LGBT rhetoric of local Trumpist politician Ryan Walters. Once again, I revise my tentative plans to return to the United States next year. Among my trans community in Naarm/Melbourne, there's consensus that it's simply not worth the risk.

In our Trumpist present, it's hard to associate the United States with concepts like freedom and opportunity and progress. In the years I've been researching the women in this book, the United States has lurched from Obama-fuelled optimism into a terrifying underworld of neo-Nazis and fascists, in which rape victims are denied abortions and trans children become refugees in their own country. While I was there in 2017, visiting archives in Washington DC and staying in Arlington, Virginia, a Unite the Right rally of assorted neo-Nazis and white supremacists in nearby Charlottesville ended with the death of counter-protestor Heather Heyer. In the aftermath, President Trump noted there were 'very fine people on both sides'.

These days, Margaret Atwood's 1985 novel *The Handmaid's Tale* increasingly feels less like a fantastical dystopia and more a glimpse of the near future. In this context, it can feel grotesque to even attach words like 'modern' and 'advanced' to a nation state that is, today, equal parts dysfunction and cruelty.

But then I remember what the United States of 1920 was really like. Jim Crow. Lynching and segregation. Black Americans denied voting rights. The Ku Klux Klan on the rise, with a fast-growing membership in the millions. Senators saying 'our business is to build up ... a white man's country'. First Nations people deemed wards of the state and disabled people forcibly sterilised.

Also, in 1920, the 19th Amendment gave women the vote – but that was only one part of a much bigger picture.

The truth is that the United States didn't suddenly stop being just and democratic in 2016. The self-serving myth of a republic committed to 'life, liberty and the pursuit of happiness' has always been at odds with cold hard facts of American life.

On one view, the Trump era is less a radical departure from a liberal norm than an amplification of tendencies always present. You could argue what Trump has done is say the quiet parts out loud. MAGA has made explicit the violence and bigotry always implicit in the project of the United States.

As Shortis puts it, Trump is 'the hideous, obscene but entirely logical result of what we might call the contradictions of American history'. He's the 'embodiment of a number of strands of American history': American exceptionalism, the 'original sin of slavery' and the 'history of structural racism and white supremacy'.

At different moments in US history, the seductive story of freedom and progress has been more or less credible. But it's always been just that: a story – a romantic narrative that papers over internal ugliness and powers the global American empire. Whatever happens in November 2024, it won't be an aberration. It will be new, quite possibly unprecedented, but also hoary with age and time. All too predictable, all too familiar. As Childish Gambino reminds us: *This is America*.

29

US WOMEN HAVE MORE FREEDOM

THE DENTIST, PERTH, 1947

After 13 years away, Dorothy Waugh hoped to see some improvement. In 1934, when the dentist was last in Australia, women's prospects had been grim. They were banished to the domestic sphere, virtually absent from public life. Parliament, business, the professions, the press – all were a sea of men. It had dismayed her, and she'd been relieved to return to Philadelphia. In the late 1930s and into the 1940s, Dorothy's dentistry career went from strength to strength. She spoke at conferences; was promoted to Assistant Professor; took home an award from the American Dental Association; consulted with the US military. Dr Waugh of Temple University was respected as an expert. Her colleagues saw beyond her skirts to recognise she had a mind of her own.

But now Dorothy was home again, this time for good. She'd crossed the Pacific aboard the *Port Wyndham*, back to the land of her birth. How much had things evolved while she'd been gone?

The world at large had changed beyond recognition. There'd been a world war, a Holocaust, an uprising against the British in India, there was even a new global body called the United Nations. Britain was in decline; the 'American Century' – declared by *Time* magazine in 1941 – had officially begun. Surely some of that upheaval had filtered down to the Antipodes. Surely things were better for women than they'd been 13 years ago.

There were some encouraging signs. Dr Waugh returned in 1947 to take up a post as Lecturer in Prosthetic Dentistry at the University of Western Australia (UWA). In Perth, on unceded Noongar land, Dorothy would teach dental prosthesis, passing on her American experience to the next generation to – as the *Argus* put it on 12 March – 'make them modern to the last degree'. This appointment was itself remarkable – she was the first woman to teach dentistry at an Australian university. As historian Hannah Forsyth has shown, women were still less than 3 per cent of the national profession – a number that had fallen, not risen, over the past three decades. But Dorothy's appointment seemed a sign that the tide was turning. It promised to be the beginning of a new era, a progressive postwar age in which the old superstitions and prejudices would be cast aside.

Before taking up her job in Perth, Dorothy passed through Melbourne to visit friends and family. While there, she urged girls to enter her profession, arguing that dentistry was – contrary to popular opinion – a natural home for women. '[T]he work is detailed, delicate and long – things that a woman is better suited to than the average man,' Dorothy explained. That week, female colleagues held a party in her honour at the Oriental Hotel. On a Thursday evening in early autumn, a dozen women dentists gathered to toast Dr Waugh, a woman who'd climbed to heights long unimaginable in their profession. She was presented with a spray of gardenias, which she pinned to her black frock. It was a night of hope and optimism, one of those moments when the arc of the universe does indeed seem to bend towards justice.

The hope lasted barely six weeks. Dorothy commenced her UWA lectureship on 15 March, at the start of the academic year. By late April, she'd resigned. When Vice-Chancellor GA Currie reported the news at University Senate, he claimed Waugh's resignation was prompted by concerns about satisfactory equipment. In his statement, Currie implied that Waugh had been difficult. Fussy. Determined to find fault. She'd been briefed before accepting the appointment, Currie stressed; she knew what she was getting into. Yet Dorothy couldn't handle it. In this official narrative, the dentist was a cosseted expat, made soft by American plenitude, undone by rudimentary conditions back home. 'She is not a pioneer', one colleague noted, implying Dorothy lacked the stomach to work on the front line.

Was this really a dispute about dental equipment? Given that Dorothy worked at Temple University for 15 years, it was out of character for her to throw in the towel at the first sign of trouble. On the contrary, all evidence points to someone who was steady. Tenacious. Not easily ruffled. A woman accustomed to swallowing everyday frustrations in pursuit of a larger goal. The Vice-Chancellor's account doesn't ring true. Dorothy had moved across the world for this job; it was a major commitment. She had every reason to make it work. Surely she wouldn't resign within a mere six weeks unless something had gone terribly wrong.

It might have been the dental equipment. But a woman being dismissed as 'difficult' by male colleagues? That's a big red flag. Dr Waugh was a mature professional used to being respected; it's easy to imagine her self-possession riled colleagues habituated to men-only spaces. Did the other lecturers feel threatened by an assertive woman in their midst? Did these men then create a hostile atmosphere? Perhaps they threw up roadblocks, undermined her authority, stonewalled attempts to secure equipment. Was Dorothy essentially forced out?

I can imagine it. It's a familiar pattern, a classic move in the misogynist playbook. If sexism was indeed the true culprit behind her resignation, it would at least have given Dorothy the satisfaction of being right. She'd argued back in 1934 that sex discrimination was worse in Australia; now here she was, proving her own point. Fifteen years at Temple; six weeks at UWA. The comparison was stark.

At any rate, by mid-1947 Dorothy had returned to Melbourne. From her rooms at 167 Collins Street, Dr Waugh hung out her shingle as a dentist. She was back at the Paris end of Collins Street, a block from where she'd first been apprenticed. Each morning, she commuted from Mt Eliza, down on the Mornington Peninsula, to her fourth-storey rooms in the heart of the city. As a Melbourne dentist, she attracted enough clients to keep practising for two decades.

To all appearances, it looked like success. A stable career, absorbing work, recognition in her hometown. But Dorothy was not content. On the contrary, she was thoroughly unimpressed. She was angry at the subordination of the nation's women, angry that Australia remained so conservative, and quite possibly angry about her own experience in Western Australia. As in 1934, this anger would fuel political action. In March 1948, a year after her return from Philadelphia, Dorothy delivered a provocative speech to the National Council of Women, Australia's premier women's organisation.

It was the first meeting of the year, held at the Melbourne Town Hall. Dorothy Waugh was the guest speaker, invited to share impressions of life abroad. Her message was straightforward, summed up in a newspaper headline: 'US Women Have More Freedom Than Ours'. Before an audience of the council's 'respectable radicals', Dorothy restated the argument she'd made in 1934. On every front, American women enjoyed 'comparative ease of life'. Their homes were more comfortable, equipped with labour-saving devices that freed up time for leisure. They were more likely to attend university or pursue activities outside the home. Even their husbands were more considerate than spouses elsewhere. Once again, Dorothy conjured a utopian America that had dubious veracity yet carried enormous rhetorical power. By gesturing towards a better world elsewhere, she urged Australian women to demand change. The speech attracted national attention, fuelling a growing narrative that the United States was a feminist model to emulate. As *The Age* summarised, 'American Women Not Housebound'.

Dorothy's feminism would not pass muster today. She was a creature of her time, with the prejudices of an affluent white woman in the heyday of White Australia. She was hampered by patriarchy; she also benefited from and upheld white supremacy. Like most of her contemporaries, she reproduced what anthropologist WEH Stanner called the 'Great Australian Silence' surrounding the dispossession of First Nations people. Her gender politics were not especially radical. True to its roots in the United States, Dorothy's feminism was focused on individual freedom and opportunity, especially the entry of fellow bourgeois white women into public life. In short, Dorothy wasn't a revolutionary; she was a proto–Girl Boss, a white liberal feminist who challenged some power structures while safeguarding others. If she was alive today, she might be CEO of Coles.

To denounce Dorothy for failing to live up to contemporary standards is anachronistic and reductive; a lazy move that turns history into self-righteous finger pointing. Yet I'm wary of reclaiming Dorothy as a forgotten feminist heroine. That kind of hagiography serves nobody. It erases an individual's full humanity, it holds them to an impossible standard, and reproduces a way of thinking that elevates some people over others. Dorothy's complex story should be a living thing – not a tribute frozen in bronze. How do we remember her fight, acknowledge her imperfect attempts to challenge the status quo, without putting her up on a pedestal?

When I get caught up in these questions, I go back to Dorothy's photograph. In a grainy *Australian Women's Weekly* image from 1947, she's wonderfully human. She's got flyaway hair, a wonky grin, bushy eyebrows, and a hat perched at such a jaunty angle it looks at risk of falling off. (Like her contemporaries Persia Campbell, Rose Cumming and Isabel Letham, Dorothy was a notorious hat enthusiast; she carried no less than 24 in her luggage.) Now in her 50s, Dorothy's face has a grandmotherly softness. Post-menopausal jowls almost swallowed by a high-neck white blouse. She looks smart and jolly and not a little bit eccentric.

This candid snapshot reminds us that Dr Dorothy B Waugh was not an idea; she cannot be reduced to abstract heroine or problematic white feminist. She was a specific individual human, with all the idiosyncrasies that involves. I suspect the photograph was taken as Dorothy disembarked from her transpacific steamer. There's a pulse of life in her expression that evokes the heightened emotions of such a moment. Do I glimpse excitement mixed with anxious anticipation? Is she perhaps a bit dazed by the crowds at the dock? Has she got one eye on finding her luggage? I'd love to be a fly on the wall as she squinted in the morning sun, proclaiming her views to the reporter. In my imaginings, she is charming and overbearing in equal measure.

Above all, Dorothy was a go-getter, a modern forever hustling to remain ahead of the times. During the war, in Philadelphia, she'd begun working with the US Navy on the manufacture of artificial eyes. Veterans were coming home from battle with missing eyes, and the techniques of prosthetic dentistry – Dr Waugh's speciality – were being employed to generate more sophisticated replacements, using plastic instead of glass. In the 1940s and 1950s, Dorothy introduced this technique in Melbourne. Alongside her dentistry practice, she pursued a side hustle in the manufacture of plastic eyes. She worked with veterans but also civilians recovering from accidents or injuries. Each eye was constructed by hand, tailor-made to the recipient, and took two days to complete. By 1950, she'd made 400 eyes, and the press proclaimed she was the only person in Australia with this skill.

In her mid-50s, Dorothy cultivated an image of herself as someone on the cutting edge. Her story hit all the high notes: plastic, science, career woman, humanitarianism – it was progress personified, a perfect good news story for a hopeful postwar age. As the plastic eye woman, a dispenser of modern marvels, Dr Dorothy Waugh defied ageism and misogyny to become a walking example of the promise of American modernity.

30

THE GREATEST AQUATIC SHOW
THE SWIMMER, SYDNEY, 1948

Isabel Letham surveyed her troupe of girls. Two dozen adolescents in matching sea-green bathing suits, white plastic waterlilies adorning their braided hair. Movie-star smiles, painted on with lipstick, beneath eyebrows plucked to a perfect arch. Here was a group of miniature Esther Williams, Sydney girls dressed up to emulate the star of the 1944 blockbuster *Bathing Beauty*. You had to look closely to notice the freckles and gangly limbs.

This was the cast of Isabel's water ballet, ready to create a spectacle at North Sydney Olympic Pool. They would move through the pool as a single organism, mesmerising the crowd with bodies arranged in formation. Normally, scruffy beach kids from the suburbs, today they were paragons of modern womanhood, disciplined athletes with glamour to burn. Isabel had made them anew.

After the final inspection, the troupe piled onto a hired truck to drive the 15 kilometres from beachside Freshwater to the pool at Milsons Point. Few of their families owned cars. It was a novelty to speed through the northern beaches, winding through neighbouring Manly, then crossing the rickety timber Spit Bridge into Mosman and Neutral Bay. Their destination was a sparkling blue rectangle, surrounded by grandstands, in the shadow of the Harbour Bridge. There a paying crowd was waiting for them.

Isabel had first discovered swimming to music in California 25 years earlier. In 1923, when she worked at Berkeley summer school, the teachers had set up poolside gramophones to improve the swimmers' grace and rhythm. Isabel subsequently replicated this technique at the City Women's Club, using music and choreography to teach an early form of synchronised swimming, then known as rhythm swimming or water ballet. Water ballet was a hot new trend in the United States, first popularised by Annette Kellerman who had launched a vaudeville career in New York in 1908, performing aquatic routines in a tank. By 1917, she was the headline act at the New York Hippodrome, accompanied by 200 'mermaids'. Over the next two decades, water ballet spread nationwide. By 1937, it had attracted the notice of impresario Billy Rose, who produced an aquacade of bathing beauties in Cleveland, and later San Francisco and New York. His star performer, Olympic swimmer Esther Williams, was recruited by Hollywood studio MGM. From the 1940s until 1955, Williams was the face of technicolour 'aquamusicals' featuring elaborate water ballets. In 1984, synchronised swimming became an Olympic sport at the Los Angeles Olympics.

Water ballet was slower to take off in Australia. Even though it was popularised by the Sydney-born Kellerman, it wasn't until the 1940s that this sport-cum-spectacle made waves in the Antipodes. Isabel was at the vanguard of the movement, one of the first to teach routines. During the late 1940s, she drew on her US experience to introduce water ballet to Sydney's northern beaches.

The Freshwater Water Babies were formed in early 1948 at the Freshwater Ladies Amateur Swim Club. The troupe was comprised of local girls who paid peppercorn fees to learn from the veteran teacher. They trained at the local ocean baths – a rectangle carved into the rocks at Freshwater Beach. In the shadow of the beach's northern headland, the girls perfected their turns and twists. Isabel set up an old gramophone at the pool's edge, although the mechanical tunes struggled to compete with the music of the wind and waves. But the important thing was to get the movements perfectly co-ordinated. When it came to water ballet, synchronisation trumped complexity. 'You can do anything,' Isabel told her troupe. 'It doesn't matter how simple it is, as long as you do it together.'

By April, they were ready. The Water Babies made their debut before a crowd of 4000 at an aquacade at North Sydney Olympic Pool, held on two consecutive evenings. The event was a fundraiser for Australia's Olympic swimming team, bound for the London games in July. It was billed in the *Sydney Morning Herald* as 'the greatest Aquatic Show ever presented', with celebrated photographer Max Dupain rolled out to record the occasion. The pool was illuminated by violet-ray lighting, while the crowd sat in darkness. Decked out in their best suits and hats, the punters were mesmerised by an evening of athletic endeavour.

Over the next two nights, Nancy Lyons broke a world record for the women's 100 yards breaststroke; Nola Rose was crowned Miss Pacific. And the Water Babies? They did Isabel proud. The Freshwater troupe outshone the competing water ballet teams, whose performers looked drab in plain swimsuits and dowdy bathing caps. Only Isabel's girls had that California flair.

Other performances soon followed. In 1949, the Water Babies did several gigs for the Australian Red Cross. Alongside choirs, an orchestra and a lifesaving exhibition, they strutted their stuff at an evening extravaganza held under lights. That year, they also hosted their own aquacade at Freshwater, using the surrounding rocks as a grandstand. Each evening, the troupe sashayed around the pool's edge in floral halter swimsuits, their waving arms tanned by the sun. Lights glowed on the water as the girls dived in with nary a splash. Isabel had injected some Hollywood glamour into a postwar city in the grips of petrol rationing and a housing shortage. In doing so, she'd also pioneered a new sport. Today, she's remembered as one of the founders of synchronised swimming in Australia.

Water ballet was a highlight of Isabel's life back in Sydney, which was otherwise an underwhelming second act that paled against her California years. The 'temporary' return to Australia in 1929 somehow became permanent. There was no conscious decision to stay, just a series of obstacles that stymied her return to California. As Isabel recovered from her fall into the San Francisco manhole, the Depression arrived to kill off any thoughts of travel. Then her mother grew frail, weakened by chronic asthma that worsened as Jeanie entered her 60s. Isabel couldn't abandon her sole surviving parent. And once World War II began, the Pacific was lousy with war ships.

Before the war came to an end, Isabel was stripped of her US citizenship. The US authorities got wind of her return to Sydney and decided she had procured her naturalisation 'illegally and by fraud'. In 1925, Isabel pledged to remain a permanent resident of the United States; yet less than five years later, she'd relocated back to Australia. The US Vice Consul in Sydney, Perry Ellis, noted that Isabel failed to register herself at the consular office and 'consistently identified herself with the Australian community'. As a result, Isabel's was a 'Fraudulent Naturalization' that must be revoked. By 1944 Isabel was back to being a British subject, a regular alien without residency rights in the United States. The door to California was slammed shut.

Back in Sydney, Isabel once more lived with her mother in beachside Freshwater, also known as Harbord. Perched on the northern beaches, between Dee Why and Manly, Harbord was a long way from the bustle of the CBD. In the early 1900s, during Isabel's youth, the suburb had been little more than a summer idyll for holidaymakers, who set up camp along the coastline. The beach was nestled between two headlands, a golden crescent licked by waves rolling in from the Pacific. On the slopes behind the ocean, the two Letham women lived in a Foam Street cottage originally built by Isabel's father. It was a humble one-storey dwelling, located in the horse paddock adjacent to her childhood home. Isabel returned to surfing and swam daily in the ocean, less than a kilometre from her front door. All the while, she taught swimming to local children, just as she had done as a teenager in the 1910s.

Isabel's teaching base was Manly Pool, an enclosed section of the harbour next to the ferry wharf at Manly Cove, that opened in 1931. With a dressing pavilion and refreshment room, water slides and diving boards, and even electric lighting, Manly Pool was a state-of-the-art beach resort. Throughout the 1930s, it attracted 250 000 visitors a year. Isabel taught around 20 students per day, charging a guinea for 10 lessons. She'd be in the water for hours on end, exposed to the elements. Burning sun, bracing winds, sudden storms. It was gruelling physical work. Isabel knew better than to complain; it was the height of the Depression, with one in three out of work, and she was fortunate to put food on the table. Even so, Isabel's new workplace was a comedown from the luxurious environs of the Women's City Club natatorium. She'd swapped heated towels and filtered water for the open ocean.

But Isabel hadn't left California behind. She stayed in contact with friends and colleagues, forging a correspondence that kept her clued into the American swimming scene. Up until her retirement in 1961, Isabel schooled her swim students in the scientific method she'd learnt in California. In the Sydney papers, she published articles about swimming pedagogy, a side hustle that brought in extra income and gave her an added platform. In her trademark assertive tone, Isabel insisted that Australia emulate the 'systematised and scientific' swimming instruction that had been 'brought to perfection abroad'.

Isabel didn't have any formal qualifications. Instead, her authority rested on a decade in California, the beating heart of the modern world. Who cared that she didn't have a degree or diploma; she'd lived overseas, in the big smoke; she knew how things were done in the places that mattered. In interwar Australia, a place with a cultural cringe so deep you could fall into it, that was enough to become an expert. Even a mere woman could command an audience if she'd won plaudits in California or London or New York.

Once again, Isabel's professional confidence did not endear her to men in the swimming world. Much like her contemporaries, the pianist Vera Bradford and dentist Dorothy Waugh, Isabel was a challenging presence – an unmarried career woman with a healthy ego, assertive demeanour and muscled athletic body. Throughout these years, Isabel was forever having public disagreements with the leadership of the Surf Life Saving Association. At the Manly Pool, male instructors undermined her work. They copied her techniques, sabotaged her pupils, criticised her teaching to parents. Their behaviour became so egregious that one instructor was even fired. Yet for all that she challenged male authority, Isabel was not a self-proclaimed feminist. She didn't think in terms of men or women, or gender roles, or patriarchal oppression. She was simply committed to a life of action. In her words, Isabel 'was always a doer. I was always a leader.'

The long days in the harbour took a toll on Isabel's body. In 1939, when she turned 40, she had been teaching at Manly for almost a decade. During the war, her teaching load ballooned, as fears about a Japanese invasion prompted a spike in demand for swimming lessons. Isabel also became a member of the Women's Australian National Service (WANS) and taught swimming to its members. The war years went by in a blur of lessons – 30 students or more a day.

By 1944, her health had disintegrated. It started with pain in her knees, then she collapsed and was admitted to hospital. The diagnosis was rheumatic fever, an inflammatory condition that emerges after untreated infection. Isabel was in hospital for three months, where she was given a new miracle drug called penicillin, only used on civilians for less than a year. It took her two years to recover. She had to re-learn to walk. The doctors warned she'd never regain full use of her hands, but in her typically defiant style, Isabel proved them wrong. She enrolled in a glove-making course, with the idea that learning a new manual task would restore her dexterity and strength. It worked, and she could also make a fine pair of gloves. By 1948, Isabel was once again striding poolside, putting the Freshwater Water Babies through their paces.

31

HOW TO WEAR A WHEELCHAIR

THE WRITER, MIAMI, 1950

In the summer of 1950, Dorothy Cottrell came out to four million readers. School was out, the trees were swathed in green and the whole season lay ahead. When a new copy of the *Saturday Evening Post* hit the newsstands in the second week of June, Dorothy was listed in the table of contents. The *Post* was the bible of middle America; a tastemaker and opinion-shaper that symbolised 'sensible' white middlebrow culture. For decades now, it had enjoyed a readership in the millions. Only the best writers were published in the *Post*, everyone knew that. After two decades in the United States, the former Queenslander was officially one of them.

It was not Dorothy's first time in the magazine. She'd published her first *Post* story in April 1947, a career highlight, that was followed up with a three-part serial in February 1948. There was a third story in March 1950. But, this latest piece was a milestone of sorts: her first personal essay, entitled 'How to Wear a Wheelchair'. Above the headline, a candid photograph of Dorothy in her wheelchair at the kitchen stove, one arm stretched over a frypan. Across the page, further photographs showed Dorothy posing with her husband, Walter. In every image, the writer was smiling. A youthful 40-something, she looked the model of a postwar housewife in her crisp white blouse, plucked eyebrows and impeccable chignon.

For decades, the writer had kept her disability private. It was her own personal business, unrelated to her work. Not something to dwell on; certainly not something to write about. Now, in this essay, Dorothy exchanged privacy for confession. Before the largest possible audience, she named herself as a disabled woman, and articulated a philosophy of disability that anticipated the 'social model' developed by disability advocates in the 1980s.

Over seven pages, the writer challenged the stigma around disability, criticising the tendency to pity or recoil from 'the handicapped'. For Dorothy, disability was not an individual tragedy but 'merely a fact of existence' that could be accommodated via environmental adjustments. It just meant some activities required 'a little extra planning'. Her life had been glorious. She'd married a good man, travelled the world, and pursued lucrative work she loved. Love, adventure, creativity, money – she had it all. 'I cannot by any stretch of the imagination picture myself as having been happier than I have been,' she told readers. 'I have had a radiantly happy life.'

To prove it, she welcomed photographer Bill Shrout into her home. Shrout, a celebrated war photojournalist and regular *Life* contributor, travelled down to Florida to document Dorothy and Walter in their residence on the outskirts of Miami. During his visit, the Cottrells showed Shrout how they'd made the home, known as Pioneer House, accessible. In the kitchen, they'd knocked the legs off the kitchen stove to make it the appropriate height. Outside, they'd installed an elevator so the writer could reach the second storey. It was a homemade device, designed and installed at a cost of only $125. As Dorothy used hand power to haul herself up, Shrout caught her laughing, her head thrown back with glee. *Here I am*, she seemed to say, *disabled and joyful – and don't you dare think the two are incompatible.* The writer was now more than a storyteller; she was a pin-up for disability pride.

Dorothy and Walter had been based in Florida since 1934. They washed up in the southern state after several years travelling around the United States. Florida was 'beautiful past almost anything on earth' – a wonderland of romantic old houses, magnolias, 'pink crepe myrtles in the dreaming mist'. The tropical climate suited them, as did the relaxed pace of life. 'I am in better health there than anywhere else,' Dorothy told family. She loved nothing better than to bathe in the balmy waters of the Florida Keys.

The only problem was the racism. Dorothy was no stranger to white supremacy. She had been raised in outback Queensland during the heyday of the White Australia policy, and had lived among Aboriginal stockhands. But the racial violence of the South was something else altogether. As Dorothy reported home in 1936, 'The Old South is ... so lovely that one can hardly believe it, but much in its people is ugly; ugliest the almost universal hatred of and persecution of the Negro.' Southerners were 'quite two hundred years behind the rest of the world – still resenting the passing of slavery'. In her experience, 'A coloured person is regarded by the Southerner as something less than human.'

Dorothy was quick to take the moral high ground in Florida and denounce the ugliness of American race hatred. But, what of the Australian variant? As was typical of white Australians in the United States, she remained silent on homegrown white supremacy – the proverbial pot calling the kettle black. Was it easier to see and denounce the racial violence of another country, than to acknowledge such horrors in one's own society? Was this quickness to condemn American racism the sign of a guilty conscience? Whatever the reason, the Great Australian Silence travelled abroad.

Despite these misgivings, Dorothy still decided to make the south her home. Throughout the 1930s and 1940s, the Cottrells embarked upon regular road trips, but they always returned to Florida. In 1939, after a decade stateside, the couple took out United States citizenship.

All the while, the Cottrells were supported by Dorothy's writing, refusing to accept money from family in Queensland. Increasingly, Dorothy focused on short fiction, which could be lucrative. The United States was home to dozens of magazines that published fiction, some of which – like the *Saturday Evening Post* – boasted subscriber numbers in the millions. By the late 1930s, as Depression conditions eased, Dorothy again began to earn good money. Her agent placed stories in *Good Housekeeping*, *Cosmopolitan* and *Nash's*. In 1936, her story 'Wilderness Orphan' was adapted for the screen. The film (titled *Orphan of the Wilderness*), produced by Sydney's Cinesound Studios and starring local starlet Gwen Munro, told the story of a boxing kangaroo who is abducted by a circus.

Ever the shrewd operator, Dorothy tailored her work to the demands of the marketplace. She published 'straight' short fiction, but also penned crime and comic shorts – genre fiction simple to churn out and easy to sell. For her, writing was a job, a profession that demanded hard graft more than creative inspiration. 'The person who wishes to write can often do so by sheer grit and sticktoitiveness [sic]', Dorothy believed. '[A] writer works. But if he likes the job he usually likes it far more than most persons like most jobs. Thus he is a lucky cuss.' She sat down at the typewriter every morning, whether the muse was calling or not. On a good day, she could write 2000 words. The consistent effort paid off. 'The starving writer has vanished,' Dorothy reported, as 'writing today is a very well-paid trade.'

These rumoured riches drew other Australians. A steady stream of writers crossed the Pacific with copy to shop around the American literary marketplace. Yet Dorothy's success was more the exception than the rule. For Australian writers, the United States was often a site of rejection and loneliness. Having been lured by a fantasy of free-flowing dollars, they experienced the harsh reality of a competitive industry that could be impenetrable to outsiders. For every success story like Dorothy, there were countless others who pinned their hopes on American fame and fortune, only to return home defeated when their savings ran out.

Although Dorothy's star had risen on the back of Australiana, this proved to be an unsustainable niche. By the late 1930s, the writer complained about a 'strange dislike of the Australian setting which is rampant amidst editors, publishers and movie makers'. Dorothy was not alone here. During World War II, there was a brief appetite for content about America's new military ally, but it was short-lived. Dorothy's initial success with *The Singing Gold* and *Tharlane* had been an anomaly. In general, American audiences could not be persuaded to care about the remote Antipodes. To keep her work marketable, Dorothy began to write about North America. Her frequent travels doubled as research. 'I always take notes of the places we pass through,' she remarked. 'Later, I will be using them for story settings.' Her story 'Hurricane Wedding', published in the *Saturday Evening Post* in March 1950, was inspired by the hurricane-plagued waters of the Cayman Islands, south of Cuba. Her 1953 book *The Silent Reefs* – Dorothy's first novel in two decades – expanded on these Caribbean themes. As ever, she demonstrated a talent for evoking place, with the *New York Times* praising the novel's 'colorful setting'.

Dorothy still hadn't returned to Australia, much to the chagrin of her Queensland family. At first, 'very desperate lack of money' prevented the Cottrells from coming home. Then, in the mid-1930s, the writer suffered a back injury that required months of recovery and inhibited travel. The outbreak of war put paid to any thoughts of crossing the Pacific. A second back injury in 1940 only exacerbated Dorothy's mobility challenges. From that point onwards, she lived in near-constant pain. Travel, and even sitting up to write, became increasingly difficult. Yet she retained her determined positivity. 'I would not trade my life for the life of any woman, living or dead,' Dorothy reflected in mid-life.

During their decades in the United States, the Cottrells inhabited a series of temporary homes. Houseboats, trailers, an old barge. In 1948, they bought Pioneer House, in the Miami suburb of Coconut Grove. For a writer who'd come to prominence via 'pioneer' novels, it was oddly fitting she'd ended up in a home with this name. In Miami, then a sleepy backwater, Dorothy was a minor celebrity. Every new publication attracted excited attention in the local press. Just as at Lake Elsinore two decades earlier, Dorothy was Miami's writer-in-residence, a cultural figure who promised to put a quiet place on the map.

Back in Australia, meanwhile, Dorothy's name was rarely uttered. She hadn't been home in decades, she no longer wrote about Australia and her debut books had been dismissed as commercial sell-outs. The writer received a brief mention in Colin Roderick's *20 Australian Novelists* (1947), which praised *The Singing Gold* as 'a skilful adaptation of autobiography to the demands of a story'. But otherwise, the local literary world had moved on. At the height of her career in the United States, Dorothy was a virtual nobody in Australia, dismissed as a 'trashy writer' who was 'moreover an expatriate'. She eventually took a trip home in 1954 but, even then, she couldn't turn things around. When Dorothy died in 1957, felled by a heart attack in Miami, the writer did not receive a single obituary in the Australian press.

32

THE TYRANNY OF AMERICAN ABSTRACTION

THE ARTIST, MELBOURNE, 1960

In the darkened hall of the National Gallery, an image was projected onto the wall. A mess of abstract forms, lines and shapes all higgledy-piggledy. Browns and greens, with the occasional spot of red. Then a new slide appeared. Pale yellow this time, with swathes of dark green and spots of pale white. The audience frowned in confusion. What were they looking at? It was difficult to make head or tail of these images. What strange new art was this?

Down the front, Mary Cecil Allen surveyed her audience, watching them take in the forms. How would they respond? Melbourne, she knew all too well, had a deep-seated suspicion towards the avant-garde. In 1935, and again during a second visit in 1950, her efforts to champion the modern move towards abstraction had been met with raised eyebrows and even outrage. Only the year before, in 1959, a group called the Antipodeans had formed in Melbourne 'to champion … the place of the image in art' and defend figurative painting against the 'tyranny' of American abstraction.

Still, Mary sensed things were changing. Eric Westbrook, the new director of the National Gallery of Victoria (NGV), was actively acquiring international contemporary art. A new dedicated art gallery was being constructed out of local bluestone on St Kilda Road. European migrants such as Georges and Mirka Mora had injected fresh energy into the local art scene, leading to the re-formation of the Contemporary Art Society (CAS) in 1953. By 1960, poet and critic Chris Wallace-Crabbe noted in the *Observer* 'much greater confidence and real sophistication than was apparent a decade ago'.

After a few months back in her hometown, Mary agreed. She told a reporter for the *Sun*, 'Australia has changed and progressed more in the past nine years than in the previous twenty.' Perhaps now, after all this time, Melbourne was finally ready to appreciate what had been happening in New York.

In the lecture hall, Mary put the befuddled audience out of their misery. The mystery slides, she explained, were images of nature. The first was a photograph of the forest floor; the second was flotsam and jetsam on the beach. Compare these, she continued, to the work of Jackson Pollock. A new slide appeared: one of Pollock's infamous action paintings. These were old news in the United States, having been exhibited since the late 1940s. But even though the artist himself was now dead, an original Pollock had not yet made its way to Melbourne, and colour reproductions were rare. For most of the audience, this was their first glimpse of the postwar American avant-garde.

Before the audience could react, Mary jumped in with an interpretation. See, she urged, how the painting resembled the abstract beauty of the natural world? Pollock's work might look like a mess, the chaotic marks of a toddler, but it was not so different from the patterns found in the forest or on the beach. If we agree that beauty resides in the latter, why not accept that beauty could also be found in action painting? On and on Mary talked, using all her skill and charm to convince her audience to see as she did.

American painting as something to admire? At the time, this was a hard pill for Australian art-lovers to swallow. Quite apart from lingering conservatism in the art world, the United States was increasingly resented as a vulgar force of cultural imperialism. It was the height of the Cold War. America was a global superpower, and Americanisation was reshaping Australian society with warp speed. Television, Hollywood, popular music, consumer products: all were turning Australia into a so-called 'Austerica'. By the early 1960s, there was growing backlash to the influence of American culture. In his iconic 1960 polemic *The Australian Ugliness*, architect Robin Boyd raged against the nation's transformation into a 'second-hand America' dominated by tawdry imitations of US styles.

In this context, Mary's attempt to champion abstract expressionism was an uphill battle. But she was a formidable advocate. In her late 60s, she remained a lithe figure with an infectious smile and the vitality of a woman half her age. Plus, as a daughter of the Melbourne establishment, a respectable spinster with polished vowels, she hardly fit the image of a brash American modern. If anyone could win over anti-American sceptics, against the pejorative associations of American culture, she could.

As Mary continued to explain Pollock at the NGV, there was a palpable shift in the room's mood. Suspicion gave way to curiosity. Heads began to nod in approval. Yes, they could see what she was saying. Yes, perhaps there was art in action painting after all. By the time she finished, the crowd could 'see the beauty in painting they had thought was just a mess'.

Afterwards, as the audience filtered into the afternoon, a bespectacled man with receding hairline and cleft chin was spotted in the crowd. Bernard Smith, a critic who lectured at the University of Melbourne, was one of the most influential voices in Australian art. He was no fan of action painting; just the previous year, Smith had been a founding member of the pro-figurative Antipodeans. Yet even this hardened anti-abstractionist was moved by Mary's arguments. As he walked down the stairs, Smith shook his head in wonder. Almost despite himself, the critic was impressed by the erudition he'd witnessed. Two years later, in his book *Australian Painting 1788–1960* – the foundation work of Australian art history – Smith paid tribute to Mary's 1960 efforts. The artist had, in a few short months in Melbourne, done much 'to make the American contribution to postwar painting better known'.

This triumph was no accident, as Mary was eminently qualified for the job. Over several decades, she'd enjoyed a ringside seat to the development of abstract expressionism in New York, her home since 1927. She'd been an intimate of Hans Hofmann, an artist renowned as 'the father of "Action" painting in the United States'. More recently, Mary had been a fixture of the art scene at Provincetown, the Cape Cod artists' colony that had, as she noted, emerged as 'the Mecca and market place for the new abstract expressionist and action painting'. Between 1934 and 1957, Hofmann taught a summer school at Provincetown, an annual event that attracted virtually every major American modernist, including Lee Krasner, Ray Eames, Jackson Pollock and Mark Rothko. In 1949, Hofmann's Provincetown circle hosted Forum 49, a ground-breaking exhibition and discussion series dedicated to the new abstractionism.

Mary was in the thick of it all. Since the 1940s, she'd been a regular visitor to the seaside town, renting a weatherboard cottage that overlooked the ocean. In 1953, newly flush with an inheritance, Mary purchased a Provincetown farmhouse called Green Bushes. From that point onwards, the art colony was her permanent home. Despite the influence of Hofmann and his acolytes, Mary was never an action painter, yet the artist was keenly interested in abstract expressionism and its philosophical underpinnings. Like many abstractionists, she was drawn to

Zen Buddhism and its ideas about unmediated experience; her favourite book was Eugen Herrigal's *Zen in the Art of Archery* (1948). In her Provincetown classes, Mary encouraged students to experiment with action painting. She taught a young Catholic priest who loved nothing better than to throw pints of paint at an enormous canvas. This priest was in good company. In August 1959, Mary reported that 'all the "action" painters are here gathered around [Hofmann] and buying houses or cottages in Provincetown'. Among them was the Chinese action painter Walasse Ting, whom Mary hosted that summer. During his visit, Ting made Mary's garden his studio. Each morning, he would lean enormous canvases against the bushes and proceed to cover them with several shades of black.

In November 1959, Mary swapped this exhilarating artistic ferment for the more sedate environs of her sisters' home in affluent Toorak. It was her third visit to Melbourne in 30 years and her first in a decade. To mark this visit, the Australian Galleries in Collingwood hosted a solo show entitled 'Men in Action' – a tongue-in-cheek allusion to action painting. 'No, I am not an Action Painter,' Mary explained, when the inevitable question was asked. 'These water colours are of *men in action*, fishermen gathering their nets, men clearing snow, making roads, in Provincetown.' The exhibition opening on 15 March was attended by over 200 people, including the Ambassador for Thailand and NGV director Eric Westbrook. Mary's old friend Maie Casey did the official honours.

Critics praised the show for its vitality and accessibility. Although the artworks retained figurative elements, they also contained the spontaneous energy and expressive style of abstract expressionism. '[T]he speed of life in America is in her paintings,' wrote Alan McCulloch in the *Herald* on 16 March. Mary's art was 'a shorthand, an elegant shorthand and one that anyone can read'. For Alan Warren in the *Sun*, the show revealed 'an artistic personality full of vigor, color and life'. All but one of the works sold, a rare achievement in an art market that still favoured conventional landscapes. This was all a far cry from Mary's experience in 1935, when her exhibition was damned in the press and the audience too scandalised to buy her art.

The rest of Mary's visit was focused on teaching. Public lectures at the NGV, a summer school for the Council of Adult Education, a workshop series for the Art Teachers' Association of Victoria. These events were attended by artists and critics, but also regular citizens with an interest in art. Mary's summer school attracted everyone from nuns and housewives to school students and businessmen. As in 1935, the artist was hailed as a masterful educator, a pedagogue no less vibrant than her artworks. She was – according to the *Sun* – 'vital, vivacious – effervescent almost ... a woman who obviously lives life at a fast pace'. In the *Herald*, the artist was declared 'one of the most vivid and eloquent personalities ever to grace an Australian lecture platform'.

Through her classes for the Art Teachers' Association, Mary influenced the next generation of art educators. One participant, Marion Scott, remembered the artist as 'an inspiring lecturer and unique art-teacher' with 'breadth of vision'. Mary was equally enthusiastic about this encounter with 'young and vital' teachers. 'I was able to see the forces that are shaping so much of the art of Australia both present and future!' she wrote.

According to conventional wisdom, Australia's introduction to abstract expressionism did not come until 1967. That year, the exhibition 'Two Decades of American Painting' brought contemporary masterpieces from New York's MoMA to Melbourne's NGV and Sydney's Art Gallery of New South Wales. This exhibition is remembered as a 'watershed moment', described by art historians Charles Green and Heather Barker in a 2013 article as 'one of the two major international exhibitions of contemporary art in the history of Australian art'.

But was the 1967 exhibition really the unprecedented introduction it has been made out to be? There is no doubt the 'Two Decades' show was influential; it helped inspire the 1968 exhibition 'The Field', a ground-breaking exhibition of contemporary Australian art. Yet, Mary was already lecturing and teaching in Melbourne to capacity crowds about the very same artists – Pollock, Hofmann, Willem de Kooning, Franz Kline, Rothko, Adolph Gottlieb, Robert Motherwell, Mark Tobey – seven years earlier. She could not show their works in the original, but she did have colour slides 'seldom reproduced or seen elsewhere'. These lectures were, in the words of friend Frances Derham, 'Melbourne's real introduction to the American Moderns'.

By the time Mary returned to Provincetown in April 1960, she was optimistic about the future of Australian art. As she wrote to Frances the following year, 'art life in Melbourne is so exciting now in so many ways and it is lovely to think'. After all these years, Mary was still an Australian citizen, and swore she would return to die at home. She was only 67 and still in fine fettle. There was no reason to think time was running out. Her Melbourne friends looked forward to a reunion in another few years.

They would, however, be disappointed. Mary never set foot in Australia again.

33

WHEN PERSIA MET POTUS
THE ECONOMIST, WASHINGTON DC, 1962

Persia was wearing a hat, of course. Of the 15 people in the room, hers was the only covered head. It was a narrow-brimmed affair, decorated with pale ribbon and a tulle veil. Black to match her simple black dress. Although hats were no longer an obligatory part of women's wardrobes, Persia had retained her passion for millinery. It was 19 July 1962, the height of a swampy Washington summer, and Persia had brought her hatted self to the White House. There, in the West Wing, the Consumer Advisory Council had just wrapped up their inaugural meeting with President John F Kennedy.

Before the meeting disbanded, they posed for a photograph to mark the occasion. The Council's eight men and six women clustered around an oval table strewn with papers and overflowing ashtrays. Kennedy stood at the centre, tanned in a dark suit. Persia was in the front row, with only Attorney General Walter Mondale between her and the president. The camera caught her looking at Kennedy, her face aglow with a warm maternal gaze. The president stood stiff, shoulders up around his ears, but Persia was slack-jawed with adoration. With a 19-year age gap, he could have been a favourite son.

He was in fact her Commander-in-Chief, and Persia was there to advise him on consumer economics. They were in the Fish Room, once President Theodore Roosevelt's office. The Australian suffragist Vida Goldstein had a private meeting with Roosevelt there in 1902. Now, exactly 60 years later, another stateside Australian had the ear of a president. Persia, a full Professor and Chair of Queens College Economics Department, was part of a new body established to bring consumer representation to the federal government for the first time.

Persia had come a long way from Nerrigundah. The idealistic country girl who believed economics could solve humanity's problems was now advisor to one of the world's most powerful men. That summer day in 1962 was the culmination of years of advocacy for an economic order that prioritised ordinary consumers. Yet the inaugural meeting of the Consumer Advisory Council was also bittersweet, as it represented a broken promise by the President. On the campaign trail in 1960, Kennedy made an election promise to create a federal Consumer Counsel. Persia was the obvious candidate for the job, boasting unparalleled experience after acting as the nation's first state Consumer Counsel in New York from 1955 to 1958. The economist was also a registered Democrat who corresponded with Jackie Kennedy and Eleanor Roosevelt. Indeed, in March 1961, the *Washington Post* reported that Professor Campbell was slated for the job. This Australian was on the verge of becoming the United States' first Consumer Counsel, a historic moment for women in politics and the consumer movement in general. With the appointment looking to be a foregone conclusion, Persia began receiving letters of congratulations.

The excitement proved premature. Once in office, Kennedy backtracked on the Consumer Counsel position, and established the Consumer Advisory Council as a compromise. Persia was still brought into the White House, but she was one of 14, a single voice on a larger body, instead of a private advisor. She'd come so close to power, but not as close as she wanted or expected.

For the next 18 months, until Kennedy's death, the Consumer Council met regularly with the president. They discussed everything from anti-trust laws to housing, medical care and trade policy. After a meeting in January 1963, the Council posed for the cameras a second time. Persia once again sported eye-catching headwear. This time, her face was shaded by a broad-brimmed black hat, decorated with an oval brooch. Around her neck was a single strand of pearls. Straight-backed in a tailored dress, Professor Campbell exuded a brisk confidence, her presence bringing to mind Hillary Rodham Clinton or Elizabeth Warren. This was a woman at ease in front of the cameras and in the company of powerful men.

Now in her mid-60s, Persia was approaching retirement age, but showed no signs of slowing down. On the contrary, she was busier and more powerful than ever. In 1962 and 1963, she wrote and hosted an educational television series called *You, the Consumer*. For the final episode in January 1963, Kennedy appeared to give his stamp of approval. 'I want to congratulate Persia Campbell ... and all who have participated in this series of programs on consumer economics,' the president said. 'Your series exemplifies the constructive use to which the great potential of television can be put, and I hope that this pioneering effort will be followed by other similar programs in other cities.'

Two years later, in 1965, Persia retired from academia and threw herself into international affairs. For the next decade, Persia 'almost lived at the United Nations'. She served as the official UN representative for the International Organization of Consumers Unions (a body Persia helped establish) and the International Federation of University Women. During these years, the economist was part of what historian Madeleine Herren calls a 'twilight zone' of female internationalists doing unacknowledged work outside formal diplomacy. Persia was a ubiquitous presence at UN headquarters, a master networker who excelled at the behind-the-scenes work of lobbying over cocktails and chance hallway encounters. As a retiree with long hours at her disposal, the economist haunted the corridors in hopes of catching delegates and officials between meetings. 'Persia was held in the highest regard and affection by all of us at the United Nations who had the pleasure of working with her,' one bureaucrat later recalled. Yet it was work that left little trace. Like many women on the international stage, Persia's influence made its mark in spaces of sociability – an ephemeral form of power whose lack of written evidence contributes to the broader marginalisation of women as historical actors.

Persia's mission was simple. She was determined to ensure the UN's development work did not lose sight of human wellbeing. At a time when rapid economic growth was entrenched as development orthodoxy, Persia continued to call for a more consumer-centred approach. 'It is not enough to get things produced,' she stressed, 'they must also be gotten into the hands of people who can use them.' Economic interventions may even do more harm than good. As early as 1953, she warned that 'rapid industrialisation might worsen rather than improve the social situation'. On occasion, her consumer advocacy had a demonstrable impact. In 1969, Persia proposed consumer amendments to the UN Declaration on Social Progress and Development that made their way into the final text.

At the same time, Persia queried the dogma of economic growth in the *International Development Review*. The *Review* was the publication of the Society for International Development, a Washington DC outfit that fashioned itself as an umbrella body for Western development professionals. From 1966, Persia wrote a regular column on UN development policy, becoming a key intermediary between high-level UN discussions and those working on the ground. The resulting articles were clinical in tone, but their partisan politics were clear. Persia repeatedly stressed the importance of 'social development' issues such as housing and food, and emphasised that increased GNP did not necessarily equate to improved social conditions. Over her tenure, the columns won what the *Review* described as a 'host of admiring and grateful readers'. The editor was 'dismayed' when, after three years, Persia's expanding workload compelled her to resign.

Persia also promoted consumer wellbeing via her work with the International Organization of Consumers Unions (IOCU). When the IOCU was founded in 1960, it was dominated by Western groups. Persia engineered a shift in focus to the developing world. During the 1960s, she spent summers in Africa, Southeast Asia and the Pacific, building local networks that resulted in a series of consumer education seminars in Tel Aviv, Jamaica and Singapore. The Jamaica seminar proved the catalyst for the Caribbean Consumer Committee; the Singapore event led to the establishment of an IOCU Asia–Pacific regional office.

In many respects, Persia personified the neo-colonialism of a self-assured white expert flying into ex-colonies to teach the locals how to live. Rather than learn about local economic practices, Persia spread the gospel of a consumer economics developed in New York. But at the same time, Persia's consumer efforts represented a feminist challenge to standard-issue economic development coming from the West. Unlike growth-oriented models focused on the male world of economic production, Persia's work ascribed value to female household labour and promoted the agency and leadership of women.

By the 1970s, the intellectual mood had caught up with Persia. The 'romance of economic development' was on the wane, and critiques of 'growthmanship' proliferated. In a much-cited article from 1972, British economist Dudley Seers asked 'Why do we confuse development with economic growth?' At the same time, 'social development' became a catchphrase of the UN's Second Development Decade. After decades of preaching a dissident message, Persia now found herself, aged 73, suddenly in step with the zeitgeist.

But she would not live to see what happened next. In March 1974, in the midst of her busy schedule, Persia suffered a fatal stroke at home in Queens. Colleagues around the world were bereft, and her children were inundated with letters of condolence. The International Council of Social Welfare feared that 'no one can take her place'.

In 2013, the year I first visited Persia's archive in New York, I spent a semester in Washington DC. At a bar one evening, I got chatting with a young man about my research. When I mentioned Persia's name, his face lit up. *Persia Campbell? Oh yeah, I know her.* He'd encountered her work in an economics degree. He spoke casually, like it was no big deal. As though it was self-evident Persia was a woman worth studying and remembering. She was part of his canon of economic thought.

The equivalent name recognition has never happened in Australia. Outside a tiny circle of feminist historians, Persia's name is met with blank stares. Over the past 15 years, I've never once encountered a non-historian who's heard of this Australian who shaped conversations at the White House and the United Nations.

It's not hard to explain this forgetting. Persia is a quadruple threat in terms of otherness: female, expatriate, Americanised and intellectual. Hardly the standard icon of settler Australia. Yet on a different view, Persia is an archetypal Australian. She was a passionate world traveller, a true creature of a nation defined by restlessness and mobility, home to 'the world's most enthusiastic travellers'. As a feminist committed to a welfarist economics, she also exemplified the progressive spirit of Australia's founding moment. Before ANZAC militarism became our 'birth of a nation' narrative, the Commonwealth was defined through what historian Clare Wright in a 2014 article calls the 'utopian ideal of a better, more peaceful, more just world based on progressive values'. You'd be hard-pressed to find a better poster child for this Australia than Persia Campbell, the reformer who dedicated her life to world peace and improved wellbeing for all humans.

What would it mean for us to tell the story of settler Australia through such an individual? How might it change things to see our nation embodied by a cosmopolitan humanitarian woman, instead of a bushranger, Gallipoli digger or male lifesaver?

If we understood our history in these terms, what possibilities for the future might emerge?

34

ISABEL'S ASHES

THE SWIMMER, SYDNEY, 2023

On a late summer morning, I catch the ferry from Circular Quay to Manly – Isabel Letham's old stomping ground and unceded Gayamagal Country. *Seven miles from Sydney, a thousand miles from care*, reads the script alongside the ferry terminal. Only yesterday the streets were turned into rivers by a torrential downpour, but this morning the heavens have cleared. The harbour city is today plucked straight from a tourism ad, a living stereotype of itself. Beneath a cloudless sky, beside an endless ocean, I grow drunk on blue. Tipsy on cobalt, absolutely legless on ultramarine. No thoughts, just sensation. Just sun-warmed flesh, fat with colour and light.

These days, the Manly Pool where Isabel taught is no longer, having been destroyed by a storm in 1974. Today, it's a harbour beach alongside the ferry terminal, a strip of gold lined with pines, one small section netted off from sharks.

After trotting across the Corso to the ocean beach, I head north along the water. It is a regular weekday, a Tuesday for workaday toil, but you wouldn't know it here. Everyone is clutching a surfboard or an ice-cream or both. There are accents from all over the world. Thongs, sunburnt shoulders, damp towels draped around necks.

At the beach's northern end, where the sand runs into cliff, the land lurches steeply upwards. Manly falls away behind me. Suddenly, the streets are quiet, full of brick bungalows baking in the sun. Within a block, the tourist mecca has become white-bread suburbia.

At the crest of the hill, Freshwater reveals itself. To an outside eye, it looks little changed from Isabel's youth. Just a cluster of houses around a swathe of beach, with enough remaining bushland to feel a world away from the city. No busy boardwalk like Manly or Bondi; no surf shops or smoothie bars. Instead the beach backs on to the original dunes, which gives way to an empty park. On the headland, I recreate a black-and-white photograph from the early 1900s. The two pictures are almost identical. More buildings now, but the shape of the landscape is the same. The waves have not noted the passing of a mere hundred years.

Across the sand is Freshwater Pool, Isabel's training ground. It's still the official headquarters of the Freshwater Amateur Swimming Club, which holds races every Saturday over summer. From here, at the beach's northern tip, you can see all the way back to Manly. Locals bake on the concrete deck, lizards in speedos, while a few heads bob up and down the lanes. Waves kiss the rocks, just metres away. Everything is gilded in the early afternoon light, sweet with the honey of settler amnesia. You can almost believe nothing bad ever happened here.

The unheated water sobers me up. Even in February, it is cold enough to send me scurrying into a brisk freestyle, arms whirling to generate heat. I only manage a few laps before retreating to my sun-warmed towel. As I shiver myself dry, I think of Isabel teaching in those waters, hour after hour, in all weather. Did she too get cold, or did her body adapt, turning fish-like, becoming a part of the landscape?

The whole scene is marked with Isabel's footprints. Freshwater was her home, her workplace, her playground. It's where she began and ended her life. But she's curiously absent from the official memory of this place. On the headland above the pool, there's a bronze statue of Duke Kahanamoku, arms outstretched aboard a surfboard. The plaque explains that Kahanamoku 'popularised surfboarding in Australia when he demonstrated his immense skills at Freshwater Beach'. Around him is a commemorative park, the ground dotted with mosaics honouring other champion surfers: Pam Burridge, Shane Bevan, Damien Hardman, Pauline Menczer. Isabel is not mentioned. Down at the surf club, there's a government plaque noting that Kahanamoku '[d]emonstrated surfing here'. Again, nothing about the woman who surfed alongside him. It's like she never even existed.

    But she's still here, quite literally in fact. In 1995, her ashes were scattered off Freshwater Beach. Surfers paddled out and threw her physical remains into the Pacific. Perhaps some of the ashes made it all the way to San Francisco. Perhaps the dissolved remnants are still circulating in this patch of surf, roiling around with the swell, gifting Isabel an afterlife of endless rides to the shore. Perhaps I even inhaled a microscopic fleck or two during my swim.

ENDINGS

The lawyer
After retiring for the second time in 1965, May Lahey remained in Los Angeles. Her former clerk Jeane Dole cared for May in her retirement, dropping by twice each day. For May's 85th birthday, Dole organised a spectacular party. On that occasion, Dole described May as 'the kind of person who will let you tell her all about something and then you later find out that she wrote the book'. May died in a local nursing home in 1984, aged 96.

The decorator
Rose Cumming died in New York City in 1968, a loss described as the 'end of an era in the decorative arts'. Afterwards, Rose's sister Eileen took over the decorating business, which she ran (alongside Ronald Grimaldi) until her death in 1982. In 2005, Dessin Fournir Collections acquired the Rose Cumming fabric and wall covering line. Today, Rose's great-niece Sarah Cumming Cecil runs Rose Cumming Design in Portland, Maine.

The swimmer
Isabel Letham lived with her mother until the latter died in 1954, and thereafter remained at the Freshwater family home. She continued to surf into her 70s and in 1993 was inducted into the Australian Surfing Hall of Fame. The swimmer lived until the ripe old age of 95, passing away in 1995 at Rayward Lodge nursing home.

The writer
After leaving Australia in 1928, Cottrell did not return until 1954. That year, she and her husband came home to take over the family station. While in Queensland, they adopted an 11-year-old called Wayne. When the Cottrells returned to Miami in 1956, Wayne went with them. Tragically, Dorothy died of a heart attack soon after, in June 1957. She was only 54. The next year, her widow and adoptive son made a permanent return to Queensland.

The artist
After returning to Provincetown in 1960, Mary Cecil Allen died suddenly in 1962, aged 68. 'Australia has lost one of its most brilliant, intelligent artists and art thinkers,' wrote Arnold Shore in *The Age*. 'How we loved her and she us!' Mary's friends organised a retrospective exhibition at the Lyceum Club. In 1963 the annual Mary Cecil Allen Memorial Lecture was established to honour her commitment to art education.

The pianist
Vera Bradford remained in Melbourne and continued playing for the ABC into the 1960s. In 1968, she established the Frankston Music Society and Orchestra and in 1980 was the subject of an ABC TV documentary. In her 90s, she moved into the Tanderra Lodge nursing home in Camberwell, where she performed for fellow residents. She died in 2004, just short of her hundredth birthday.

The economist
Persia Campbell kept working until the end, dying of a fatal stroke in March 1974, a few days short of her 76th birthday. After the *New York Times* published a eulogy, tributes poured forth from Buenos Aires, Auckland, Geneva, London and Washington DC.

The health guru
In Perth, Alice Caporn continued teaching American 'food science'. One of her students was Dorothea Snook, a woman who ended up as Perth's pre-eminent naturopath and practised into the 1990s. Alice remained a walking advertisement for her regime until the last. She'd long boasted that she'd 'live to 100'. As it turned out, she almost made it. She died in 1969, aged 93.

The dentist
After returning to Melbourne in 1947, Dorothy Waugh worked as a Collins Street dentist until the late 1960s. She retired to Queenscliff, on the western edge of Melbourne's Port Phillip Bay. Dorothy died in 1983, aged 89.

The nurse
After marrying Sidney Nolan in 1948, Cynthia Reed accompanied the artist on his travels and developed a new career as a travel writer. She published five works of travelogue, including *Open Negative* (1967) – an account of travelling in the United States between 1959 and 1961. Following years of ill health, she died by suicide in a London hotel in 1976.

NOTES

Introduction: Light years ahead
1. 'I can't describe': 'Impressions of New York: Miss Allen's Impressions', *Argus* (Melbourne), 9 December 1927, 18.
2. 'extraordinarily stimulating': 'The American Scene: Miss Mary Allen Returns', *Argus* (Melbourne), 20 July 1935, 24.
2. 'unfortunate addiction to modernism': 'Modern Art – Another View', *Age*, 23 August 1935, 10.
6. 'Australia is still': 'Women in the Antipodes', *Sydney Morning Herald*, 8 December 1921, 5.
7. 'matriarchate': Helen Jerome, *The Secret of Woman*, New York: Boni and Liveright, 1923, 62, 67–68. See also 'Women Should Tell Australia's Story to Woman-Ruled US', *Argus* (Melbourne), 17 October 1944, 7; Theresa Moore to mother, 27 September 1949 & 22 November 1950, box 3, Papers of Theresa Moore, c.1940–1988, MS ACC02.093, National Library of Australia, Canberra.
7. 'I shall never forget': Kate Jennings, 'Everywhere and Nowhere', *National Library Magazine*, December 2010, 24.
8. 'realise what we are missing': Theresa Moore to mother, 2 December 1950, box 3, Papers of Theresa Moore.

Chapter 1: Seeking fame and fortune in America
This chapter draws on material in Shirley Lahey, *The Laheys: Pioneers, Settlers and Sawmillers*, Taringa, Qld: Shirley Lahey, 2003.
13. 'mocked her habit': 'A Canungra girl was a US judge', *Sun* (Sydney), 2 May 1943, 2.
13. 'But now she steels herself': 'Girl in America', *Brisbane Courier*, 26 July 1911, 17.
15. 'bullocky': 'Women Can Excel at Law', *Mercury* (Hobart), 29 April 1947, 10.
16. 'to seek fame and fortune in America': 'Girl in America'.
18. 'like a package': 'A Career that Began with a Whipping', *Los Angeles Times*, 13 June 1973, 14.
20. first woman admitted: 'Called to the Bar', *Brisbane Courier*, 4 October 1929, 24.
22. 'What wonderful people Americans are': 'Girl in America'.

Chapter 2: The vocation of glamour

This chapter draws on the Rose Cumming, Russell L Cecil and affiliated families photographs and papers, 1870s–2012, PR 393, New York Historical Society; Rose Cumming, 'A Door Always Open', in *The Finest Rooms by America's Great Decorators*, Katharine Tweed (ed.), New York: Viking, 1964, 43–53; Adam Lewis, *The Great Lady Decorators: the women who defined interior design, 1870–1955*, New York: Rizzoli, 2009; Jeffrey Simpson, *Rose Cumming: Design Inspiration*, New York: Rizzoli, 2012.

27 'I'm perfectly useless': Cumming, 'A Door Always Open', 44.
28 'She was like Coco Chanel': Thomas Britt quoted in Simpson, *Rose Cumming*, 21.
30 'wild to get away': Eileen Cecil quoted in 'Rose Cumming Chintzes – Honoring the Past', *New York Times Magazine*, 28 September 1980.
30 'greatest love': Cumming, 'A Door Always Open', 44.
31 'When I was a girl': 'A Fabulous New York Home', *Sunday Herald* (Sydney), 26 July 1953, 21.
35 'Miss Rose Cumming is considered': 'Australian Women Abroad', *Sunday Times* (Perth), 5 June 1921.

Chapter 3: Freshwater mermaid does Hollywood

This chapter draws on material in the Papers of Isabel Letham, 1860–1995, Warringah Local Studies Collection, Dee Why Library, Sydney; Yves Rees, 'Isabel Ramsay Letham (1899–1995)', *Australian Dictionary of Biography*, National Centre of Biography, Australian National University, published online 2019, <adb.anu.edu.au/biography/letham-isabel-ramsay-27062>; and Phil Jarratt, *That Summer at Boomerang*, Melbourne: Hardie Grant Books, 2014.

Unless otherwise indicated, quotations come from Isabel Letham interviewed by Roslyn Cahill, 1986, Letham Papers.

38 'Yes, this is my first visit': 'Australian Surf Champion takes a Dip at Waikiki', *Honolulu Star-Bulletin*, 12 September 1918, 2.
40 'Freshwater mermaid': 'A Sydney Sea-Gull: Athletic Girl Who Rides the Waves at 15 Miles an Hour', *Sunday Times* (Sydney), 18 August 1918, 13.
40 'surf queen': Ed Moriarty, 'Diana of the Waves: She Gained Fame as Surf Queen in Home of Great Swimmers', *Los Angeles Record*, 14 October 1919.
40 'If Honolulu is a sample': 'Australian Champion Surf-Board Rider is Charmed with Honolulu', *Honolulu Star-Bulletin*, 14 September 1918, 4.
41 Jay's epistles: Mike Jay to Isabel Letham, 15 February 1919, Letham Papers.
48 'young Diana of the waves': Ed Moriarty, 'Diana of the Waves'.

Chapter 4 Decorator to the stars

This chapter draws on the Rose Cumming, Russell L Cecil and affiliated families photographs and papers, 1870s–2012, PR 393, New York Historical Society; Rose Cumming, 'A Door Always Open', in *The Finest Rooms by America's Great Decorators*, Katharine Tweed (ed.), New York: Viking,

1964, 43–53; Adam Lewis, *The Great Lady Decorators: the women who defined interior design, 1870–1955*, New York: Rizzoli, 2009; Jeffrey Simpson, *Rose Cumming: Design Inspiration*, New York: Rizzoli, 2012.
50 'absolute necessity': 'How Girls Have Made Money', *Boston Globe*, 18 March 1923, 41.
50 'statuesque beauty': *Daily News* (New York), 26 Oct 1923, 21.
51 'I always felt Dorothy': Joanne Creveling quoted in Simpson, *Rose Cumming*, 94.
52 'radiant': *Daily News* (New York), 27 September 1923, 13.
53 Peggy Guggenheim rented: Angelica Zander Rudenstine, 'Chronology,' *Getty Research Journal*, no. 9 (2017):1–25.
53 'Venetian opulence': 'Color Rhythm', undated magazine feature, folder 26, box 1, Cumming Papers.
54 'strict Christian conduct': 'DeMille Tries to Hold Human Nature in Check for 7 Years', *Variety*, 15 June 1927, 5.
55 'ever-present military bearing': handwritten caption, folder 28, box 1, Cumming Papers.
56 'makes every woman look beautiful': Cumming, 'A Door Always Open', 51.
56 'narrow old brownstone': Rose Cumming, 'An Old Brownstone Building Transformed', *Arts & Decoration*, May 1928, 60.
57 'within an inch of their lives': Cumming, 'A Door Always Open', 44.
57 'cows browse': Rose Cumming quoted in Lewis, *The Great Lady Decorators*, 136.

Chapter 6: Getting modern with natation

This chapter draws on material in the Papers of Isabel Letham, 1860–1995, Warringah Local Studies Collection, Dee Why Library, Sydney; Yves Rees, 'Isabel Ramsay Letham (1899–1995)', *Australian Dictionary of Biography*, National Centre of Biography, Australian National University, published online 2019, <adb.anu.edu.au/biography/letham-isabel-ramsay-27062>; and Phil Jarratt, *That Summer at Boomerang*, Melbourne: Hardie Grant Books, 2014.

Unless otherwise specified, quotations come from Isabel Letham interviewed by Roslyn Cahill, March 1986, Letham Papers.

67 'very capable teacher': Isabel Letham reference from Clara Roseby, Principal of Kambala, Rose Bay, 23 August 1918, Letham Papers.
69 'Pageant of Mermaids': 'Girl Swimmers Participate in Water Pageant', *Oakland Tribune*, 28 July 1923, 10.
71 '[Isabel] herself is an example': 'Miss Letham's Methods', undated news clipping, Letham Papers.
73 'one of the foremost swimming instructors': *San Francisco Examiner*, June 1926, Letham Papers.
74 'enable women to live more abundantly': Marie Hicks Healy, 'Why a City Club?' 1, no. 2 *Women's City Club Magazine of San Francisco* (1927):5.

Chapter 7: A new comet in fiction

This chapter draws upon materials in the Dorothy Cottrell Archive, no. 178, James Cook University, Toowoomba – especially an unpublished biography: Barbara Ross, 'Prepared for the journey: a life of the Australian writer Dorothy Cottrell', DC/1/10; the Papers of Dorothy Cottrell (Cottrell Papers), 1929–1970, MS 6085, National Library of Australia, Canberra; and the Ularunda and the Elmina Stations Collection (UES Collection), 1877–1955, Deposit 14, Noel Butlin Archives Centre, Australian National University, Canberra.

Unless otherwise indicated, quotations are from Barbara Ross, 'Prepared for the journey: a life of the Australian writer Dorothy Cottrell'.

76 'Glad to publish': Telegram to Mrs WM Cottrell, 16 April 1927, box 2, folder added 6/7/81, Cottrell Papers.
77 'abnormally successful first effort': EC Fletcher to George Story, 19 April 1927, 14/3/12, UES Collection.
78 'nearly died of joy': Dorothy Cottrell to Mary Gilmore, 17 April 1927, quoted in Ross, 149.
80 'unnecessary duplicity': EC Fletcher to George Story, 16 February 1923, 14/3/12, UES Collection.
80 'if they choose to make a tradgy [sic]': Dorothy Cottrell to Lavinia Fletcher, 10 July 1923, quoted in Ross, 116–17.
81 'Dossie's book': EC Fletcher to Edwin, 7 April 1929, 14/3/13, UES Collection.
81 'shaking with fright': Dorothy Cottrell quoted in Ross, 136–37.
81 literary 'genius': Mary Gilmore, 'Dorothy Cottrell: Australia's New Writer', *Sydney Morning Herald*, 27 October 1928, 13.
82 'from the back of beyond': Barton W Currie, 'Editorial', *Ladies' Home Journal*, December 1927.
82 'make a heap of money': EC Fletcher to George Story, 20 June 1927, 14/3/12, UES Collection.
82 'sensational rise to fame': 'Sydney Girl's Sensational Rise to Fame', *Smith's Weekly* (Sydney), 23 July 1927, 1.
84 'iniquitous taxation': EC Fletcher to George Story, 4 December 1927, 13/3/12, UES Collection.
84 'awfully keen': Dorothy Cottrell to Mary Gilmore, quoted in Ross, 183.
84 'mere fact of geographical distance': Eric Mills case file, 1936, Case No: 36145/006–05, Immigration Arrival Investigation Case Files, RG 85, National Archives and Records Administration, San Francisco.
84 'quota restrictions': Anne Rees, '"Treated Like Chinamen": United States immigration restriction and white British subjects', *Journal of Global History* 14, no. 2 (2019):239–60.
86 'stand up in the great world': Mary Gilmore, 'Dorothy Cottrell and Her Books', *Sydney Mail*, 7 November 1928, 17.
86 Dorothy was the thief: Ross, 165–70.

Chapter 8: A city of dreams

This chapter draws on material from Anne Rees, 'Mary Cecil Allen: Modernism and Modernity in Melbourne, 1935–1960', *emaj* no. 5 (2010):1–36; Eileen Chanin & Steven Miller, *Awakening: Four Lives in Art*, Adelaide: Wakefield Press, 2015; the Mary Cecil Allen Papers at the Archives of American Art, Smithsonian Institute, Washington DC; the Frances Derham Papers at the University of Melbourne Archives; and the Allen Family Papers, MS 9320, State Library of Victoria.

87   'It is a wonderful experience': 'Impressions of New York: Miss Allen's Impressions', *Argus* (Melbourne), 9 December 1927, 18.
87   'More than anywhere else': An Artist Sees New York', *Herald* (Melbourne), 14 January 1928, 17.
89   'virile and compelling': 'Miss Mary Allen in New York', *Australasian* (Melbourne), 2 March 1929, 17.
90   'how we students': 'Personal Notes on Mary Cecil Allen', Frances Derham Papers, 3.
90   'nourishment for the minds': untitled news clipping, folder 3, Mary Cecil Allen Papers.
90   'an apostle of art': 'Program of the 1963 Mary Cecil Allen Memorial Lecture', Frances Derham Papers.
91   'supreme mastery': 'Miss Mary Allen's Guide Lecture', *Age* (Melbourne), 6 September 1926, 14.
91   'create nothing but monsters': Notes for a Lecture on Modern Art, Box 1/5, Allen Family Papers.
92   'the modern manner': 'Australian Woman Painter Exhibits in New York', *Daily Standard* (Brisbane), 7 May 1930, 2.
93   'strong and silent': Alfred Brookes quoted in 'Personal Notes on Mary Cecil Allen', Frances Derham Papers, 10.
95   'because she felt restricted': Alfred Brookes quoted in 'Personal Notes on Mary Cecil Allen', 9.
95   'city of dreams': 'The American Scene: Miss Mary Allen Returns', *Argus* (Melbourne), 20 July 1935, 24.
96   'the life of a single woman': Allen quoted in 'Biography of Mary Cecil Allen', Frances Derham Papers, 49.

Chapter 9: We do not teach ladies

This chapter draws on material in the Papers of Isabel Letham, 1860–1995, Warringah Local Studies Collection, Dee Why Library, Sydney; the *Women's City Club Magazine of San Francisco*, 1927–29; Yves Rees, 'Isabel Ramsay Letham (1899–1995)', *Australian Dictionary of Biography*, National Centre of Biography, Australian National University, published online 2019, <adb.anu.edu.au/biography/letham-isabel-ramsay-27062>.
Unless otherwise indicated, quotations come from Isabel Letham interviewed by Roslyn Cahill, March 1986, Letham Papers.

99 'opportunities were high for women': Isabel Letham interviewed by Terry Eldridge, 1980, Letham Papers.
100 'medicinal value': *Women's City Club Magazine of San Francisco* 1, no. 3 (1927):45; and 1 no. 5 (1927):35.
100 One of Isabel's success stories: Alma C Bennett, 'Swim?', *Women's City Club Magazine of San Francisco* 3, no. 5 (1929):20.
101 'swimming hostess': 'Swimming Notes', *Women's City Club Magazine of San Francisco* 2, no. 4 (1928):29.
104 'efficient and loyal service': Women's City Club of San Francisco to Isabel Letham, 22 March 1929, Letham Papers.

Chapter 10: An atmosphere for excellence

This chapter draws on Ivor Morgan, 'A Memoir of Vera Bradford, Master Pianist', *History Australia* 3, no. 2 (2006):53.1–53.7. The letters and interviews quoted in this chapter come from the personal papers of Vera Bradford, private collection.

Unless otherwise indicated, quotations come from an 'Interview with Vera Bradford', 25 September 1988, contained in the personal papers. The interviewer and place are not recorded.

110 'music centre of the world': 'Merle Robertson Back Home', *Mail* (Adelaide), 27 April 1935, 15.
110 'best teachers': 'Effort to Help Pianist', *News* (Adelaide), 3 September 1936, 11.
115 'a brilliant future': Ivy Crane Wilson to Vera Bradford, Los Angeles, 29 March 1933.

Chapter 11: Our only woman judge

This chapter draws on material in Shirley Lahey, *The Laheys: Pioneers, Settlers and Sawmillers*, Taringa, Qld: Shirley Lahey, 2003.

119 'I have not found anyone': 'Municipal Judges Named', *Los Angeles Times*, 26 December 1928, 17.
119 'credit to her sex': Alma Whitaker, 'Successful Career in Law', *Los Angeles Times*, 13 March 1933, 20.
119 'most generally popular appointment': 'Our Only Woman Judge', *Herald* (Melbourne), 4 October 1934, 25.
120 'widely and favorably known': 'Municipal Judges Named'.
120 'possess intellects of a fine caliber': 'Another Woman Judge', *Los Angeles Evening-Post Record*, 4 January 1929, 14.
120 'Our Only Woman Judge': *Herald* (Melbourne), 4 October 1934, 25.
120 'one of few women judges': *Chronicle* (Adelaide), 12 Aril 1934, 28.
125 'almost starved': 'Career that Began with a Whipping', *Los Angeles Times*, 13 June 1973, 14.
125 Judge Stephens expressed regret: 'Cupid's Loss to be Court's Gain', *Los Angeles Times*, 27 December 1928, 20.

127 'perfectly nice, normal young woman': Alma Whitaker, 'Successful Career in Law', *Los Angeles Times*, 13 March 1933, 20.
127 'Though sometimes classed as "half a woman"': 'New Woman Judge Keen, Modest', *Los Angeles Evening Post-Record*, 9 March 1929, 2.

Chapter 13: The religion of progress

This chapter draws on Allis R Wolfe, *Persia Campbell: Portrait of a Consumer Activist*, Mount Vernon: NY: Consumers Union Foundation, 1981; and the Persia Campbell Papers, Consumer Union Archive, New York.

136 'Most of us who remained': 'Intellectual History', c. 1953, folder 9, box 1, series II, Campbell Papers.
136 'economic matters': 'Intellectual History'.
137 'ethical questions': RF Irvine, *The Place of the Social Sciences in the Modern University*, Sydney: Angus & Robertson, 1914, 21.
137 'I have never met': Helena Swanwick, *I Have Been Young*, London: Victor Gollanz, 1935, 358.
138 'Miss Campbell reads a lot': Lilian Knowles report, 16 October 1923, Persia Campbell file, LSE Archives.
138 'already a legend': Letter of condolence from Allan GB Fisher, Middlesex, 22 March 1974, folder 9, box 1, series VI, Campbell Papers.
138 'The standards of living': *Sydney Morning Herald*, 8 March 1929, 5.
139 'politically a Radical': Graham Wallas to William Beveridge, 19 April 1926, Persia Campbell file, LSE Archives.
140 'I have worked closely': Letter of condolence from Charles S Ascher, 3 March 1974, folder 9, box 1, series VI, Campbell Papers.

Chapter 14: Boom to bust

This chapter draws upon materials in the Dorothy Cottrell Archive, no. 178, James Cook University, Toowoomba; the Papers of Dorothy Cottrell (Cottrell Papers), 1929–1970, MS 6085, National Library of Australia (NLA), Canberra; and the Ularunda and the Elmina Stations Collection (UES Collection), 1877–1955, Deposit 14, Noel Butlin Archives Centre, Australian National University, Canberra; Walter Cottrell interviewed by Barbara Ross, 1979, ORAL TRC 986, NLA.

Unless otherwise specified, quotes are from Dorothy Cottrell's correspondence in Box 2, Folder added 6.7.81, Cottrell Papers.

145 'grandiose ideas': Walter Cottrell, 'Some explanation of the bald outline of our movements in the States', n.d., Folder added 22.10.84, Cottrell Papers.
145 'the world seemed teeming': Walter Cottrell, 'Some explanation of the bald outline of our movements in the States', n.d., Folder added 22.10.84, Cottrell Papers.
145 '[o]ne of the books': Elsie Ford, 'Book Chats', *Galt Herald* (Galt, CA), 14 June 1929, 5.
145 'Australian background': 'Singing Gold', *News and Observer* (Raleigh, NC), 13 January 1929, 34.

145 bestseller of 1929: *Lake Elsinore Valley Sun-Tribune*, 10 April 1930, 5.
146 'spent a staggering amount': Dorothy Cottrell to family, 2 April 1930, Box 2, Folder added 6.7.81, Cottrell Papers.
146 'a great novel of Australian life': *Los Angeles Times*, 14 June 1930, 18.
146 'epic quality': *Daily Times* (Davenport, Iowa), 17 May 1930, 3.
146 'tremendous in its scope': *Philadelphia Inquirer*, 21 June 1930, 10.
147 'well-known writers': *San Francisco Examiner*, 16 February 1930, 52.
147 'the biggest advertisement': 'Cripple's Pluck', *Evening News* (Sydney), 31 October 1929, 14.
148 'sturdy pioneer race': 'Tharlane', *Oakland Tribune*, 8 June 1930, 80.
150 'handyman, bell boy': Walter Cottrell, Chronology of Dorothy Cottrell's life, n.d., Folder added 22.10.84, Cottrell Papers.
151 'That was why': Walter Cottrell, 'Some explanation of the bald outline of our movements in the States', n.d., Folder added 22.10.84, Cottrell Papers.

Chapter 15: People over profits
This chapter draws on Anne Rees, 'Lessons from Australia: Persia Campbell and the International Afterlives of Federation-Era Welfarism', *Australian Historical Studies* 48, no. 4 (2017):519–35; Allis R Wolfe, *Persia Campbell: Portrait of a Consumer Activist*, Mount Vernon: NY: Consumers Union Foundation, 1981; and the Persia Campbell Papers, Consumer Union Archive, New York.
152 stopped at number 175: Persia Campbell, 'Neva as a Person', memorial service speech, 9 December 1958, folder 58, box 4, series V, Campbell Papers.
155 'Australia will always be': 'Australian Research Worker Marries American', *News* (Adelaide), 30 October 1931, 4.
156 'consumer-minded': 'Intellectual History', c.1953, folder 9, box 1, series II, Campbell Papers.
157 'it would have been impossible': Wolfe, *Persia Campbell*, 10.
157 'some study of Australian experiences': 'Fixing a Minimum Wage', 1933, folder 49, box 4, series V, Campbell Papers.

Chapter 16: Why should we hate each other?
This chapter draws on Ivor Morgan, 'A Memoir of Vera Bradford, Master Pianist', *History Australia* 3, no. 2 (2006):53.1–53.7.
The letters and interviews quoted come from the personal papers of Vera Bradford, private collection.
162 'cultural internationalism': Akira Iriye, *Cultural Internationalism and World Order*, Baltimore & London: Johns Hopkins University Press, 1997.
163 'As these young men and women': Rockefeller quoted in Liping Bu, 'Cultural Understanding and World Peace: The Role of Private Institutions in the Interwar Years', *Peace & Change* 24, no. 2 (1999):157.
164 'The most fantastic six years': Interview with Vera Bradford, 25 September 1988.

164 'deported the jazz band': Deirdre O'Connell, 'Contesting White Australia: Black American Jazz Musicians in a White Man's Country', *Australian Historical Studies* 47, no. 2 (2016):241–58.
166 'big things' ahead: Esther Strote to Vera Bradford, Chicago, c. January 1934.

Chapter 17: A philosophy of nakedness
This chapter draws on Yves Rees, 'The fight for the white stuff: the ongoing machinations of the milk wars', *Griffith Review 78: A Matter of Taste*, November 2022, 115–26; Greta Puls, *Gut Instinct: Mrs Snook's Diet*, Greta Puls, 2017.
168 'full of vitamins': 'Nudism, with Reservations, is Found in DC Resort Area', *Evening Star* (Washington DC), 2 July 1933, 17.
170 'successful living': 'Larger Life League Principles Are Explained in Statement', *Evening Star* (Washington DC), 13 August 1933, 16.
170 'indecent exposure': 'Advocate of Nudism Resigns as Views Arouse League Row', *Evening Star* (Washington DC), 31 July 1933, 2.
171 'In every movement': 'Pioneer in Nudism Discovers Her Theories Misunderstood', *Evening Star* (Washington DC), 1 August 1933, 17.
171 'philosophy of nakedness': Alice M Caporn, *Sex Intelligence*, Boston: Radiant Health Publishers, 1934, 25; 'Nudist Camp Idea Fails for Washington', *Daily News* (New York), 2 August 1933, 36.
171 'It seems some people': 'Pioneer in Nudism Discovers Her Theories Misunderstood'.
172 'It is not difficult': Alice M. Caporn, *Awake, Christian Scientists!*, Boston: Four Seas Company, 1921, 313.
173 'redemption narrative': 'De Profundis', *Modern Living* 1, no. 6 (June 1939):7.
174 'the ideal climate': 'Founding a Colony in British Honduras', *Chronicle* (Adelaide), 3 February 1938, 54.
174 'pernicious perversion': Caporn, *Sex Intelligence*, 26.

Chapter 18: From colonial girl to fierce feminist
176 'holding a meeting': 'Women Citizens', *Argus* (Melbourne), 15 August 1934, 15.
177 'it seems to me that Australia': Franklin quoted in Jill Roe, *Stella Miles Franklin: A Biography*, Sydney: Fourth Estate, 2008, 263.
178 '135 women dentists': Hannah Forsyth, 'Reconsidering Women's Role in the Professionalisation of the Economy: Evidence from the Australian Census, 1881–1947', *Australian Economic History Review* 59, no. 1 (2019):69.
179 'The number of women dentists': Forsyth, 'Reconsidering Women's Role', 70.
181 'one of only three women dentists': 'University Life in America', *Age*, 18 July 1934, 13.

183 'The fact that I was a woman': 'Women Citizens', *Argus* (Melbourne), 15 August 1934, 15.

Chapter 19: The Yanks are on the right track

This chapter draws on ME McGuire, *Cynthia Nolan: A Biography*, Melbourne: Melbourne Books, 2016; Cynthia Reed, *Lucky Alphonse*, Melbourne: Reed & Harris, 1944; Cynthia Nolan, *A Bride for St Thomas*, London: Constable, 1970.

The correspondence cited in this chapter is from Papers of John and Sunday Reed, box 2, file 8, MS 13186, State Library of Victoria, Melbourne.

185 'Inside the laboratory': The following scene and quote are taken from Reed, *Lucky Alphonse*, 24, 27.
186 'Johns Hopkins wouldn't admit Cynthia': Cynthia Reed to John and Sunday Reed, Los Angeles and Chicago, summer 1935.
188 'from moral to professional authority': Angela Woollacott, 'From Moral to Professional Authority: Secularism, Social Work, and Middle-Class Women's Self-Construction in World War I Britain', *Journal of Women's History*, 10, no. 2 (1998):85–111.
189 'to go to America': Midwives & Nurses Miss Stella Pines' Activities, 1930–1935, A1928, 660/9, National Archives of Australia, Canberra.
193 'its greyness, its bloodlessness': Reed, *Lucky Alphonse*, 60.

Chapter 20: An unfortunate addiction to modernism

This chapter draws on material from Anne Rees, 'Mary Cecil Allen: Modernism and Modernity in Melbourne, 1935–1960', *emaj* no. 5 (2010): 1–36; Eileen Chanin & Steven Miller, *Awakening: Four Lives in Art*, Adelaide: Wakefield Press, 2015; the Mary Cecil Allen Papers at the Archives of American Art, Smithsonian Institute, Washington DC; the Frances Derham Papers at the University of Melbourne Archives; and the Allen Family Papers, MS 9320, State Library of Victoria.

Unless otherwise indicated, Frances Derham quotations come from a copy of her 'Biography of Mary Cecil Allen', in the Frances Derham papers.

197 'immense crowd': 'Personal and Social – Melbourne', *The Home*, 1 October 1935, 8.
198 'chief topic of conversation': 'Melbourne Chatter', *Bulletin*, 28 August 1935, 43.
199 'very naïve': 'Modern Art Defended', *Age* (Melbourne), 26 August 1935, 11.
200 'bizarre and mocking': Untitled news clipping, c. 1935, folder 3, Mary Cecil Allen Papers.
200 'the dead hand of European decadence': Lionel Lindsay, *Addled Art*, Sydney and London: Angus & Robertson, 1942, x, 16.
201 'Yankee-trained woman': Untitled news clipping, c.1935, folder 3, Mary Cecil Allen Papers.

202 'the most American thing in America': Roosevelt cited in Kenneth G Hance, 'The Contemporary Lecture Platform', *Quarterly Journal of Speech* 30, no. 1 (1944):41.
202 'appeared grotesque and without meaning': 'Modern Art: Distortion Defended', *Argus* (Melbourne), 27 August 1935, 10.
202 'Modern drawing does not': 'Miss Mary Allen Talks on Art', *Argus* (Melbourne), 13 August 1935, 10.
202 'perhaps the finest painting': 'Miss Mary Allen Talks on Art'.
203 'direct link to Europe': Yves Rees, 'Friday essay: the Melbourne bookshop that ignited Australian modernism', *The Conversation*, 22 May 2020.
203 'first time that Cubism': 'Melbourne Today', *Advertiser* (Adelaide), 17 October 1935, 8.
203 'It was surprising': 'Women Painters Entertain Miss Allen', *Argus* (Melbourne), 10 October 1935, 15.
204 'Clever women in America': 'Australian Pictures for New York', *Advertiser* (Adelaide), 17 June 1936, 8.
204 'the American institution': 'School of Painting to be Established at Gisborne', unknown newspaper, 10 January 1936, folder 3, Mary Cecil Allen Papers.
204 'kind of priestess': Frances Burke in 'Personal Notes on Mary Cecil Allen', Frances Derham Papers.
205 'so large that many people': 'Art in Schools: National Gallery Lecture', *Argus* (Melbourne), 9 July 1936, 13.
205 'magical light and colour': 'Australian Pictures for New York', *Advertiser* (Adelaide), 17 June 1936, 8.

Chapter 21: The pernicious virus of American hooey
This chapter draws on Yves Rees, 'The fight for the white stuff: the ongoing machinations of the milk wars', *Griffith Review 78: A Matter of Taste*, November 2022, 115–26; Greta Puls, *Gut Instinct: Mrs Snook's Diet*, Greta Puls, 2017.
Unless otherwise specified, quotes are from Alice Caporn's lifestyle magazine, *Modern Living* 1: no. 6 (June 1939).
207 'recharging the human dynamo': 'Nudism, with Reservations, is Found in DC Resort Area', *Evening Star* (Washington DC), 24 July 1933, 17.
207 'famous American Authority': *Sunday Times* (Perth), 7 August 1938, 17.
207 'advanced American views': 'Dietetics and Sunbathing', *West Australian* (Perth), 10 November 1937, 7.
210 'Everyone who is really modern': 'American Diet: Fruits and Salads Prominent', *West Australian* (Perth), 9 December 1938, 7.
210 'the application of dietetics': 'Dietetics and Sunbathing'.
211 'Why Cow's Milk': Alice M Caporn, 'Healthy Children Will Combat Disease Naturally', *Mail* (Adelaide), 25 December 1937, 4.
211 'in chemical analysis': WH Taylor, 'Cow's Milk as Food', *West Australian* (Perth), 16 May 1939, 15.

212 'key to proper nutrition': 'Dietetic Bunk Exposed', *Sunday Times* (Perth), 4 June 1939, 2.
212 'Australians are sterile': 'Fantastic Food Fads Further Exposed', *Sunday Times* (Perth), 11 June 1939, 3.
213 'milk faddist': 'Dietetic Bunk Exposed'.
213 'recognised health authorities': 'Fantastic Food Fads Further Exposed'.
214 'We congratulate America': 'Uncle Sam leads with salads', *Daily News* (Perth), 16 January 1950, 8.

Chapter 22: Hard to take after America
This chapter draws on ME McGuire, *Cynthia Nolan: A Biography*, Melbourne: Melbourne Books, 2016; Cynthia Reed, *Lucky Alphonse*, Melbourne: Reed & Harris, 1944; Cynthia Nolan, *A Bride for St Thomas*, London: Constable, 1970.
The correspondence cited is from Papers of John and Sunday Reed, box 2, file 8, MS 13186, State Library of Victoria, Melbourne.
The Theresa Moore quotes are taken from diary and letters in box 3, Papers of Theresa Moore, c.1940–1988, MS ACC02.093, National Library of Australia, Canberra.
215 'You are not in America now': Nolan, *A Bride for St Thomas*, 33, 60. See also Reed, *Lucky Alphonse*, 55–56, 124.
215 'Life here seemed peaceful': Reed, *Lucky Alphonse*, 40.
215 'After America how small': Nolan, *A Bride for St Thomas*, 38. See also Reed, *Lucky Alphonse*, 60.
220 'I was going to the United States': Board transcript, 23 August 1927, 55383/028A, RG 85, National Archives and Records Administration, Washington DC.

Chapter 23: Making Australia modern
This chapter draws on Ivor Morgan, 'A Memoir of Vera Bradford, Master Pianist', *History Australia* 3, no. 2 (2006):53.1–53.7. The letters and interviews quoted below come from the personal papers of Vera Bradford, private collection.
223 'longing for [her]': Besta Brown to Vera Bradford, Chicago, 7 January 1935.
223 'future plans': Alexander Raab to Vera Bradford, Berkeley, CA, 26 November 1936.
224 'she told the Hubers': Lucile Huber to Vera Bradford, Chicago, 18 November 1938.
225 'complete control in piano-playing': 'Pianist Discusses New Technique', *Argus* (Melbourne), 30 August 1945, 10; 'The "Weight Technique" and "Finger Technique"', *Sydney Morning Herald*, 13 May 1944, 6.
225 'excluded from the school choir': Author interview with Pam Usher, Melbourne, December 2019.
226 'payment was "ridiculous"': 'Pianist's Break with ABC', *Argus* (Melbourne), 16 September 1944, 5.

226 'Vera had "been paid"': 'Manager defends ABC policy', *Mercury* (Hobart), 18 September 1944, 7.
227 'Margaret Holden made her debut': 'Teacher sees student on way to fame', *Argus* (Melbourne), 10 February 1950, 12.
227 'The most fantastic six years': Interview with Vera Bradford, 25 September 1988.

Chapter 24: Lessons from Australia
This chapter draws on Anne Rees, 'Lessons from Australia: Persia Campbell and the International Afterlives of Federation-Era Welfarism', *Australian Historical Studies* 48, no. 4 (2017):519–35; Allis R Wolfe, *Persia Campbell: Portrait of a Consumer Activist*, Mount Vernon, NY: Consumers Union Foundation, 1981; the Persia Campbell Papers, Consumer Union Archive, New York.

229 'People who are able': *Investigation of Concentration of Economic Power: Letter Transmitting a Preliminary Report*, Washington DC: US Government Printing Office, 1939, 1.
229 'At 2.40 pm': *Verbatim Record of the Proceedings of the Temporary National Economic Committee*, vol. 3, Washington DC: Bureau of National Affairs, 1939, 295–303.
231 'established professionally': Persia Campbell to Sydney Campbell, n.d., folder 5, box 1, series VI, Campbell Papers.
231 'male chauvinism': Wolfe, *Persia Campbell*, 68.
231 'disgraceful situation': Queens colleague to Persia Campbell, 8 April 1954, folder 11, box 1, series VI, Campbell Papers.
232 'imaginative and inquiring mind': Persia Campbell to George School, 23 December 1950, folder 5, box 1, series VI, Campbell Papers.
233 'beneath their professional considerations': Persia Campbell to Dr Davis, 20 September 1945, folder 9, box 1, series VI, Campbell Papers.
233 'minimum wage system': 'Why a 75-cent minimum wage?' c.1949, folder 60, box 4, series V, Campbell Papers.
234 'a long experience in Australia': 'Project outline', folder 8, box 1, series III, Campbell Papers.
234 'deeply interested': Persia Campbell to Elbridge Sibley, 12 January 1949, folder 8, box 1, series III, Campbell Papers.
235 'one of the leaders of FAO work': James Howard to Ernst Schwarz, 7 December 1950, folder 2, box 1, series IV, Campbell Papers.
235 'raised levels of living': Persia Campbell to James Howard, 31 October 1949, folder 1, box 1, series IV, Campbell Papers.
235 'the consumer point of view': Persia Campbell, 'Consumer Politics in Action: A Case Study of Consumer Representation, State of New York 1955–58', folder 69, box 5, series V, Campbell Papers.
236 'She was before her time': Wolfe, *Persia Campbell*, 22.

Chapter 25: Anti-English and pro-American
This chapter draws on ME McGuire, *Cynthia Nolan: A Biography*, Melbourne: Melbourne Books, 2016; Cynthia Reed, *Lucky Alphonse*, Melbourne: Reed & Harris, 1944; Cynthia Nolan, *A Bride for St Thomas*, London: Constable, 1970.

238 'It was satisfying': Reed, *Lucky Alphonse*, 214–19.
239 'she reported her marriage': 'Miss Cynthia Reed Married in USA', *Herald* (Melbourne), 4 December 1940, 13.
240 'shot out of the sky': McGuire, *Cynthia Nolan*, 127.
241 'anti-English and pro-American': McGuire, *Cynthia Nolan*, 140.

Chapter 26: Selling Australia
This chapter draws on the Rose Cumming, Russell L Cecil and affiliated families photographs and papers, 1870s–2012, PR 393, New York Historical Society; Rose Cumming, 'A Door Always Open', in *The Finest Rooms By America's Great Decorators*, Katharine Tweed (ed.), New York: Viking, 1964, 43–53; Adam Lewis, *The Great Lady Decorators: the women who defined interior design, 1870–1955*, New York: Rizzoli, 2009; Jeffrey Simpson, *Rose Cumming: Design Inspiration*, New York: Rizzoli, 2012. The discussion of the Australian Society of New York and its Anzac Day dinner draws on Yves Rees, 'Gumtree Skyscrapers and Takeaway Flat Whites: Anzac in the United States', *Journal of Australian Studies* 47, no. 4 (2023):736–51.

244 'From Australia I send': 'Comrades in Arms', *Age*, 27 April 1942, 3.
245 'pioneering days': Anzac Dinner program, 24 April 1942, folder 1, box 1, Cumming Papers.
246 'Australians don't really seek': Shirley Duncan interviewed by Yves Rees, 10 June 2014.
248 'a shopkeeper at heart': Cumming, 'A Door Always Open', 44.
248 'The Depression almost smashed Rose': Eileen Cumming quoted in Simpson, *Rose Cumming*, 115.
249 'quite a figure in New York': Mr Cantor obituary, folder 24, box 1, Cumming Papers.
249 'a live landmark': Eleanor Stark, 'The Passing of an Era', *Home Furnishing Daily*, 1 April 1968.
249 'vaccination party': *Tribune* (Sydney), 29 April 1947, 4.
250 'old, worn and outmoded': 'Bernadotte Seeks to Void His NY Lease', *Sun* (Baltimore), 28 May 1947, 3.
250 'People from all over': Karl Freund, 'The Brownstone House of Rose Cumming', folder 15, box 1, Cumming Papers.

Chapter 27: A better world for women
This chapter draws on material in Shirley Lahey, *The Laheys: Pioneers, Settlers and Sawmillers*, Taringa, Qld: Shirley Lahey, 2003.

Unless otherwise specified, quotes are drawn from this source.
251 'You agree that a woman's place': 'Recent Broadcasts', *Equal Rights* 31, no. 4 (1945):12.
254 'analytical, logical and inductive': John Steven McGroarty, *History of Los Angeles County*, Chicago & New York: American Historical Society, 1923, 178–79.
255 Harlow appeared in Judge Lahey's courtroom: 'Jean Harlow in Probate Court', *Cornell Daily Sun* 53, no. 44, 15 November 1932.
257 'She represents woman': 'Judge May Lahey Honoured by Two Clubs at Luncheon', *Los Angeles Times*, 28 February 1947, 15.
257 'Everybody knows that women': 'Women can Excel at Law', *Mercury* (Hobart), 29 April 1947, 10.
259 'Ariel felt it would': Justice Mildred L Lillie, oral history interview, 1989–1990, LA Law Library, Los Angeles.

Chapter 29: US women have more freedom
265 '[T]he work is detailed': 'Woman Dentist will Teach New Methods', *Daily News* (Perth), 10 March 1947, 4.
265 When Vice-Chancellor GA Currie: 'Lecturer Resigns', *West Australian* (Perth), 22 April 1947, 6.
266 'She is not a pioneer': 'Lecturer Resigns', *West Australian* (Perth), 22 April 1947, 6.
267 'US Women Have More Freedom': 'US Women Have More Freedom than Ours', *Daily News* (Perth), 13 March 1948, 8.
267 'respectable radicals': Marian Quartly and Judith Smart, *Respectable Radicals: A history of the National Council of Women Australia, 1896–2006*, Melbourne: Monash University Publishing, 2015.
267 'comparative ease of life': 'The Life of Melbourne', *Argus* (Melbourne), 12 March 1948, 7.
270 the only person in Australia: 'Melbourne Woman Makes Plastic Eyes', *Argus* (Melbourne), 14 December 1948, 2; 'New Artificial Eye that Moves in Coordination', *West Australian* (Perth), 18 March 1950, 15.

Chapter 30: The greatest aquatic show
This chapter draws on material in the Papers of Isabel Letham, 1860–1995, Warringah Local Studies Collection, Dee Why Library, Sydney; Yves Rees, 'Isabel Ramsay Letham (1899–1995)', *Australian Dictionary of Biography*, National Centre of Biography, Australian National University, published online 2019, <adb.anu.edu.au/biography/letham-isabel-ramsay-27062>; and Phil Jarratt, *That Summer at Boomerang*, Melbourne: Hardie Grant Books, 2014.
272 Isabel was at the vanguard: Bill Myatt, 'Miss Surfboard Girl of 1915', *Everybody's Magazine*, 1963; Margaret Bardwell to Isabel Letham, 26 December 1962, Letham Papers.

273 'You can do anything': Isabel Letham interviewed by Roslyn Cahill, 1986, Letham Papers.
274 'illegally and by fraud': Statement by US Attorney Frank J Hennessy and Report of Fraudulent Naturalization by Perry Ellis (US Vice Consul, Sydney), June 1944, Letham Papers.
275 'systematised and scientific': Isabel Letham, 'Swimming', *North West Champion* (Moree), 24 October 1935, 1.
276 'was always a doer': Paulene Turner, 'Queen of the king tide catches her last wave', *Sydney Morning Herald*, 13 February 1986, 12.

Chapter 31: How to wear a wheelchair

This chapter draws upon materials in the Dorothy Cottrell Archive, no. 178, James Cook University, Toowoomba; the Papers of Dorothy Cottrell (Cottrell Papers), 1929–1970, MS 6085, National Library of Australia, Canberra; and the Ularunda and the Elmina Stations Collection (UES Collection), 1877–1955, Deposit 14, Noel Butlin Archives Centre, Australian National University, Canberra.

Unless otherwise specified, quotations are from Dorothy Cottrell's correspondence to family in box 2, folder added 6/7/81, Cottrell Papers.

281 'The person who wishes to write': Dorothy Cottrell, undated notes on writing, c.1950s, DC/4/22, Cottrell Archive.
283 'I would not trade my life': Dorothy Cottrell, undated typed note, DC/4/22, Cottrell Archive.
283 'trashy writer': Barbara Ross, 'Encounters with Dorothy Cottrell', DC/1/6, Cottrell Archive.

Chapter 32: The tyranny of American abstraction

This chapter draws on material from Anne Rees, 'Mary Cecil Allen: Modernism and Modernity in Melbourne, 1935–1960', *emaj* no. 5 (2010):1–36; the Mary Cecil Allen Papers at the Archives of American Art, Smithsonian Institute, Washington DC; the Frances Derham Papers at the University of Melbourne Archives; and the Allen Family Papers, MS9320, State Library of Victoria.

284 'to champion': *Antipodeans: 4th – 15th Aug. 1959*, Melbourne: Spotlight Press, 1959.
286 'Austerica': Geoffrey Serle, 'Godzone: Austerica Unlimited?' *Meanjin Quarterly*, no. 4 (1967):237–50.
286 'see the beauty': 'Biography of Mary Cecil Allen', Frances Derham Papers, 69.
287 'the father of "Action" painting': Mary Cecil Allen, 'Notes on Hans Hofmann's Teaching', *CAS Broadsheet*, May 1962, 4–7.
287 'the Mecca and market place': Mary Cecil Allen to Frances Derham, Provincetown, 11 September 1959, Frances Derham Papers.
288 'all the "action" painters are here': Mary Cecil Allen to Frances Derham, Provincetown, 7 August 1959, Frances Derham Papers.

288 'No, I am not an Action Painter': Allen quoted in 'Biography of Mary Cecil Allen', Frances Derham Papers, 66.
289 'an inspiring lecturer': Marion Scott, *Viewpoints and Vanishing Points: the Mary Cecil Allen Memorial Lecture 1964*, Melbourne: Art Teachers' Association of Victoria, 1964.
289 'young and vital': Allen quoted in 'Biography of Mary Cecil Allen', Frances Derham Papers, 66–67.
290 'seldom reproduced': Mary Cecil Allen to Frances Derham, Provincetown, 7 August 1959, Frances Derham Papers.
290 'Melbourne's real introduction': 'Biography of Mary Cecil Allen', Frances Derham Papers, 67.

Chapter 33: When Persia met POTUS
This chapter draws on Anne Rees, 'Lessons from Australia: Persia Campbell and the International Afterlives of Federation-Era Welfarism', *Australian Historical Studies* 48, no. 4 (2017):519–35; Allis R Wolfe, *Persia Campbell: Portrait of a Consumer Activist*, Mount Vernon, NY: Consumers Union Foundation, 1981; the Persia Campbell Papers, Consumer Union Archive, New York.
293 'almost lived at the United Nations': Colston Warne eulogy, 23 March 1974, folder of biographical sketches, box 1, series VI, Campbell Papers.
294 'Persia was held in the highest regard': Condolence letter from NGO Section of UN, 6 March 1974, folder 9, box 1, series VI, Campbell Papers.
294 'It is not enough': 'FAO Sixth Session', 1951, folder 20, box 2, series V, Campbell Papers.
294 'rapid industrialisation': Pan Pacific Women's Association *Bulletin*, November 1953, folder 299, box 36, series IV, Campbell Papers.
295 'romance of economic development': David Engerman, 'The Romance of Economic Development and New Histories of the Cold War', *Diplomatic History* 28, no. 1 (2004):23–54.
296 'no one can take her place': Condolence letter from International Council of Social Welfare, 6 March 1974, folder 9, box 1, series VI, Campbell Papers.

SELECT BIBLIOGRAPHY

Akami, Tomoko. *Internationalizing the Pacific: The United States, Japan and the Institute of Pacific Relations in War and Peace, 1919–1945*. London & New York: Routledge, 2002.
Allen, Mary Cecil. *The Mirror of the Passing World*. New York: WW Norton & Co, 1928.
—— *Painters of the Modern Mind*. New York: WW Norton & Co, 1929.
Alomes, Stephen. *When London Calls: The Expatriation of Australian Creative Artists to London*. Cambridge: Cambridge University Press, 1999.
Arrowsmith, Robyn. 'Australian WWII War Brides in America: Their Memories and Experiences'. PhD thesis, Macquarie University, 2010.
Bell, Philip, & Roger Bell. *Implicated: The United States in Australia*. Melbourne: Oxford University Press, 1993.
—— (eds). *Americanization and Australia*. Sydney: UNSW Press, 1998.
Bennett, Bruce, & Anne Pender. *From a Distant Shore: Australian Writers in Britain, 1820–2012*. Melbourne: Monash University Publishing, 2013.
Bier, Lisa. *Fighting the Current: The Rise of American Women's Swimming, 1870–1926*. London: McFarland & Co, 2011.
Bongiorno, Frank. 'In this world and the next: political modernity and unorthodox religion in Australia, 1880–1930', *ACH: The Journal of the History of Culture in Australia*, nos 24–25 (2006).
Boyd, Robin. *The Australian Ugliness*. Melbourne: Cheshire, 1960.
Bridge, Carl, Robert Crawford, & David Dunstan (eds). *Australians in Britain: The Twentieth-Century Experience*. Melbourne: Monash University ePress, 2009.
Britain, Ian. *Once an Australian: Journeys with Barry Humphries, Clive James, Germaine Greer and Robert Hughes*. Melbourne: Oxford University Press, 1997.
Bryant, Mary Nell. 'English Language Publication and the British Traditional Market Agreement'. *Library Quarterly* 49, no. 4 (1979):371–98.
Bu, Liping. 'Cultural Understanding and World Peace: The Roles of Private Institutions in the Interwar Years'. *Peace & Change* 24, no. 2 (1999):148–71.
Burdett, Basil. 'Modern Art in Melbourne', *Art in Australia*, no. 73, 1938, 17.
Butler, Rex, & ADS Donaldson. 'Against Provincialism: Australian–American Connections, 1900–2000'. *Journal of Australian Studies* 36, no. 3 (2012):291–307.
Campbell, Persia. *Consumer Representation in the New Deal*. New York: Columbia University Press, 1940.

—— *The Consumer Interest: A Study in Consumer Economics.* New York: Harper & Bros, 1949.
Caporn, Alice. *Awake, Christian Scientists!.* Boston: Four Seas Company, 1921.
—— *Sex Intelligence.* Boston: Radiant Health Publishers, 1934.
Carter, David, & Roger Osborne. *Australian Books and Authors in the American Marketplace, 1840s–1940s.* Sydney: Sydney University Press, 2018.
Chanin, Eileen, & Steven Miller. *Awakenings: Four Lives in Art.* Adelaide: Wakefield Press, 2015.
Collins, Diane. *Hollywood Down Under: Australians at the Movies, 1896 to the Present.* Sydney: Angus & Robertson, 1987.
Conor, Liz. *The Spectacular Modern Woman: Feminine Visibility in the 1920s.* Bloomington & Indianapolis: Indiana University Press, 2004.
Cottrell, Dorothy. *The Singing Gold.* Boston & New York: Houghton Mifflin Company, 1929.
—— *Tharlane.* Boston & New York: Houghton Mifflin Company, 1930.
Cumming, Rose. 'A Door Always Open'. In *The Finest Rooms by America's Great Decorators*, Katharine Tweed (ed.), 43–53. New York: Viking, 1964.
Curran, James, & Stuart Ward. *The Unknown Nation: Australia After Empire.* Melbourne: Melbourne University Press, 2010.
Dawood, Azra. 'Building "brotherhood": John D Rockefeller Jr and the foundations of the New York City's International Student House'. *Journal of Architecture*, 24, no. 7 (2019):898–924.
Deacon, Desley. 'Cosmopolitans at Home: Judith Anderson and the American Aspirations of JC Williamson Stock Company Members, 1897–1918'. In *Impact of the Modern: Vernacular Modernities in Australia, 1870s–1960s*, Robert Dixon & Veronica Kelly (eds), 202–22. Sydney: Sydney University Press, 2008.
—— 'Location! Location! Location! Mind Maps and Theatrical Circuits in Australian Transnational History'. *History Australia* 5, no. 3 (2008):81.1–81.16.
—— 'From Victorian Accomplishment to Modern Profession: Elocution Takes Judith Anderson, Sylvia Bremer and Dorothy Cumming to Hollywood, 1912–1918', *Australasian Journal of Victorian Studies* 18, no. 1 (2013):40–65.
—— *Judith Anderson: Australian star, first lady of the American stage.* Melbourne: Kerr Publishing, 2019.
Dixon, Robert, & Veronica Kelly (eds). *Impact of the Modern: Vernacular Modernities in Australia, 1870s–1960s.* Sydney: Sydney University Press, 2008.
Drachman, Virginia C. *Sisters in Law: Women Lawyers in Modern American History.* Cambridge, MA: Harvard University Press, 1998.
Elliot, Sumner Locke. *Fairyland.* Melbourne: Text, 2013.
Engerman, David. 'The Romance of Economic Development and New Histories of the Cold War'. *Diplomatic History* 28, no. 1 (2004):23–54.

Esau, Erika. *Images of the Pacific Rim: Australia and California, 1850–1935*. Sydney: Power Publications, 2011.

Fitzgerald, Tanya, Diane Kirkby, & Caroline Jordan. 'Lines of Exchange: Australian and New Zealand Women on Carnegie and Fulbright Programme Awards, c.1930s–1980s'. *History of Education* (2024):1–21.

Forsyth, Hannah. 'Reconsidering Women's Role in the Professionalisation of the Economy: Evidence from the Australian Census, 1881–1947'. *Australian Economic History Review* 59, no. 1 (2019):55–79.

Green, Charles, & Heather Barker. 'The Watershed: Two Decades of American Painting at the National Gallery of Victoria'. *National Gallery of Victoria Art Journal* 1, no. 50 (2011):64–77.

Hallett, Hilary A. *Go West, Young Women! The Rise of Early Hollywood*. Berkeley: University of California Press, 2013.

Hance, Kenneth G. 'The Contemporary Lecture Platform'. *Quarterly Journal of Speech* 30, no. 1 (1944):41–47.

Hayball, Doris. *Strawberries in the Jam: Being Intimate Notes about Interesting People*. Melbourne: Sunsphere Press, 1940.

Herren, Madeleine. 'Gender and International Relations through the Lens of the League of Nations', in *Women, Diplomacy and International Politics since 1500*, Glenda Sluga and Carolyn James (eds), New York: Routledge, 2016.

Hughes, Robert. *The Art of Australia*. Ringwood, Vic: Penguin, 1970.

Iriye, Akira. *Cultural Internationalism and World Order*. Baltimore and London: Johns Hopkins University Press, 1997.

Irvine, RF. *The Place of the Social Sciences in the Modern University*. Sydney: Angus & Robertson, 1914.

Jarratt, Phil. *That Summer at Boomerang*. Melbourne: Hardie Grant Books, 2014.

Jenner, Dorothy Gordon. *Darlings, I've Had a Ball*. Sydney: Ure Smith, 1975.

Jerome, Helen. *The Secret of Woman*. New York: Boni and Liveright, 1923.

Kirkby, Diane. *Alice Henry: The Power of Pen and Voice*. Cambridge: Cambridge University Press, 1991.

Kramer, Paul A. 'Is the World Our Campus? International Students and US Global Power in the Long Twentieth Century'. *Diplomatic History* 33, no. 5 (2009):775–806.

Langmore, Diane. *Glittering Surfaces: A Life of Maie Casey*. Sydney: Allen & Unwin, 1977.

—— 'In Search of Maie Casey'. *Victorian Historical Journal*, 69, no. 1 (1998):4–13.

Lahey, Shirley. *The Laheys: Pioneer Settlers and Sawmillers*. Taringa, Qld: Shirley Lahey, 2003.

Lake, Marilyn. *Progressive New World: How Settler Colonialism and Transpacific Exchange Shaped American Reform*. Harvard: Harvard University Press, 2019.

Lake, Marilyn, & Henry Reynolds. *Drawing the Global Colour Line: White Men's Countries and the Question of Racial Equality*. Cambridge: Cambridge University Press, 2008.

Levy, Shawn. *The Castle on Sunset: Love, Fame, Death and Scandal at Hollywood's Chateau Marmont*. New York: Knopf Doubleday, 2020.
Lewis, Adam. *The Great Lady Decorators: the women who defined interior design, 1870–1955*. New York: Rizzoli, 2009.
Lindsay, Lionel. *Addled Art*. Sydney & London: Angus and Robertson, 1942.
Luckins, Tanja. 'Historiographic Foodways: A Survey of Food and Drink Histories in Australia'. *History Compass* 11, no. 8 (2013):551–60.
Macdonald, Angela. 'Hollywood Bound: A History of Australians in Hollywood to 1970'. PhD thesis, University of Sydney, 2001.
MacDonald, JS. *Australian Painting Desiderata*. Melbourne: Lothian Publishing Company, 1958.
Magarey, Susan, & Kerrie Round. *Roma the First: A Biography of Dame Roma Mitchell*. Kent Town, SA: Wakefield Press, 2007.
Martin, Sylvia. 'Between the Covers'. *Lesbians on the Loose* 8, no. 8 (1997):34.
Matthews, Jill Julius. *Dance Hall & Picture Palace: Sydney's Romance with Modernity*. Sydney: Currency Press, 2005.
May, Bridget. 'Nancy Vincent McClelland (1877–1959): Professionalizing Interior Decoration in the Early Twentieth Century'. *Journal of Design History* 21, no. 1 (2008):59–74.
Meaney, Neville. 'Britishness and Australia: Some Reflections'. *Journal of Imperial and Commonwealth History* 31, no. 2 (2003):121–35.
Megaw, M Ruth. 'Undiplomatic Channels: Australian Representation in the United States, 1918–39'. *Australian Historical Studies* 15, no. 60 (1973):610–30.
McGuire, ME. *Cynthia Nolan: A Biography*. Melbourne: Melbourne Books, 2016.
McWilliams, Carey. *Southern California: An Island on the Land*. Salt Lake City: Peregrine Smith Books, 1973.
Mickenberg, Julia L. *American Girls in Red Russia: Chasing the Soviet Dream*. Chicago: University of Chicago Press, 2017.
Modjeska, Drusilla. *Exiles at Home: Australian Women Writers, 1925–1945*. London: Sirius, 1981.
Morgan, Ivor. 'A Memoir of Vera Bradford, Master Pianist'. *History Australia* 3, no. 2 (2006):53.1–53.7.
Morton, Peter. *Lusting for London: Australian Expatriate Writers at the Hub of Empire, 1870–1950*. New York: Palgrave Macmillan, 2011.
Ninham, Sally. *A Cohort of Pioneers: Australian Postgraduate Students and American Postgraduate Degrees, 1949–1964*. Ballan, Vic: Connor Court Publishing, 2011.
Nolan, Cynthia. *Open Negative: An American Memoir*. London: Macmillan, 1967.
——*A Bride for St Thomas*. London: Constable, 1970.
O'Connell, Deirdre. 'Contesting White Australia: Black American Jazz Musicians in a White Man's Country'. *Australian Historical Studies* 47, no. 2 (2016):241–58.

Osborne, Roger. 'A National Interest in an International Market: The Circulation of Magazines in Australia during the 1920s'. *History Australia* 5, no. 3 (2008):75.1–75.16.

Owens, Larry. 'Patents, the "Frontiers" of American Invention and the Monopoly Committee of 1939: Anatomy of a Discourse'. *Technology and Culture* 32, no. 4 (1991):1076–93.

Paisley, Fiona. *Glamour in the Pacific: Cultural Internationalism and Race Politics in the Women's Pan-Pacific*. Honolulu: University of Hawai'i Press, 2009.

Pesman, Ros. *Duty Free: Australian Women Abroad*. Melbourne: Oxford University Press, 1996.

Pietsch, Tamson. 'Many Rhodes: Travelling Scholarships and Imperial Citizenship in the British Academic World, 1880–1940'. *History of Education* 40, no. 6 (2011):723–39.

—— 'Tools of the Trade: The Interwar Fight for Control of Dentistry in Australia', in *The First World War, the Universities and the Professions in Australia, 1914–1939*, Kate Darian-Smith & James Waghorne (eds), Melbourne: Melbourne University Press, 2019.

Puls, Greta. *Gut Instinct: Mrs Snook's Diet*. Greta Puls, 2017.

Putnis, Peter. 'International News Agencies, News-Flow, and the USA–Australia Relationship from the 1920s till the End of the Second World War'. *Media History* 18, no. 3–4 (2012):1–19.

Quartly, Marian, & Judith Smart. *Respectable Radicals: A history of the National Council of Women Australia, 1896–2006*. Melbourne: Monash University Publishing, 2015.

Reed, Cynthia. *Lucky Alphonse*. Melbourne: Reed & Harris, 1944.

Rees, Anne. 'Mary Cecil Allen: Modernism and Modernity in Melbourne, 1935–60'. *emaj*, no. 5 (2010):1–36

—— '"Australians Who Come over Here Are Apt to Consider Themselves Quite Large People": The Body and Australian Identity in Interwar London'. *Australian Historical Studies* 44, no. 3 (2013):405–22.

—— '"Bursting with New Ideas": Australian Women Professionals and American Study Tours, 1930–1960'. *History Australia* 13, no. 3 (2016):382–98.

—— 'Stepping through the Silver Screen: Australian Women Encounter America, 1930s–1950s'. *Journeys* 17, no. 2 (2016):49–73.

—— 'Travelling to Tomorrow: Australian Women in the United States, 1910–1960'. PhD thesis, Australian National University, 2016.

—— '"A Season in Hell": Australian Women, Modernity and the Hustle of New York, 1910–1960'. *Pacific Historical Review* 86, no. 4 (2017):632–60.

—— 'Lessons from Australia: Persia Campbell and the International Afterlives of Federation-Era Welfarism', *Australian Historical Studies* 48, no. 4 (2017):519–35.

—— 'Rebel Handmaidens: Transpacific Histories and the Limits of Transnationalism' in Anna Clark, Alecia Simmonds & Anne Rees (eds),

Transnationalism, Nationalism and Australian History. London: Palgrave, 2017.

—— 'Reading Australian Modernity: Unsettled Settlers and Cultures of Mobility'. *History Compass* 15, no. 11 (2017):1–13.

—— 'A War of Card Indexes: From Political Economy to Economic Science', in *The First World War, the Universities and the Professions in Australia, 1914–1939*, Kate Darian-Smith & James Waghorne (eds), Melbourne: Melbourne University Press, 2019.

—— '"Treated Like Chinamen": United States Immigration Restriction and White British Subjects'. *Journal of Global History* 14, no. 2 (2019):239–60.

Rees, Yves. 'From Socialists to Technocrats: The Depoliticisation of Australian Economics', *Australian Historical Studies* 50, no. 4 (2019):463–82.

—— 'Making Waves across the Pacific: Women, Radio Broadcasting and Australian–U.S. Connections'. *Feminist Media Histories* 5, no. 3 (2019):85–113.

—— 'Moving on Up: Economic Opportunism, Trans-Pacific Mobility and Non-Elite Internationalism'. *Journal of Australian Studies* 43, no. 4 (2019):464–78.

—— 'Sojourns: A New Category of Female Mobility', *Gender & History* 31, no. 3 (2019):717–36.

—— 'Friday essay: the Melbourne bookshop that ignited Australian modernism'. *The Conversation*, 22 May 2020.

—— 'The fight for the white stuff: the ongoing machinations of the milk wars'. *Griffith Review 78: A Matter of Taste*, November 2022, 115–26.

—— 'Gumtree Skyscrapers and Takeaway Flat Whites: Anzac in the United States'. *Journal of Australian Studies* 47, no. 4 (2023):736–51.

Riseman, Noah. *Transgender Australia: A History Since 1910*. Melbourne: Melbourne University Press, 2023.

Robinson, WW. *Lawyers of Los Angeles: A History of the Los Angeles Bar Association and of the Bar of Los Angeles County*. Los Angeles: Los Angeles Bar Association, 1959.

Roderick, Colin. *20 Australian Novelists*. Sydney & London: Angus & Robertson, 1947.

Roe, Jill. 'Australian Women in America, from Miles Franklin to Jill Ker Conway'. In *Approaching Australia: Papers from the Harvard Australian Studies Symposium*, Harold Bolitho & Chris Wallace-Crabbe (eds), 139–58. Cambridge, MA: Harvard University Committee on Australian Studies, 1998.

—— '"Testimonies from the Field": The Coming of Christian Science to Australia, c.1890–1910'. *Journal of Religious History* 22, no. 3 (1998):304–19.

—— *Stella Miles Franklin: A Biography*. London, New York, Sydney & Auckland: Fourth Estate, 2010.

Rosenberg, Emily S. *Spreading the American Dream: American Economic and Cultural Expansion*. New York: Hill & Wang, 1982.

—— 'Consuming Women: Images of "Americanization" in the American Century'. *Diplomatic History* 23, no. 3 (1999):479–97.
Rupp, Leila J, & Verta A. Taylor. *Survival in the Doldrums: The American Women's Rights Movement, 1945 to the 1960s*. New York: Oxford University Press, 1987.
Russell, R Lynette. *From Nightingale to Now: Nurse Education in Australia*. Sydney: WB Saunders, 1990.
Santich, Barbara. *What the Doctors Ordered: 150 Years of Dietary Advice in Australia*. Melbourne: Hyland House, 1995.
Scharf, Lois, & Joan M Jensen (eds). *Decades of Discontent: The Women's Movement, 1920–1940*. Westport, CT: Greenwood Press, 1983.
Scott, Anne Firor. *Natural Allies: Women's Associations in American History*. Urbana & Chicago: University of Illinois Press, 1993.
Seers, Dudley. 'What Are We Trying to Measure?', *Journal of Development Studies* 8, no. 3 (1972):21.
Serle, Geoffrey. 'Godzone: Austerica Unlimited?', *Meanjin Quarterly*, no. 4 (1967):237–50.
Shortis, Emma. *Our Exceptional Friend: Australia's fatal alliance with the United States*. Melbourne: Hardie Grant, 2021.
Simpson, Jeffrey. *Rose Cumming: Design Inspiration*. New York: Rizzoli, 2012.
Siracusa, Joseph M, & David G Coleman. *Australia Looks to America: Australian–American Relations since Pearl Harbor*. Claremont: Regina Books, 2006.
Smith, Bernard. *Australian Painting 1788–1960*. Melbourne: Oxford University Press, 1962.
Sobocinska, Agnieszka. *Visiting the Neighbours: Australians in Asia*. Sydney: NewSouth Publishing, 2014.
Stanner, WEH. *After the Dreaming: The Boyer Lectures 1968*. Sydney: ABC, 1969.
Steel, Frances. 'Lines Across the Sea: Trans-Pacific Passenger Shipping in the Age of Steam'. In *The Routledge History of Western Empires*, Robert Aldrich & Kirsten McKenzie (eds), 315–29. London & New York: Routledge, 2014.
—— '"The 'Missing Link'": Space, Race, and Transoceanic Ties in the Settler-Colonial Pacific'. *Transfers* 5, no. 3 (2015):49–67.
—— 'Re-Routing Empire? Steam-Age Circulations and the Making of an Anglo Pacific, c.1850–90'. *Australian Historical Studies* 46, no. 3 (2015):356–73.
Stephensen, PR. *Mental Rubbish from Overseas*. Sydney: Cultural Defence Committee, 1935.
Swanwick, Helena. *I Have Been Young*. London: Victor Gollanz, 1935.
Sydnor, Synthia. 'A History of Synchronized Swimming'. *Journal of Sport History* 25, no. 2 (1998):252–67.
Tate, Audrey. *Fair Comment: The Life of Pat Jarrett, 1911–1990*. Melbourne: Melbourne University Press, 1996.
Veit, Helen Zoe. *Modern Food, Moral Food: Self-Control, Science, and the Rise of Modern American Eating in the Early Twentieth Century*. Chapel Hill: University of North Carolina Press, 2013.

Wallace, Chris. 'I was more "dinkum" than had been anticipated': Noël Coward's 1940 Tour of Australia, 'Waving the Wartime Flag for Britain'. Modern British Studies Conference, University of Birmingham, 4 July 2019.

Wallace-Crabbe, Chris. 'Inspecting "The Schools"', *Observer*, 16 April 1960, 19.

Ward, Stuart. *Australia and the British Embrace: The Demise of the Imperial Ideal*. Melbourne: Melbourne University Press, 2001.

Waterhouse, Richard. *From Minstrel Show to Vaudeville: The Australian Popular Stage, 1788–1914*. Sydney: UNSW Press, 1990.

Weinbaum, Alys Eve et al. (eds). *The Modern Girl Around the World: Consumption, Modernity, and Globalization*. Durham & London: Duke University Press, 2008.

White, Richard. '"Americanization" and Popular Culture in Australia'. *Teaching History*, no. 12 (1978):3–21.

—— '"A Backwater Awash": The Australian Experience of Americanization'. *Theory, Culture & Society*, no. 3 (1983):108–22.

Wolfe, Allis R. *Persia Campbell: Portrait of a Consumer Activist*. Mount Vernon, NY: Consumers Union Foundation, 1981.

Woollacott, Angela. 'From Moral to Professional Authority: Secularism, Social Work, and Middle-Class Women's Self-Construction in World War I Britain'. *Journal of Women's History* 10, no. 2 (1998):85–111.

—— *To Try Her Fortune in London: Australian Women, Colonialism and Modernity*. New York: Oxford University Press, 2001.

—— 'Rose Quong Becomes Chinese: An Australian in London and New York'. *Australian Historical Studies* 38, no. 129 (2007):16–31.

—— *Race and the Modern Exotic: Three 'Australian' Women on Global Display*. Melbourne: Monash University Publishing, 2011.

Wright, Clare. '"A Splendid Object Lesson": A Transnational Perspective on the Birth of the Australian Nation'. *Journal of Women's History* 26, no. 4 (2014):12–36.

—— *You Daughters of Freedom: The Australians Who Won the Vote and Inspired the World*. Melbourne: Text, 2019.

ACKNOWLEDGMENTS

This book was researched and written on the stolen lands of First Peoples from around Turtle Island and the continent known as Australia. I pay my respects to Elders past and present and any First Peoples reading this book. I am grateful to walk on Country that you have tended for millennia. I pay especial respects to the Wurundjeri people of the Kulin Nation, on whose Country most of this book was written. Other parts were written on Gadigal land and Dharug land. A core tenet of this book is that Australia and the United States are twin settler nations, built on white supremacy, and linked by shared structures of colonial violence and racism. As a historian of these two nations, and a white settler, I am committed to working for justice for First Peoples and challenging colonial oppression on these continents and around the world. Always was, always will be. Free Palestine.

This book had its genesis back in 2008, when I stumbled upon a *Meanjin* article about Mary Cecil Allen in the stacks of the University of Melbourne's Baillieu Library. In the intervening sixteen years, I have accrued countless debts. Thank you to colleagues, friends and interlocutors at the ANU, where this project had its first iteration, especially Angela Woollacott, Desley Deacon, Carolyn Strange, Jill Matthews and Daniel McNamara. This early research was supported by an Australian Postgraduate Award and Endeavour Research Fellowship from the Australian federal government. Thank you to Glenda Sluga at the University of Sydney, for supporting my work on Persia Campbell and Australian economics. Thanks also to Sydney colleagues Tamson Pietsch, Anna Clark, Sophie Loy-Wilson and Alecia Simmonds. At La Trobe University, where I've worked since 2017, I've been blessed with likeminded colleagues who've been nothing but supportive over some tumultuous years. Thank you especially to Clare Wright, Kat Ellinghaus, Emma Robertson, Katie Holmes, Tim Minchin, Tim Jones, Nadia Rhook, Roland Burke, Ruth Gamble, Ruth Morgan, Nikita Vanderbyl, Claudia Haake, Jennifer Jones, Bernard Keo, Diane Kirkby, Nick Bisley, Quinn Eades, Matt Smith and Lauren Gawne.

This project has been supported by several institutions, including Varuna: The National Writers House, Georgetown University, the Australian Academy of the Humanities, and the Australian Historical Association. The ideas in this book have been developed through articles published in many peer-reviewed journals, including *Australian Historical Studies*, *History Australia*, *Gender & History*, *Journal of Australian Studies*, *Journal of Global History*, *Feminist Media Histories*, *Pacific Historical Review* and *History Compass*. I am enormously indebted to the editors and peer-reviewers of those journals, who volunteer endless hours of unpaid labour to the collective pursuit of building knowledge. Thank you for your (often invisible and unacknowledged) commitment to scholarship. Thanks also to *Griffith Review* and *Meanjin* for publishing early versions of some ideas presented here.

History making is a collective endeavour. This book is built on the work of countless historians who've gone before. Thank you especially to Marilyn Lake, Angela Woollacott, Clare Wright, Jill Matthews, Desley Deacon, Fiona Paisley and Ian Tyrrell. You're all intellectual giants and it's been an honour to know you and your work. This book is also the product of many years in libraries and archives, only a small fraction of which are named in the endnotes. To all the library staff and archivists who helped me along the way, across Australia, the United States and Britain – thank you for sharing your labour and expertise. A huge thank you also to Pam and Jim Usher, for welcoming me into your home and trusting me with the Vera Bradford archive.

Acknowledgments

I've had a crush on NewSouth Publishing for years. Since working together on this book, that crush has blossomed into a full-blown romance. It's been a career highlight to work with this team of kickass professionals, all with enormous brains and bigger hearts. Thank you especially to publisher Elspeth Menzies, project editor Paul O'Beirne, copyeditor Victoria Chance and publicist Kat Rajwar. You're the best in the biz.

To Clare Wright – beloved friend, colleague, podcast co-host, and comrade. Your fingerprints are all over this book. Thank you for inspiring me to stop imagining a thousand foes. To my literary agent Jacinta di Mase – thank you for believing in this book and helping it reach the biggest possible audience. Thanks to my Rees and Lansdowne families, who've always been superlative cheerleaders of my adventures in the archive. Especial thanks to my mother Robyn Lansdowne, whose brilliant mind has been a cherished source of intellectual companionship over the life of this project. You first taught me to think, and I treasure that we're still testing ideas with each other.

To my Naarm queer writing group – Sam Elkin, Jasper Peach, Jonathan Butler, Savannah Hollis, Jack Nicholls, Tim Loveday. Thank you for friendship, comradery, invaluable feedback, and the inspiration of your own writing. Thank you to the Hysterians – Alexandra Roginski, Alexis Bergantz and Sandro Antonello. We've been on this wild ride for over a decade, and we keep showing up for each other. You'll always be my hivemind for any and every history conundrum (though I continue to disagree with your taste in nineteenth-century men). Thanks also to my now defunct ECR writing group – Alexandra Roginski, Kyle Harvey, Alexis Bergantz, Ben Huf, James Keating, Kathryn Ticehurst, Sandro Antonello. To the Melbourne Frontrunners – thanks for the runs, coffee and community. To the Salty Slags and swim coach Jason Bryce – thanks for the companionship in cold-water madness. You're the best damn fun and I love being a bit bonkers with y'all.

Thank you to other friends who nourish my soul and keep me laughing, especially Kristine Ziwica (and Esme, Isla, Richard and Harry), Clancy Reid, Sam Elkin and Gemma Cafarella, Ben Huf, Sally Stuart, Clementine Ford, Louisa Lim, Reid Dearson, Beejay Silcox, Bram Presser, Eleanor Jackson, Cheryl Leavy, Simon Westcott, Anjali Nihalchand, Astrid Edwards, Liz Errol, Neela Janakiramanan, Frankie and Aude Yeats. To Zelda, Arabella and Delphi – thank you for joyful distraction. And biggest gratitude to Kristy Yeats, for the world-remaking gift of your spirit. Thank you for teaching me all the things you can't learn inside a book.

INDEX

Aboriginal
    Aboriginals Ordinance 86
    Gadigal 1
    Gayamagal 298
    Lee, Barbara Cherry 86
    Leigh, Cherie 86
    May 86
    Ngunnawal 31
    Noongar 265
    stockhands 280
    Wurundjeri i, ix, 111
    Yugambeh 15, 17
    Yuin 135
    see also First Nations
    see also Indigenous people
Adelaide, SA 121, 240
    Advertiser 202, 314
    Chronicle 120, 309, 312
    Mail 309, 314
    News 309, 311
Albany, WA 235
Allen, Ada 89
Allen, Beatrice 89
Allen, Edith Margaret 89
Allen, Harry 89
Anderson, Judith 29, 322
'Andrea', Dorothy Jenner 6, 10
Anglican 186
Anzac 296
    Anzacs and Americans 244, 326
    Day 244–45, 317
    Dinner 243–45, 247, 317
    gathering 247
Aquitania 1, 88
Arizona, USA 13, 20, 122, 261
Art Students League 92
Arts & Decoration 56, 306
Atkinson, Dr Everitt 212, 214

Atlantic, crossing the 1, 29, 88, 107, 110, 153, 240
Atyeo, Sam 190, 201, 240
Australian Federation of University Women 203
Australian Women Board Riders Association 45
Australian Women's National Club 203
Australian Women's Weekly 86, 269

Ballet, water 271–74
Banfield, EJ 80
Bennett, Alma C 100–01, 309
Bennett, Enid 32
Bennett, Suzanne 242, 247
Berengaria 50
Berkeley, University of California, USA 67–72, 163, 271, 315
Bern, Paul 255
Bernadotte, Carl Johan 249–50, 317
Bisexual 94
Bondi, NSW 97–98, 299
Boston, USA 82, 172–74, 207, 312
    Globe 51, 306
Bride for St Thomas, A 193, 216, 219, 313, 315, 317
Brisbane, QLD 14–17, 22–23, 77, 79, 82, 85,
    Courier 304
    Daily Standard 308
British Columbia, Canada 16, 42
Broadway, NY, USA 14, 19–20, 22, 30, 87, 121, 135, 243
Brookes, Alfred 308
Brookes, Herbert 93, 200
Brookes, Ivy 2, 93, 197, 200
Bryn Mawr College, USA 138, 153

Burdett, Basil 206
Burke, Frances 94, 204, 314
Burridge, Pam 45, 300

California Daughters of the British Empire state convention 125
Calvert Beach, USA 168–69
Cambridge, UK 142, 215
Canada 3, 15, 129, 179, 242
Canberra, ACT 218
Canungra, QLD 15, 22, 305
Capitalism 34, 131, 230
Caribbean 234, 240, 282, 295
Caribbean Consumer Committee 295
Carnegie 142, 323
    Corporation 141
    Trust, The 88
Catholic 186, 288
    St Josephs, Chicago, USA 186
    see also Christian
Cecil, Dr Russell LaFayette 52–53
Chateau Marmont, USA 123, 257, 324
Chauvinism 231, 316
Chesapeake Bay, USA 168, 170, 174, 208
Chicago Musical College 106–09, 114, 161, 223–24
China 57, 160, 162, 164–65
Chinese
    decor 50, 53, 248
    migration 24, 137
    people 72, 137, 164–65, 288, 307, 326
    robe 249
    thesis on 137–38
Christian 3, 54–55, 112, 114, 122, 169–70, 209–10, 306
    see also Church
Christian Science 172, 207, 210, 312, 322, 326
Church 52, 79, 101, 112, 114, 122, 153–54, 161, 172, 185, 203, 255
    see also Christian
Cinema 5, 22, 32, 54, 163

Cisgender 64, 131
Columbia University, USA 89, 157, 174
Committee
    Anzac Dinner 243
    Caribbean Consumer 295
    Consumer Advisory 155
    Monopoly 229, 325
    National Association of Consumers 232
    Nude sunbathing 171
    Senate 228
    Temporary National Economic 229, 316
Communism 182, 230
Conference
    Chicago 257
    Consumers National Federation 157
    Food and Agriculture Organization 235
    High Cost of Living 157
    Institute of Pacific Relations 142–43
    London Naval 134
    Paris Peace 136
Consumer Council 235–36
Consumers National Federation 157, 229–30, 232
Coo-ee Clarion 245, 247
Costanoan 18
    see also First Nations
Country Women's Association 203
Crowninshield, Frank 26–32, 36, 51
Cultural imperialism 141, 285

Deardorff, Neva 152–55
Debut
    book 146, 240, 283
    Chicago Symphony Orchestra 161
    concert 227, 316
    debutante 28, 208
    screen and film 29, 32
    water ballet 273

DeMille, Cecil B 54, 247
Democrat 235–36, 261, 292
DePaul University, USA 185, 191
Disability 78, 101–03, 256, 263, 279
Discrimination 5, 19, 125, 183, 252, 267
Divorce 16, 54, 123, 126, 153, 252, 259

Earthquake 68, 70, 151
Elliot, Sumner Locke 4
Elocution 1, 27, 186, 210, 322
Elopement 79–80, 82
Episcopalian 154
  see also Christian

Fairbanks, Douglas 53
Fashion 2, 9, 18, 32, 34, 50, 86, 100, 201, 210, 218
Feminism
  and interior decoration 58
  and postcolonial theory 61
  American 7, 120, 126, 181–82, 188, 201, 213, 231, 252–53, 295–96
  Australian 8, 44, 60–61, 172, 176–78, 203
  white liberal 268–69
  see also Deardoff, Neva
First Nations 7, 18, 24, 33, 86, 177, 205, 245, 263, 268
  see also Aboriginal
  see also Indigenous
Fitzgerald, F Scott 26, 53, 123
Florida, USA 159, 208, 279–81
Fundraising 26, 74, 109, 247, 256, 273

Gabrielino 18
  see also First Nations
  see also Indigenous people
Gallery
  Art Gallery of New South Wales 289
  Contemporary Art Gallery, New York 92
  Cynthia Reed Gallery 190, 201, 240
  Fine Art Society gallery 90, 197–98
  National Gallery Art School 1
  National Gallery of Victoria 88–90, 198–206, 284, 286, 288–89, 314
Gallipoli 9, 28, 243, 297
German people 27, 92, 161, 220
Germany 68, 160, 162
Gillies, Florence 88
Gilmore, Mary 81–86, 147, 307
Gisborne, VIC 204, 314
Goldstein, Vida 158, 172, 291
Good Housekeeping 230, 281
Goulburn, NSW 31, 54, 59
Graduation 19, 25, 46, 108, 174, 180–81, 232
Grainger, Percy 107–10, 114, 227
  Fellowship 107, 113
  Museum 222, 224
Greig, Flos 20

Hairdressing 47, 49, 65–66
Hallett, Hilary 18, 21, 34
Hawai'i, USA 15, 38–42, 68
Hofmann, Hans 92, 287–88, 290, 319
Honolulu Star-Bulletin 38, 40, 305
Hoover, Herbert 16–18, 144
Houghton Mifflin 82, 145–46
House & Garden 28, 58

India 160–62, 164–65, 264
Indigenous people 139, 165, 245
  see also Aboriginal
  see also First Nations
International House 160–66
Interwar 4, 95, 127, 210, 276, 311
Irish 13–16, 23, 122, 178
Irvine, Robert 137, 157, 310
Italy 50, 88, 220

Jamaica 295
Japan 17, 42, 134, 160, 162, 165, 276

Japanese people 42, 134, 164
Jay, Mike 38, 40–41, 305
Jenner, Dorothy 6, 10
Jennings, Helen 7, 304
Jerome, Helen 7, 304

Kahanamoku, Duke 38–40, 45, 72, 299
Kahn, Otto 35–36, 249
Kellerman, Annette 67, 272
Kennedy, John F 291–93

Ladies' Home Journal 76–77, 82–83, 144, 146, 307
League for the Larger Life 169–70, 312
Lenape 180
   see also First Nations
Leslie, Lilie 32
Lewis, Adam 305–06, 317
Lewis, Dr. James Monahan 178–79
Lillie, Mildred L 257, 259, 318
Lindsay, Daryl 206
Lindsay, Lionel 199, 313
Lindsay, William 17
London School of Economics 137–38, 176
Los Angeles Law Library 20–21
Lovely, Louise 32
Lucky Alphonse 189–93, 216, 218–20, 238–41, 313, 315, 317
Lyceum Club 203–04, 302

Mackie, Lyba Sheffield 69
Madison Avenue, USA 35, 50, 56–57, 94, 248
Makura 15
Manhattan 220–21
Manhattan, NY, USA x, 3, 29, 43, 91, 95, 138, 158, 239
Manly, NSW 97, 99, 271, 274–76, 298–99
Mariposa 181, 183, 188, 190
Massacre 15
Melba, Dame Nellie 2

Melba Hall 222
Melbourn Conservatorium 108–09, 222–25, 227
Mermaids 38, 40, 272, 305, 307
Methodist 31, 161, 178, 214
   see also Christian
Miami, USA 279, 283, 302
Misogyny 5, 7, 62, 266, 270
Modern Health Colony 174–75
Modern Living 209, 211, 312, 314
Montaukett 33
   see also First Nations
   see also Indigenous people
Monterey 200
Morgan, Ivor 225, 309, 311, 315
Museum ix–x
   Metropolitan 89, 202
   Of Modern Art 56
   Roerich 93
   Whitney 152
   see also Grainger

Natation 67, 69, 71, 74–75, 275
National Association of Consumers 232
National League for Women's Service 73
Naturopath 173, 214, 303
New Thought 169–70, 172, 210
New York Times 36, 52, 54, 89, 93, 247, 282, 302, 305
Niagara 29, 38, 42, 45, 85–86, 110
Nightingale Model 189, 215, 217, 241
Nonbinary 63–64, 262
NSW Industrial Commission 138, 156–57
Nudism iii, 3, 169–71, 174, 208, 312, 314

Ohlone 18
   see also First Nations
   see also Indigenous people
Olympics 39, 103, 154, 272–73
Oval Office 3, 7
Oxford, UK 142

Pageant of Mermaids 69–70, 306
Payne Whitney Clinic 237–40
Peacock, Lady 176–77, 183
Penguin 151
Pennsylvania, USA 77, 138, 179–81, 232, 259, 261
Phi Delta Delta 23
Philippoff, Colonel Georges 55–56
Pink-collar 18, 34, 46
Piscataway 169
   see also First Nations
   see also Indigenous people
Playground Commission 71–74, 99
Prosthetic dentistry 181, 265, 269

Quaker 152, 232
Queer 62–64, 93–95, 130–31

Raab, Alexander 114–15, 161, 222–24, 315
Racism 72, 84, 137, 147, 192, 263, 280
Radiant Health 174, 312
Republican 16, 119, 144, 242, 261
Rockefeller, John D 163, 311
   Foundation 135, 141–43, 152, 163
Roosevelt, Eleanor 140, 292
Roosevelt, President Theodore 155–56, 202, 229, 243, 291–92
Royal Art Society 79
Russia 55, 72, 182
Russian people 43, 53, 108, 114, 182, 246

Scandal 71, 79, 164, 169, 174, 198, 203–04, 208, 289
Scholarship 15, 107–08, 110, 114, 121, 137, 142
Segregation 263
Sexism 5, 99, 182, 266
Sexuality 94–95, 174
Shinnecock 33
   see also First Nations
   see also Indigenous people

Siberia Maru 134
Singapore 129, 243, 295
Singing Gold, The 82–83, 144–46, 149, 282–83, 310
Smallpox 249
Smithsonian Institute 308, 313, 319
Snook, Dorothea 303, 312, 314
Socialism 81, 137, 156
Sonoma 75
Sorority 23, 256
Stolen Generations 86
Streeton, Arthur 91, 199
Suffrage 17, 23, 124, 137, 158, 291
Surf Life Saving Association of Australia 99, 103, 276
Swanwick, Helena 137, 310
Sydney Harbour 1, 44, 79

Tajo Building 19–21, 121
Tataviam 18
   see also First Nations
Tharlane 146, 149, 282, 311
Tongva 18
   see also First Nations
   see also Indigenous people
Trans 62–64, 131, 133, 262

Ularunda station, QLD 76–80, 82, 84, 86, 307, 310, 319
University of Southern California, USA 17–19, 21, 23, 25, 46
Usher, Pam 111–13

Vancouver, Canada 15, 122
Vanderbilts 52, 242, 248
   Hotel 42–43
Vanity Fair 26, 32, 51
Variety 54, 306
Ventura 47, 49
Victorian Women Citizens' Movement 176–77, 183–84

Waikiki, USA 38–42, 305
Waldorf Astoria 43, 242
Wallace-Crabbe, Chris 285

Wanamaker's 30
Westbrook, Eric 284, 288
White Australia policy 24
Whitney Museum 152
Willebrandt, Mabel Walker 123–24, 257
Women of colour 24

Women's City Club of San Francisco 73–74, 100, 104, 275, 306, 308–09
Woollacott, Angela x, 67, 313

Zen Buddhism 287
Zen in the Art of Archery 288

www.ingramcontent.com/pod-product-compliance
Ingram Content Group UK Ltd.
Pitfield, Milton Keynes, MK11 3LW, UK
UKHW041302180426